SPANISH MYSTICISM

A PRELIMINARY SURVEY

BY

E. ALLISON PEERS, M.A.

SOMETIME SCHOLAR OF CHRIST'S COLLEGE, CAMBRIDGE
GILMOUR PROFESSOR OF SPANISH IN THE UNIVERSITY OF LIVERPOOL

METHUEN & CO. LTD.
36 ESSEX STREET W.C.
LONDON

First Published in 1924

TO

MY WIFE

PREFACE

THIS book is a short "Introduction" to a subject the vastness of which would require many volumes to do it justice. Some account is given of the nature of Spanish Mysticism and of the works of the greatest of the many mystical writers who figure in Spanish literature in and about the sixteenth century. For the rest, the author has been content to select a few representative passages from thirteen such authors and to let them speak for themselves.

This selection is of necessity small and many notable writers are entirely unrepresented in it. But it will serve to make known a few of their contemporaries in a country where only the two greatest—St. Teresa and St. John of the Cross—are read, and it may perhaps arouse enough interest to lead to the translation of the complete works of many others. Ramón Lull, whose *Book of the Lover and the Beloved* is accessible in English,[1] has been omitted from the anthology as being a Majorcan who wrote in Catalan. In a complete history of Spanish Mysticism he would, however, be given an important place.

Not only passages describing the Mystic Way and the life and experiences of the proficient have been chosen for translation; rather, a selection has been

[1] *The Book of the Lover and the Beloved*, S.P.C.K., 1923.

made which includes much that is mystical only in the wider sense. Exposition, autobiography, and spiritual correspondence—to take but three examples—have been given their place, for the spirit which pervades them all is the same.

The biographical and bibliographical notes prefixed to the selections from each author are in no case exhaustive. The same may be said of a few footnotes which have been added to the text for the sake of readers who have not access to the Vulgate. Apart from these, only one or two obscure passages have been annotated.

The two greatest poems of St. John of the Cross have already been admirably translated by Mr. Arthur Symons, and the present writer, who could not hope to better them, is deeply indebted to their author for permission to reproduce them in this collection. To the Benedictines of Stanbrook grateful acknowledgment must be made for the right to reprint their version of some lines from St. Teresa. Mr. Aubrey F. G. Bell has generously sanctioned, not only the publication, but in a few places the adaptation, of some translations, as yet unpublished by him, from Fray Luis de León.

To Miss Marion Young and Miss L. J. Gardiner the author's thanks are due for their help in reading through large portions of the book in manuscript.

E. A. P.

THE UNIVERSITY, LIVERPOOL,
September, 1924

CONTENTS

CONTENTS

PART I

AN INTRODUCTION TO SPANISH MYSTICISM

CHAPTER I

ESPAÑA MÍSTICA

NO thoughtful traveller can spend many weeks in Spain without perceiving that mysticism is inborn in its people. Neither the cosmopolitan tone of the great cities, nor the lusty paganism which, even in the smallest towns, invades the most solemn of holy-days, can destroy in his spirit the sense that in this nation flows the undercurrent of mystic life. Nor can he for long be content to look upon the Spain of legend—of the "black legend" which has done so much in our own land to obscure the greatness of the country which is its victim. He may well become convinced that the soul of Spain is its mystic self, and wish to trace its expression through history, literature, or art, or even to seek for it in the daily activities and aspirations of the Spanish people in this twentieth century. But, if he should prefer the easier task of delving into that vast wealth of literature which Spanish mysticism gave to the service of religion, he will find in these pages some guide to its barely explored treasures.

It is no exaggeration, but literal truth, to assert that the mystical writings of the Golden Age alone can be numbered by the thousand.[1] Even in Spain, the significance of such riches has not yet been fully realised. The piety of a Franciscan brother gives us a worthy edition of Fray Juan de los Angeles ; a modern Academician edits Estella's Meditations for the people ; and a still more modern journalist rediscovers Fray Luis de

---

[1] Menéndez y Pelayo estimates them at three thousand, and if we interpret the word 'mystical' widely the estimate is by no means of improbable truth.

3

Granada. But for all that is being done, far more remains to be accomplished. Few of the mystical classics are accessible to the unlearned reader, in comparison with the greater number of those which elude at times even the scholar's researches. And, as a compatriot of Rousselot's said in 1908,[1] many have declared his study of Spanish Mysticism to be inadequate, as indeed it is, but none has written a work that can supersede it—though, for a Spaniard, this should be no impossible task. The statement still remains a true one.

In England, where three hundred years ago one great Spanish mystic[2] was read, translated and adapted for general use, little more is known now than then of the great company to which he belonged. St. Teresa and St. John of the Cross, it is true, are accessible in English to all, but by almost every modern writer on mysticism in the language they have been treated as the sole representatives in Spain of the literature which they so greatly enriched. It would be painful, though easy enough, to cite examples of this neglect. Rather would we seek to indicate—since in a book of these dimensions no more is possible—how much the neglect has cost.

None who reflect on the course of Spanish history will wonder that the Mystic Roll in Spain is a long one. Her early national story is that of age-long devotion to an ideal, and in such an atmosphere mysticism breathes its native air. One has but to think of the eight centuries preceding the Reconquest of the Moors' last citadel, of the scattered remnant driven northwards to those Asturian highlands which no conqueror can call his own, of the victory of Pelayo and his little band over the invaders who would have harried them out of existence, of the formation of that "contemptible" little kingdom which was to come out from its northern fastnesses, to grow and extend its bounds, knowing no rest, living through centuries with one vehement, fixed desire, to win back Greater

---

[1] A. Morel-Fatio, in *Bulletin Hispanique*.

[2] Luis de Granada. The British Museum has fourteen English translations of parts of this writer's works, the majority of them dating from the sixteenth or early seventeenth century.

Spain,—*for the Cross.* Through the mists of legend and the clear light of history we may follow that narrative and mark the slow, successive stages of the Reconquest. The statesmanship of Alfonso I,—the exploits of the historical Cid—reverses like the Battle of Alarcón—astounding victories such as Las Navas de Tolosa—disruptions causing weakness — alliances bringing strength—finally the union of Castile and Leon preluding the recapture, first of Cordoba, and then of the great Sevilla. (And still we are but in the thirteenth century!) The century of stagnation—the great defeat of the Salado— the reign of Alfonso XI—the successful siege of Algeciras: one step more. Once again a century of civil strife and arrest of progress : then the last great act of the long drama—the union of Aragon and Castile—the appearance of the Christian armies in the Vega of Granada—the success of Baeza—the final onslaught on Granada itself—and that proud 2nd of January, 1492, when the Catholic Monarchs rode in triumph into the city.

Small wonder if, long before this drama of reconquest was over, one factor in the complex Spanish temperament was fixed for all time. For close upon eight hundred years a nation had been moulding its self-consciousness by pressing forward undauntedly towards the goal of its desire. And its devotion to the ideal was never to leave it; its ardent passion for the Cross was never to fade. It was for ever to be up in arms, intolerant of its foes, and therefore prone to violence and excess.[1] These traits suggest that peculiar blend of fanaticism and mysticism, which for good or for evil have ever marked the religious life of Spain.

Space forbids a discussion of how far the conquered race helped to mould the character of the conquerors. Angel Ganivet would find in the involuntary fusion of the two peoples a solution which many, more instinctively perhaps than

---

[1] Masdeu was right after all when he said of his fellow-countrymen: "Son los más firmes defensores de la religión y los maestros de la ascética; hombres devotos; y si pecan por exceso, es con alguna inclinación a la superstición, pero no a la impiedad." (*Historia crítica de España y de la cultura española,* 1783, Vol. I, pp. 261-2.)

scientifically, reject.   To him the Romancero is a symbol of a
greater whole :—

From this popular poetry, at once Arabic and Christian,—the
Arabic element not deadening the Christian, but giving it greater
brilliancy of tone—arose the most striking tendencies of the
religious spirit of Spain : to wit, poetic exaltation, or mysticism,
and fanaticism, which was the exaltation of action.

The Mysticism was, as it were, a sanctification of African
sensuality ; the fanaticism was a reversion against ourselves, after
the Reconquest, of the fury which had accumulated during eight
centuries of strife.[1]

Whether or no, with the historian Altamira, we reject this
theory,—and whether or no for his reasons [2]—we cannot but
recognise the fundamentally mystical element in the Spanish
temperament for centuries before it found orthodox religious
expression in the products of the cloister.   Few would hesitate
to grant this concession, and for our purpose it is the one fact
essential.

Let who will not grant it go to Spain—and, as we have
already implied, there is no surer path to an understanding of
our subject.   Once there, let him consider its earliest works of
art,—above all, the sermons in its stones, reflecting what mystic
energy there was in those flights of the human soul which gave
to Spain her majestic cathedrals—Toledo the rich, Salamanca
the strong, León the fair, Oviedo the divine, and Sevilla the
great.   Sevilla above all, concerning which its founders said :
" Let us build so magnificent a temple that in ages to come
men shall think us to have been mad."   When genius courted
that saying has ever been the time of its truest greatness.

Of the earliest expression of the mystical spirit, contemporary with those great days, nothing can be said in this
volume, so infinitely more important is the period which

---

[1] *Idearium español*, p. 15.

[2] *Psicología del pueblo español*, 2nd ed., p. 105.   " El hecho de haber sido
la mística, en el Renacimiento, una importación alemana sobre la clase de otros
precedentes clásicos y medioevales . . . " is a reason which we cannot admit, as
will be seen.   The author's next point, that the mysticism of Spain in the Middle
Ages is rooted in Moslem philosophy, is on the other hand quite tenable.

followed later. This great age of Spanish mysticism began with curious suddenness in the first years of the sixteenth century—the age pre-eminently of Spanish conquest, prosperity and genius. That this should be the case was supremely fitting. Many writers, in England as elsewhere, have refuted the vulgar error that the individual mystic is as a rule of an unpractical temperament, that he is of necessity,—or even that he is commonly—a dreamer and a recluse.[1] A recent writer on education has said : " It is men who have practised meditation, and have in that supreme activity made the muscles of their minds at once firm and lissome, who can turn themselves . . . to the distracting engagements of the world, set them in a pattern, give them with order unity, and endure them with unfaltering courage." [2] One has but to intensify that thought, to lift it to a higher plane, and the secret of the mystic's practical strength lies revealed.

But is it always realised that what is true of the individual is true of the epoch also? That to the great ages of mysticism the nations in whose bosoms the germ has been formed, and who have brought it to life and maturity, can look for the times of their greatest prosperity, for their most cherished 'practical' achievements, as well as for the birth or growth of their greatest poets, painters, dramatists, sculptors, artists, thinkers and statesmen? Such at least is often true, and it is true in the history of Spain.

Let the reader for a moment consider that great age which began with the Conquest of Granada. The year 1491, which saw the last agony of Moslem rule in Spain, saw also the birth

---

[1] *E.g.* W. R. Inge: *Christian Mysticism*, 5th ed. 1921, pp. xi-xii. Evelyn Underhill : *The Life of the Spirit and the Life of To-Day*, 1922, pp. 42-3, etc., etc. Francisco de Osuna, on this matter, makes the striking comment : Los ejercitados, aun en las obras manuales de por casa, están tan recogidos y puestos con Dios como los nuevos cuando están muy de rodillas en secreto lugar. (*Tercer Abecedario Espiritual*, Trat. VI, Cap. 5.) And quite apart from this there is the truth expressed in Traherne's famous couplet :

> A man that seemeth idle to the view
> Of others, may the Greatest Business do.

[2] E. T. Campagnac : *Society and Solitude*, 1922, p. 225.

of a man (Ignatius Loyola) who was to create a spiritual army more powerful than that whose task was done. The voyages of Columbus, let us remember, the expeditions of Pizarro, and the vast American discoveries, were contemporary with the formation of that same religious army, and with the far-reaching reform in the Order of Carmel. How often might St. Ignatius' *Ite, omnia inflammate et accendite* have been repeated as a god-speed before warfare profane! For civil life merged easily into the life of religion : is not Felipe II, soldier and statesman, immortalised by the sombre pile of the Escorial? was not the name of Reyes Católicos given to the greatest monarchs of Spain?

In literature, it is the same story. Even apart from the greatest of the mystics, who by secular standards rank high, this period in which they flourished saw the greatest literary triumphs that Spain has known, and in fields as diverse as possible. It was no purely ecstatic age, but that same full-blooded one which gave us hearty works of fiction like *Lazarillo de Tormes*, the exceedingly secular as well as the sacred plays of Lope de Vega and Calderón, the sonnets and eclogues of Garcilaso, the florid art of Herrera, the later dramas of Tirso de Molina and Alarcón, and that one master-work which alone would make a century great, in which the story-teller's supreme art blends with a prodigious knowledge of human nature—the *Don Quijote* of Cervantes.[1]

The Prado will remind us of another sphere in which the Golden Age, of Mysticism and Letters alike, was a great one. There hang the Morales, the Navarretes, and the Herreras ; there one may ponder on the *bizarreries* which stamp the strangely speaking canvasses of El Greco, the fervid asceticism of a Zurbarán, the infinite sympathy of a Murillo, the eternal appeal of the greatest of them all—Velázquez. Nor can one forget, even standing among those glories, that the vast *retablo* of the Conception which is the pride of Salamanca[2] was painted

---

[1] *Cf.* again Ganivet (*op. cit.* p. 161) who connects Don Quijote, by implication, with the Spanish Mystics, and presents him as the type of the post-conquest Spaniard.

[2] It hangs in the Convento de las Agustinas Recoletas.

by Ribera but a generation after the death of Salamanca's greatest son, while his greatest mystic work was still new.

These are but indications of the splendours of the hundred years in which Mysticism bloomed and flowered again and again in the domain of Spanish literature. The products of that time in even one of many fields furnish material enough for a life of study: here we have been unable to do more than merely point to their existence, before passing on to our main subject.

CHAPTER II

THE PRECURSORS OF ST. TERESA

IT is as attractive as it is appropriate to begin our survey of the greatest mystics with Fray Hernando de Talavera.[1] Born as early as 1428, trained and educated in the North, he became in middle age confessor and director to Queen Isabella, accompanied the Christian armies southwards, and played no small part in the Conquest of Granada. To him, when Granada fell, was assigned the honour of bearing the standard of the Cross, and planting it on the highest of Alhambra's towers. He became, as of right, chief pastor of the conquerors, and Archbishop of Granada. Who could have better claim to stand at the head of this long line of Spanish mystics than one so aptly representing both the Reconquest itself and a city whose sons have been called the most mystical of all the sons of mystic Spain?[2]

Yet there is strictly speaking but little that is mystical in the writings of Fray Hernando. He must stand, not at the head of those now to come, but midway between them and those earlier authors not now to be noticed. If he can be considered historically as ushering in the mystical school, it is as one of many ascetic and moral writers in whose works here and there may be caught a flash of mystic wisdom. His "Brief form of Confession," his manual for communicants, and, even more, his "profitable treatise" upon seemliness in dress,[3]

[1] Cf. Nueva Biblioteca de Autores Españoles, Vol. XVI, Madrid, 1911, where he is given primacy of place in the collection.

[2] Angel Ganivet: Granada la Bella, Madrid, 1905, p. 53 : "Lo místico es lo español, y los granadinos somos los más místicos de todos los españoles."

[3] "Breve forma de confesar," etc., "En qué manera se debe haber la persona que ha de comulgar," "De vestir y de calzar, etc.," and "Tratado de lo que significan las ceremonias de la misa" are reprinted in N.B.A.E., XVI, pp. 1-93.

are the practical works of a practical director of souls,—"manuals for the million" they might be called to-day—intended as they are not for the few but for the many. Hardly different is the shorter treatise, addressed to a noble lady on the right use of time;[1] all its eloquence and ardour, its wealth of illustration and metaphor cannot be said to raise it, for more than a brief moment, above the bare level of asceticism.

With Fray Hernando must be classed Alejo de Venegas,[2] a shadowy figure of whom little more is known than can be gathered from his writings. One of the earliest Spanish champions of the familiar mother tongue, he attracts us here less by his *Treatise of Orthography* and the curious glossary which is readily accessible in Spanish,[3] than by his best-known work, the *Agony of the Passage of Death* (1537).[4]

In this treatise Alejo de Venegas seldom appears as a mystic, except in the sense in which that title may be claimed by every true believer whose life is hid with Christ in God. The Christian is described as "united by grace with Christ," his life on earth is a "long martyrdom," to die is but to throw off this mortal body, and the life of the blessed is figured as that of company (rather than oneness) with God. Ideas such as these the expositor develops in the somewhat crude, anthropomorphic fashion of the age. As the reader soon discovers, he is a theologian always, a practical teacher most of the time, and a mystic, in the strictest sense, hardly ever. Eloquent and stirring passages he has in plenty, but none which can with justice be quoted at any length in this survey.

Alonso de Orozco, whose life, but for a space of nine years, spans the entire length of the sixteenth century, also wrote many books which are not primarily mystical. The *Garden of Prayer* is a treatise on the nature and power of vocal prayer and the supreme example of it left by Jesus Christ. The *Spiritual Betrothal* is an exposition, written for nuns, of their

---

[1] *N.B.A.E.*, XVI, pp. 94-103.   [2] Also written Vanegas.
[3] *N.B.A.E.*, XVI, pp. 259-318.
[4] *Ibid.*, pp. 105-258: *Agonia del tránsito de la muerte.* His other important work is entitled *Diferencias de libros que hay en el Universo* (1540).

three vows.   The lengthy *Memorial of Holy Love*, though full
of the spirit which animates the true mystic, is not concerned
with the higher states of prayer.   Of works like the *Treatise
on Confession*, *Examination of the Conscience* and *Rule of
Christian Life* the titles speak for themselves.   Even the
avowedly mystical *History of the Queen of Sheba*, in which not
only that narrative, but many another passage from the Old
Testament, is interpreted as expounding the higher religious
life, deals mainly with the lower states in that life and not with
the less common experiences and the goal of Union.   The
most advanced of Orozco's many treatises which we have seen
is the *Mount of Contemplation*, a sequel to the *Garden of
Prayer*.   This is by no means his most original or characteristic work, but for our purpose it is of great importance.
Written in dialogue form, it describes the four *jornadas* or
stages of the Mystic Life, of which the highest is the " contemplation of God in Himself."   That it is not altogether con-
vincing, that it smacks of reading more than of experience, we
may freely allow.   But we have also to take account of the
busy and active life which its author led.   Between preaching
and writing, he had little chance of that peace and rest of
which, like a later Augustinian, Luis de León, he so eloquently
wrote.[1]   And the duties of his calling led him towards ascetic
rather than mystic writing.

A special interest attaches to Alonso de Orozco, of which
a few words may be added here.   Late in the last century,
a manuscript of his was found in the Augustinian convent of
San Felipe el Real, Madrid, which appeared to be the rough
sketch of an unwritten work entitled *Of Nine Names of Christ*.
This title suggests at once that of the well-known work of
Orozco's great fellow-Augustinian, which we shall presently
describe,[2] and when the notes were printed[3] it became clear

---

[1] *Cf.* for example the extracts from Orozco (pp. 53 ff.) and Luis de León
(pp. 157 ff.) below.

[2] See p. 38.

[3] See the Augustinian review, *La Cuidad de Dios*, Vols. XVI, XVII. *passim*,
and also our Bibliography, pp. 175, 259 below.

that there was an equally strong resemblance in substance. That Luis de León's masterpiece owed something to this sketch is at least possible, since the two Augustinians undoubtedly had personal relations with each other. It is also possible that conversations between them, which each recorded independently in his own fashion, may have been the basis of the later *Names of Christ*, in which case we may read both the works of Orozco, and the passages ascribed to Luis de León's character ' Juliano,' with a new interest.[1]

These early authors, mainly ascetics, bring us at length to the years when the greatest Spanish mystics were beginning to write. It has already been said that their works fall naturally into no set divisions, and that, in deviating from an order which is approximately chronological, there is practically no gain. The outstanding figure in the long line of mystics, however, is that of St. Teresa, and it is no affectation, but the strictest fidelity to truth, to assign to her a position of pre-eminence in this survey. Further, to study the chief of the early mystics of her century is to study those men whose works she read, and dwelt upon, as her own *Life* tells, during the formative years of her career.[2]

Of these, incomparably the greatest is Francisco de Osuna, whose *Third Spiritual Alphabet*,[3] her earliest mystical guide, a devoutly minded relative gave her when she was still young.

[1] The conclusions of Conrado Muiños Saenz, which later contributions to the question have not, in our judgment, affected, are, in his own words, as follows :—
Resulta que *evidentemente*, *Los Nombres de Cristo* de Fr. Luis de León, y del Beato Alonso de Orozco tienen entre sí íntimas e innegables relaciones ; que *probablemente*, el opúsculo del Santo de San Felipe sirvió de pauta en gran parte para el clásico libro del Maestro salmantino ; que *seguramente* el Marcelo que en él nos dejó tan hermosas enseñanzas es el mismo Fr. Luis de León ; que *verosímilmente* en Juliano está representado el Beato Alonso de Orozco, y en Sabino *tal vez* el P. Alfonso de Mendoza. (*La Ciudad de Dios*, XVII, 550.)

[2] See A. Morel-Fatio : " Les lectures de Ste. Thérèse," in *Bulletin Hispanique*, 1908, pp. 17-67.

[3] *Tercer Abecedario Espiritual*, in *N.B.A.E.*, XVI, pp. 319-587, the edition here quoted. The book is called an " alphabet" because the title of each chapter begins with a letter of the alphabet in turn. But the apparent artificiality is hardly noticeable in the treatise, less so by far than the prayers with alliterative petitions which sometimes startle the modern reader.

Osuna's exposition of the "prayer of recollection" led her to
the state which she calls the "prayer of quiet."[1]   "I delighted
in that book exceedingly," she says, "and determined to follow
the mystic road (*aquel camino*) with all my strength . . .
taking the book as my guide, for I found no human guide—
that is, no confessor—who could understand me."[1]

"The principal cause which moved me to write this book,"
says Osuna, "was to bring to the general notice of all the
exercise of recollection."[2]   Unfortunately he has little gift for
orderly exposition, and not only is it long before he reaches his
main theme,[3] but he leaves it again and returns to it without
due progression.   One has to search through his book to
profit by it, but in the search much profit is to be found.

For, apart from its want of system, it is an admirable guide
for those who are setting out on the Mystic Way, and need
much direction.   Were it translated into our own language, it
might well be as closely and as frequently read as the works
of St. Teresa herself.   One can readily understand how that
saint, as a girl untutored in the school of contemplation, made
it her chief companion, and drank in its temperate yet lofty
teaching.   For its greatness largely consists in this : that even
while its author is writing in simple fashion of the rudiments
of Christian virtue or the elements of a holy life, he is carried
up into the heights and his thought is transfigured before us.
Never losing sight of his goal, writing ever for those "who in
purity of spirit *would attain to God*,"[4] he can at once instruct
and inspire, exhort and kindle, encourage and reprove.   The
proficient, without weariness, may read his counsels to the unlearned ; the beginner, struggling upward, may contemplate the
heights of the perfect life, yet not turn from them in dejection,
believing them to be beyond his eventual reach.

No mystic, surely, has spent more loving care upon the
preparation of the aspirant, nor dealt more tenderly, yet more

---

[1] *Libro de su vida*, Cap. IV.   Her copy of the *Abecedario* is still to be seen
at Avila.

[2] *Tercer Abecedario Espiritual*, Trat. VIII, Cap. 1.   [3] Trat. VI.

[4] Title of Trat. I, Cap. 1, *cf.* Trat. X, Cap. 5.

faithfully, with the dreaded negations of the purgative way.
From the "three things necessary to quiet contemplation"[1]
we may pass to learn of the "vigilance we must have over
ourselves"[2] and the "guarding of our hearts."[3] Following
this road, we come to the night of sense, with its "disengaging
of the soul and emptying it of all created things."[4] We are
told how the seeker must be deaf, and blind and dumb, "but
ever meek."[5] And the advantage of this methodless manner
of exposition is that the writer can go back at will, as his in-
stinct prompts him, to underline those counsels which his
learners are most in danger of forgetting. "But ever meek"!
How many a time, in the *Alphabet*, does such a phrase as this,
or as "with quietude of spirit," give us halt for reflection and
for rest!

In such a context we light suddenly upon the chapters
which treat of the "prayer of recollection."[6] Fray Francisco
exhausts his power of words in his efforts to convey its greatness. "It is the coming of the Lord to the soul. . . . It is
friendship or the opening of the devout heart to Christ. . . .
It is a spiritual ascension with Christ. . . . It is the third
heaven to which the contemplative soul is caught up. . . . And
wherefore should I say more?"[7]

We may not linger over the counsels which he gives upon
the practice of this high degree of prayer. He has much to
say, and the discursiveness of his manner draws it out unduly.
But his intense spirituality pervades all; St. Teresa must have
learned much from his warnings against striving for "sweetness" and "interior joys,"[8] from his disregard of the external
accompaniments of the mystic life, from the clearness with
which his gaze is fixed upon the Goal.[9] "Desire thy Beloved
ever."[10] Know Him through His creatures, indeed,—"for all

---

[1] Trat. XV, Cap. 5. [2] Trat. I, Cap. 1.
[3] Trat. IV, Caps. 1-5. [4] *Ibid.*, Cap. 1. [5] Trat. III.
[6] By this phrase, which he uses somewhat loosely, is sometimes meant the
mystic life as a whole, at others a particular stage of it, corresponding approximately to the Prayer of Quiet.
[7] Trat. VI, Cap. 3. [8] *E.g.* Trat. V, Cap. 2.
[9] *E.g.* Prólogo, Trat. V, Cap. 2, etc. [10] Trat. XI, Cap. 4.

created things are a ladder by which the feet of the wise
ascend to God "[1]—but strive continually to be one with Him,
"considering that He is the end of all thy works and desires."[2]
"Then shall He be ever with thee as the Star was with the
Magi and the North is with the mariner."[3]   Thus after much
striving shalt thou reach "the summit of contemplation, where
striving is no more but all is rest."[4]

Of this state Osuna says little; on the life of the proficient,
too, he dwells but now and again, though some of these
passages are the most moving and inspiring in the book.[5]   The
fact is that for all his learning—which, unlike some of his
contemporaries, he never parades[6]—he writes from living
experience, as contemplative and director both.   He is less
concerned to write of the rare heights of Carmel for the few
than to mark out the path to them for the many.   If St. Teresa,
of the elect, surpasses him, we can never forget, as we read his
glowing words, that when they first kindled her heart she was
still of that great company not yet made perfect.

Another early book which guided St. Teresa, and which
links its author with those who prepared the way for her, is
the *Ascent of Mount Zion*,[7] the work of Bernardino de Laredo.
This book she read at a time when she was seeking to describe
and understand her mystical experiences, and was greatly
perplexed and troubled because she could neither find words to
express herself nor even translate her experiences into terms of
thought.   Laredo's description of the higher states of prayer
came like a flood of light upon her self-questionings: these
favours were what God had granted to herself.[8]

A very slight acquaintance with the *Ascent of Mount Zion*

---

[1] Prólogo. *Cf.* Trat. XXII, Cap. 5.

[2] Trat. XXII, Cap. 5.   [3] *Ibid.*

[4] Trat. III, Cap. 2.   [5] *E.g.* Trat. XVIII, Cap. 3.

[6] Besides a deep and extensive knowledge of the Bible and a more than
ordinary acquaintance with the Fathers, he shows a familiarity with the works of
Gerson, whom he frequently quotes, and thus furnishes one example of that
foreign influence upon Spanish mysticism which has sometimes, and quite wrongly,
been denied.

[7] *Subida del monte Sion por la vía contemplativa.*

[8] *Libro de su vida*, Cap. XXIII.

(of which, unfortunately, there is no modern edition) suffices to
show that its author was a genuine contemplative. For all his
repetitions, the occasional obscurity of his style, the frequency
of his digressions and the ample use which he makes of the
Fathers, he speaks with his own voice, and with the quiet
authority of experience. And so his book, or at the least that
part of it which tells of the "reverencing of God in quiet
contemplation," deserves to be read and pondered.

This part consists of the third and final book,[1] the subject
of which—"that the Ascent of Mount Zion exceeds that of all
other mountains"—alone justifies the title of the treatise. In
it Laredo devotes himself to the subject of contemplation, which
he defines as the "prayer of the soul alone in its pure and
essential substance, apart entirely from its lower powers."
This is the "better part,"—the Way of Mary. And once he
has made clear what its nature is, he makes an elaborate
analysis, as befits one who was a physician as well as a religious,
of the growth of the spirit during the course of the contemplative life : of its joys, its hindrances, its troubles—of the sleep of its
powers—of the perils of 'unreal contemplation'—of the spirit's
true passivity. If he says less than some of those who succeeded
him upon the spirit's final haven of Union in the Beloved, we
may well believe that it is but for lack of words.

A very different writer from Laredo is S. Pedro de Alcántara,
the details of whose life of marvellous austerity are well known.
In his day he was widely read, as indeed in some places
he is still. "Blessed Theresia his ghostly child"[2] is among
the witnesses to his popularity. "He is the author of several
little books on prayer," she says, "written in the vernacular,
and now in common use; for as one who has had long practice

---

[1] Book I, which comments upon the theme "that the life of Christ is the cross of
Christ," is preparatory, while Book II is principally concerned with Meditation.
These two books are approximately twice the length of the third.

[2] The phrase is from an English edition of his chief work, published in
Brussels in 1632, as

A Golden Treatise of Mentall Praier,

With diverse spirituall rules and directions, no lesse profitable than necessarie for
all sortes of people.

2

in prayer he wrote very profitably for those who are given to it." [1]

The *Treatise of Prayer and Meditation* is essentially a book for the people,—"brief and compendious," so the preface tells us, and intended for the poor to buy who are unable to afford the large and costly books that were then the only ones published. It is written "with clarity," but perhaps it is rather its brevity and fervour that have commended it to generations of would-be contemplatives. The English edition, three centuries old but twice reissued, gives the book the distinct and well-merited title of *A Golden Treatise*, and says of the Saint, as little known to English readers then as now; "His eies were sparklinge tokens of the fire of diuine love which was in his soule." As we read the pages of the treatise, even apart from the additional devotions put there by later Spanish piety, we can feel the influence of that ardent soul still.

Of Juan de Avila, the "Apostle of Andalucía," it is peculiarly difficult to write in a brief survey like the present. Essentially a missionary, endowed with a severely practical nature, and brought by his work into close and continual contact with immature souls,[2] he could hardly have written much for the proficient : such was not his vocation. And yet we can recognise in him many, perhaps all, of the characteristics of that great mystical school which is now forming. As we read his *Spiritual Letters* we are struck by the reserve with which he speaks of mental prayer : we feel that here is a great mystic indeed, but one tied down to the ground and unable to soar. The *Audi, filia* (" Hearken, O daughter "), which found favour with the great St. Ignatius Loyola, himself spiritual soldier and mystic both, confirms the impression. When, in its later chapters, some traces of mysticism appear, it is with every sign of restraint. Yet the " Rich Cabinet full of Spirituall Jewells " [3] has some treasures for the mystic if they are not

---

[1] *Libro de su vida*, Cap. XXX.

[2] " It is not the clapping of handes which he begs," says the English edition (1620) of the *Audi, filia ;* "he shoots at no less than the souls of men."

[3] Sub-title of the 1620 translation (see Bibliography, p. 200).

intended for him alone.   How could it be otherwise of one
who wrote from such heights as he himself had reached, and
wrote from the heart, under the divine inspiration of love?
His works, said a contemporary biographer (and once more we
quote them in the quaintly figured language of the English
translation):

were not so much the issue of a studious and speculative brayne, as of a bleeding and boyling hart.   Boyling,
through the love of God; and bleeding, for the sins of the
world.

And again:

It is the leste wonder if his words were like so many·burn-
ing coales, which might serve to seare those soules which are
full of festred soares; and to set such others as are found, on
fire, with the love of Almighty God.[1]

These passages, in their original language, were written by
one who was himself far more widely read in England[2] than
Juan de Avila, and is undoubtedly the greatest of all those who
may be described as St. Teresa's precursors: Fray Luis de
Granada.   In this Dominican friar we have not only an orator
and teacher, an ascetic and a moralist of tremendous force, a
literary figure of no mean stature, but also a mystic, at least by
gleams and flashes.   Though so much of his life was spent in
Portugal, Fray Luis' name brings us back to that great city of
his birth, Granada, so full of significance for our theme.   His
life, as viewed from the twentieth century, was uneventful, and
it is hard to imagine oneself back in the time when his oratory
was known in half Europe.   But even to-day his work is full
of power, though he is known rather by the *Sinner's Guide*
than by the semi-mystical *Memorial of the Christian Life* and
its *Additions*.

Unlike the great majority of his Spanish contemporaries
Luis de Granada is something of a Nature-mystic, one who,
far from despising created things or thrusting them from him

---

[1] Preface to the above edition.
[2] See, *e.g.*, J. G. Underhill: *Spanish Literature in the England of the
Tudors*, New York and London, 1899.

as hindrances to spiritual progress, uses them at times as means
of rising to higher planes of experience.   So widely was he
read in our country in the sixteenth and seventeenth centuries
that he may well have inspired men like Vaughan and Crashaw,
with whom he has much in common.[1]   Be that as it may—for
such a question requires more careful investigation than can be
given to it here—his attitude to Nature is exactly mirrored in
lines like those of Vaughan's well-known prayer :—

> Grant I may so
> Thy steps track here below,
>
> That in these masques and shadows I may see
> Thy sacred way ;
> And by those hid ascents climb to that day
> Which breaks from Thee,
> Who art in all things, though invisibly.[2]

Few Spaniards have loved the sights and sounds of Nature
more intensely than this Dominican friar.   The glories of
moonlight or of a starlight night are his common theme ;
hardly less frequently does he describe the smiling countryside
in summer and the woods in springtime.   But his most eloquent
passages are those in which he speaks of the sea : now at rest,
hardly stirred by the merest breath of wind, its tiny waves gently
lapping the shore, now lashed into rage, its billows parting and
revealing chasms beneath.   " All this pictures to us the fury of
the Divine wrath, and the greatness of that power which can
raise and still such tempests when He pleases."

It is beside the point to write more of the stylistic virtues
of Fray Luis, or to show with what skill and effect he employs
his love of Nature to add force and vividness to his moral and
ascetic writings.   " His single aim," says his biographer Muñoz
again and again, " was to lead souls to heaven " ; into this task
he put all his talents and his powers.

But he wrote too, though in a secondary degree, for the
journeyer on the Mystic Way ; and when Muñoz tells us of his

---

[1] He was translated by Francis Meres among others.   It seems probable
that Donne knew the *Sinner's Guide* at least of Fray Luis' works.

[2] " I walk'd the other day to spend my hour. . . ."

love of solitude we are doubtless at the secret of some of his
most inspired passages. These will be found principally in
the *Book of Prayer and Meditation*, in the *Memorial of the
Christian Life* and in the *Additions* to the latter book. Most
readers will wish to read these books as written, irrespective of
the mystical or non-mystical nature of particular passages, but
those who so prefer may excerpt chapters from each work,
which, when put together, give an adequate, if not a complete
account of the Mystic Life.

Few, Fray Luis admits,—or rather, emphasises—can even
hope to attain to the summit of that life [1] : " to give up all but
God and to be joined in spirit with Him in continual and most
ardent love." [2] Precisely what this happy state may be Fray Luis
can hardly be said to make clear, and only in a more detailed
study could his description of it be adequately discussed. But
from his predecessors in mystical theology he takes such terms
as "the transformation of the soul in God Himself," [3] though
he does not, like his successors in Spain, apply the even bolder
phrases, such as those which speak of " deification."

The road to such a lofty goal is described at length,
though more is said of the essential qualities of the mystic—
humility, perseverance, and the like—than of the actual self-
training which he needs. Occasionally we find passages like
the following,—true enough but insufficient to serve as a guide
for the aspirant.

First this love brings with it a knowledge by experience
of the goodness, sweetness and nobility of God ; through the
which knowledge comes a wondrous enkindling of the will, and
this leads to a marvellous joy ; from the joy comes a very ardent
desire after God, from the desire a new satiety, from the satiety
an inebriation, whence a security and a perfect repose in God,
in Whom the soul has its rest and spiritual Sabbath. [4]

Any reader of these books will see that Fray Luis says

---

[1] *Memorial, etc.*, Tratado VII.
[2] *Introducción del Símbolo de la Fe* (Obras IX, 86).
[3] *Adiciones, ed. cit.*, p. 31.
[4] *Memorial, etc., ed. cit.* p. 539.

little of purgation in direct connection with the mystical life.
It may even be thought that he presents that life as essentially
positive—as a life of continuous desire and perhaps of continual achievement.   But if purgation is not made a distinct
stage in the progression towards Union it is only because in
Fray Luis' mind and writings the purgative life is another
name for life itself.   Some of the greatest Spanish mystics are
for ever warning their readers against over-indulgence in self-
mortification.   Not so Luis de Granada.   Whether in exhorta-
tion or exposition, he is continually to be found insisting upon
the necessity for bodily discipline, for the aspirant and the
proficient alike.   " Nada es lo que nada cuesta," is his text :
" that which costs us nothing is worth nothing." [1]   And he
even goes so far as to say of the typical exercises of self-
mortification : " Seldom is devotion found apart from these
exercises, or the exercises without devotion." [2]   It will readily
be understood that the mysticism of so thorough an ascetic
needs to assign no place of its own to purgation, for this is ever
with him.

[1] *Memorial, etc., ed. cit.*, p. 558.
[2] *Libro de la oración y meditación, ed. cit.*, pp. 317-18.

CHAPTER III

THE CARMELITE SAINTS

SO we come to the two greatest of all the Castilian mystics, —and first to Teresa de Jesús, foundress, mystic and saint, reformer of the Order of Carmel, and unquestionably the greatest woman in the history of Spanish Literature, if not in the history of Spain. The good fortune which has preserved her correspondence during the last twenty years of her life allows us to remove the trappings of the saint and to see and reverence the woman's form beneath. From the letters,—so natural, practical and intimate, yet so deeply spiritual—we should hardly suspect the mystic, still less the gilded figure of tradition whose vile body was the subject of more posthumous and repulsive " honours " than one can think about with comfort. She stands revealed in them as a woman of amazing common-sense with a turn for business and a considerable gift of quiet humour. Martha and Mary have seldom been so well combined as in the personality of St. Teresa.

The combination is seen at its best in the mystic writings. Her autobiography presents the mystic life as she knew it in 1562,—and how striking it is that the succeeding years, during which she was leading the busy life of a foundress, were those in which she travelled longest and farthest on the Mystic Road ! The first similitude which she employs to describe the life of the contemplative is that of the watered garden :

It seems to me that the garden can be watered in four ways : by taking water from a well, which costs us much labour; or by a water-wheel and buckets, when the water is drawn by a windlass—I have drawn it thus at times : it is less laborious than the other way, and gives more water ;—or by a stream or a brook, which waters the ground much better, for it becomes more thoroughly saturated, and there is less need to water it often, and the gardener's labour is much less ; or by showers of rain, when the Lord Himself waters it without any labour of ours, and this way is incomparably the best.[1]

In the exposition of this similitude occurs the description of that " Prayer of Quiet " which she learned largely from Francisco de Osuna, though a later and more adequate account of it is found in the *Mansions*, written in the year 1577. In this book St. Teresa describes her pilgrim's progress towards the goal of Union as that of a traveller walking through the several rooms of a palace till he reaches the innermost of all :

I shall think of our soul as of a castle, formed of a single diamond or of a transparent crystal, in which are many rooms, just as in Heaven there are many mansions. . . . Some of these are above, others below, others on either side ; and in the centre, in the midst of them all, is the chiefest of them, where many things most secret pass between God and the soul.[2]

In the final chapters of the *Mansions* St. Teresa exhausts her storehouses of metaphor as she endeavours to describe the bliss of the Unitive Life,—the Marriage of the Soul and the Divine Lover. But St. Teresa never forgets that these experiences are for the few, and in her earlier chapters she spends equal care in describing the outer Mansions, where most of those who read her books must of necessity be content to stay. The postulants for admission into the castle precincts, we read, are "still very worldly" and have only "some" desire to do well.[3] The first Mansions, accordingly, are of Humility ; the second, of the Practice of Prayer ; the third of Meditation and Exemplary Life, the farthest point reached by any but the mystically-minded. In the fourth Mansion we have the Prayer of Quiet, in which the soul is at rest and near our Lord, and the faculties of the soul, " by quiet contemplation, are able to realise in Whose Presence they are."[4]

[1] *Libro de su vida*, XI, 4.   [2] *Moradas*, I, i.   [3] *Ibid.*, I, ii.
[4] *Ibid.*, IV, ii.   Cf. *Conceptos del Amor de Dios*, IV, i, and *Camino de Perfección*, XXXI, 1.

Those who would learn more of St. Teresa's experience of the Prayer of Quiet may find it in her equally well-known *Way of Perfection* written not long after the *Book of Her Life*. The highest states of prayer, however, are most graphically described in the *Mansions*. The fifth Mansions speak of the Prayer of Union,—or, as other writers term it, the Spiritual Betrothal—in which the soul is asleep, "both to the things of this world and to itself,"[1] but which is an experience of brief duration only. The sixth Mansions represent a state of greater favours still, but also of great spiritual affliction, the soul being "wounded with love for her Spouse,"[2] and the Bridegroom receiving her plaints with silence.[3] After the space of many chapters St. Teresa at last leads us into the innermost Presence, and we read of the Marriage of the Soul and her Divine Lover. This is no passing experience, but one which remains for ever. It is complete transformation and complete Union : "it may be called another Heaven."[4]

As she writes of these intimate experiences the practical woman, the rude verse-writer, the homely prose stylist is transformed, by the very ardour of her white-hot zeal, into the most eloquent of inspired contemplatives.

> From thence,
> I learn'd to know that Love is eloquence,

says Crashaw of her, truly. Yet the glory of St. Teresa is that all her ecstasies and raptures, all the rare joys of her ascent of Mount Carmel do not hinder, but rather inspire her to help those who are still on the lower slopes, and struggling upward. Patient mother, as she was, of her spiritual children, she is the patient instructress of those who while drinking of her "brim-fill'd bowls of fierce desire" find the way of attainment beyond them. She directs their lives, as few other writers can, to "the true Orient, Christ." And for that age as for this she did well. It may not be summed up by the number or the greatness of its mystic sons.

---

[1] *Moradas*, V, i.   [2] *Ibid.*, VI, i.
[3] *Ibid.*, VI, i., ii.   [4] *Ibid.*, VII, i.

It preferred an arid treatise on the vanity of the world to a
golden book of *Meditations on the Love of God*.[1] It knew
Luis de Granada as orator and ascetic, but not as mystic.
And Juan de Avila did well to write for it a book of popular
devotion, reserving for a few intimate friends the letters in
which he permitted himself to write of the Mystic Life.

What could such an age have to say to the most ethereal of the
Spanish mystics? For so we may call St. Teresa's friend and
disciple, fellow reformer and fellow sufferer, known familiarly
in this country as St. John of the Cross. This great writer
reached heights unknown either before or since in Spain : we
may doubt if his finest raptures have been, or can be, surpassed.
Primarily, he is a poet, and as such is among the first in
Spanish literature. And nearly all his work centres round
three of his own poems : *On a dark night, Where art Thou
hid ?* and *O Living Flame of Love.*

In his long prose commentaries on these poems he gives
the fullest and most eloquent description of the Mystic Way to
be found in the language. From the spiritual awakening of
the pilgrim,—the first stage of all—we follow him (in the *Dark
Night of the Soul*) through the phases of reflection and meditation to the point where he sets his foot firmly upon the contemplative path.

The House of Sense is left behind, and the soul is plunged
into that Night of Purgation which gives the first book its
name :

> Upon an obscure night,
> Fevered with love in love's anxiety,
> (O hapless, happy plight !)
> I went, none seeing me,
> Forth from my house where all things quiet be.
>
> .   .   .   .
>
> Blest night of wandering,
> In secret, where by none might I be spied,
> Nor I see anything ;
> Without a light or guide,
> Save that which in my heart burnt in my side.[2]

[1] See under Diego de Estella, pp. 34-5 below.
[2] From Mr. Arthur Symons' translation.

The realistic chapters which describe the Dark Night must be read by all those who would study San Juan de la Cruz, for they are intensely characteristic of his teaching. Not less so is the second period of darkness, that Dark Night of the Spirit which succeeds the state of Illumination (that is, the Spiritual Betrothal) and must be passed through by all who would know the mysteries of complete Union. One thinks of Vaughan's well-known lines:

> There is in God—some say—
> A deep but dazzling darkness ; as men here
> Say it is late and dusky, because they
> See not all clear.
> O for that Night ! where I in Him
> Might live invisible and dim !

But the Dark Night of the Spirit, as conceived by St. John of the Cross, is something more terrible than this "Divine darkness" which is familiar to all readers of mystical literature. In it "the spirit is purified and laid bare, to be disposed and made ready for union in love with God." [1] The full light of the Divine Wisdom beats upon the soul not yet perfected. She sees naught but the blackness of her own wretched state, and, most of all, she is afflicted by "what seems to her a clear perception that God has abandoned her—that He utterly loathes her and has cast her into darkness. The thought of abandonment by God is a great and a grievous affliction. . . . All this, and even more, the soul feels now, for with fearful apprehension she dreads that it will be so with her for ever." [2]

Yet even through so dreadful a Night, the soul presses forward, on fire with the love of God, and considering only how she may reach Him, till at length she reaches the goal of Union —the "Spiritual Marriage."

Lofty as is this state, St. John of the Cross enters boldly upon the description of it, and to the intellect at least he makes clear how great are its glories. "It is a complete transformation of the soul in the Beloved, whereby each surrenders to the

---

[1] *Noche Oscura*, I, viii.   [2] *Ibid.*, II, vi.

other the entire possession of itself in the consummation of Love's union; herein the soul becomes divine—becomes God, by participation in God—so far, that is, as in this life may be possible." [1]   The union of the two—of lover and Beloved—is more real even than that of two candle-flames, or of two rays of the sun.

A superficial reading of San Juan de la Cruz is sufficient to show how he differs from St. Teresa.   He has little of her human and humorous solicitude for the weaker brethren, and her ever-keen sense of their limitations.   He starts from a higher level, and never once looks down.   He speaks " wisdom among them that are perfect . . . the wisdom of God in a mystery, even the hidden wisdom."   But if he mounts with ease through mists of doubt to heights above the clouds which none but he (or so to the wondering reader it seems) has ever trod, he tells from those heights, so simply and convincingly, of things too sacred for common words, that one scarcely realises, in reading, their divine nature.

Pre-eminent as a mystic, St. John of the Cross is equally so, as has been suggested above, as a lyric poet.   None before nor since has drawn such music from a language so exquisitely musical, while appealing to the imagination and the emotions of all those to whom religion and poetry are more than names. The opening lines of the *Dark Night* are surely unsurpassed and unsurpassable for sheer beauty.   Hardly inferior to that poem is the *Spiritual Canticle*, that song of the wandering lover, which combines with its wealth of mystical significance the most delicate sensibility towards Nature.   We hear the " sounding cataracts," the rustling of the gentlest breeze, the song of the nightingale, the trickling of the stream ; feel the breath of the wind stirred by the cedars, the still, silent evening, the deep calm of night, the howling storm and the driving rain ; catch the perfume of the lily, the rose, the fragrant ambar ; see the woods and meadows, the islands of an undiscovered sea, the deserted valleys, the forests infested by wild beasts, the wounded stag panting on the hillside, the dove finding her mate

[1] *Cántico* XXII.

safe by the grassy banks. The third of the greatest lyrics, *O Living Flame of Love*, is equally rich in meaning, and makes equal use of imagery, but of the imagery of light. Throbbing ceaselessly through it is that flame which wounds, and, as it wounds, heals. Shedding soft radiance over it are the seven strangely beauteous lamps with which God pierces the deep caverns of feeling that He may perfectly illumine the perfect soul :

> O lamps of fire that shined
> With so intense a light,
> That those deep caverns where the senses live,
> Which were obscure and blind,
> Now with strange glories bright,
> Both heat and light to his belovèd give.
>
> With how benign intent
> Rememberest thou my breast
> Where thou alone abidest secretly,
> And in thy sweet ascent,
> With glory and good possessed,
> How delicately thou teachest love to me ! [1]

[1] From Mr. Arthur Symons' translation.

CHAPTER IV

THE LATER MYSTICS

FAR below the Carmelite Saints, yet so high as in any other age to be pre-eminent, come three writers somewhat later in date, each of whom made important contributions to mystical literature. First of these is the Augustinian Pedro Malón de Chaide, whose beautiful work entitled *The Conversion of the Magdalen* was only published, after his death, in 1592, though it had been written many years previously.[1]

Malón de Chaide was a poet—a fact which is as manifest in his prose, as in the verse translations of psalms and in the "divine songs" which he intersperses in his treatise, apologising quite needlessly for doing so. As we read those few sonnets, which he modestly describes as "not the choicest nor most skilfully penned in the world"[2] we wish that he might have given us more. But his prose, if somewhat unequal, is vigorous and effective in its attack, fertile, and, indeed, often brilliant in exposition. Were it more moderate and restrained, Malón de Chaide might take a place beside his greatest contemporaries in pure literature.

The *Conversion of the Magdalen* is avowedly a popular book, composed "to be put into the hands of the vulgar" as a counter-attraction to the profane works of fiction then so much in vogue. "A little girl who can hardly walk will have a *Diana* in her pocket,"[1] says the author. And to "amend the great harm which many of these books may do,"[3] this book and others like it have been written. One would not, then,

---

[1] *Conversión de la Magdalena : Prólogo.*
[2] *Ibid.* [3] *Ibid.*

expect to find in it the themes of the *Mansions* or of the *Dark Night of the Soul*. Much that is expressed in those books may indeed be read into it and illuminated by it, but it will not be studied for its descriptions of mystic experience any more than for its philosophical digressions or its literary style. Its supreme attractions are in the mystical spirit which inspires it, in its warmth and colour, and the ardour with which it relates and interprets the tenderest, most human and most moving of narratives. These have won for it, and rightly, a place in the affections of Spain.

To those who identify St. Mary Magdalene with the sister of Martha and Lazarus, and with the "woman that was a sinner" who anointed the feet of Christ in Simon's house, she cannot but be the New Testament symbol of the mystic. It is significant that the Catholic Church, which has appointed, as the Gospel of her Feast, the story of the anointing, has chosen for the Lesson that panegyric of love which is the greatest glory of the Song of Songs, and the starting-point of the mystic's progress.[1] So the expositor of that Gospel (for such an exposition the book really is) begins his task with a discourse upon divine love, which is little more than an anthology of the greatest things which have been said upon it by the inspired writers and by the Fathers.[2]

It would take overmuch space to write of all the mystical and semi-mystical themes of which Fray Pedro treats: the sufficiency and power of love, the conception of God as the Universal centre and the nature of Union are the chief. As to Union, he holds opinions of its essence far less lofty than those of St. Teresa and San Juan de la Cruz. But his picture of Mary, after the Saviour's death, seeking a desert place where she may live alone with her Beloved, and later ascending to the place whither He has gone, with Him continually to dwell, is hardly, on its own plane, surpassable. It is certain that many will learn as much from this book about the Mystic Way as

---

[1] *Cant.* III, 1-5, and (the passage referred to) VIII, 6-7.
[2] *Conversión de la Magdalena*, Parte 1ª, § 1.

from those authors who have devoted themselves entirely to writing of it.

Malón de Chaide is sometimes termed by Spanish writers the "metaphysician of love": the Franciscan, Juan de los Ángeles, who has been called its psychologist and moralist,[1] may therefore conveniently be compared with him. An Andalucian, he has been eulogised for the softness and sweetness of his style, in terms which, typically southern, lose their force when translated into our own language.[2] But he can be severe and rugged enough on occasion. More noteworthy even than his vast erudition is the keenness of the insight into human nature which leaves few honest readers unscathed: the passages on *amor propio*,[3] for example, and the dialogue on Introversion in the *Conquest*,[4] are among Spanish students of mysticism as well known as they deserve. Constantly quoting Gerson, Ruysbroeck and Tauler, he is among the few Spaniards of his age to be directly influenced by contemporary foreign mysticism. But he never ceases for a moment to be Spanish. As striking as his learning and his style is the vivid imagination which his suave manner re-enforces. He is full of unforgettable phrases: the very titles of his treatises invite one to read him: *The Garden of the Faithful Soul, The Conquest of the Kingdom of God* (how full of meaning that phrase to sixteenth-century Spain!), *A Spiritual Strife between God and the Soul, The Triumphs of the Love of God.* . . .

The *Conquest* is a series of dialogues between a spiritual director and his disciple, treating of the interior life. Part of it deals with the duties of self-control incumbent upon every Christian, with the subject of penitence, and with the Passion

---

[1] Rousselot, *op. cit.*, p. 114.

[2] Particularly I think of Menéndez Pelayo's oft-quoted phrase: " Uno de los más suaves y regalados prosistas castellanos, cuya oración es río de leche y miel." (*Cf. Ideas estéticas*, 2nd ed., 1896, pp. 131-6.) *Cf.* also contemporary and other testimonies collected by Fr. Jaime Sala (ed. *N.B.A.E.*, pp. li ff.). Notably that of Juan Molina who describes Fr. Juan as " sacando suavemente para los fieles de la Iglesia miel de la piedra y aceite de la durísima roca, esto es, de la corteza de su letra desgranar con sus manos las espigas y darles a comer con gran contentamiento la médula espiritual que entraña."

[3] *Lucha Espiritual*, I, 15-17.

[4] *Conquista del Reino de Dios*, Diálogos IX, X.

and Death of Christ. The more properly mystical chapters
occur here and there within the work ; there is, in fact, no well-
marked progression from one dialogue to another. That which
describes the four gates to the Kingdom is particularly rich in
meaning, and the dialogues on introversion (IX, X) and contemplative exercises (VIII), are equally so, while other passages
such as that which is here translated on " The Soul's Intimacy "[1]
take us into heights which few have scaled. The *Manual of
Perfect Life*, as its title may be thought to imply, is mainly
ascetic. Written in the same dialogue form as the *Conquest*, it
deals mainly with such matters as friendships, carnal temptations, deadly sin, vocal prayer and meditation. But it also
speaks, with a directness and a detail which recall St. Teresa's
Mansions, of the lower stages of the mystical life and of
aspiration to the life of union, if not its realisation. The
Spiritual Strife is described in its sub-title as " revealing the
greatness and the triumphs of love, and showing forth that most
excellent way of the affections." Its prologue says that its aim
is "to show that for the soul that would approach God and
unite itself with Him in spirit, there is no other way than by
love, whose property is to transform the lover into the object of
his love, and to bring about the straitest unity." Accordingly
Fray Juan deals first with the nature of love, its conflict and its
wounds, its privileges and joys, and the intimacies to which it
leads. Among the many traits of interest in this book is a
chapter on the Divine Darkness, which, however, is written
mainly out of an acquaintance with the classical writers upon
that subject.

Omitting the mainly doctrinal *Garden of the Soul*, the long
commentary on the *Song of Songs*, and a number of minor
works, we come to the *Triumphs of the Love of God*. This is
perhaps Fray Juan's masterpiece. Starting from the individual
soul he describes its nature, its powers and passions, and especially the degrees and depths of its capability for love, before
saying anything of his true subject. Such a procedure is full

---

[1] See p. 136 below.

3

of meaning as illustrating both Fray Juan's own temperament
and the psychological tendencies of Spanish mysticism in
general.   From the point now reached he passes to the subject
of the mystic's love for God, his desire for union and transformation, and the way of mental prayer which if followed will bring
the few who may reach it to their goal.   The treatise is one of
the most valuable which Spain has produced.   While never
marking out the mystic road as exactly as does St. Teresa,
Juan de los Ángeles deals in detail, and in something like a
true progression, with each of its stages.   Nor does he forget
the beginner, his chapters on the Blessed Sacrament, on ejacu-
latory prayer, on the ordering of one's devotions and the like
being written as well for the wayfaring man as for the proficient.
The appeal of the book, nevertheless, is primarily to the mystic,
whose fervent love, which inspires it, it cannot but in its turn
inspire.

The third of the mystics slightly later in date than St.
Teresa is Diego de Estella, who, not alone of Spanish mystics,
influenced St. François de Sales.   Of his books two only are still
generally read, even by his own countrymen.   One of these is
a treatise on the Vanity of the World, which in its author's own
age—even in his lifetime—was translated into English as the
Contempt of the World and the Vanity thereof.   The other,
which has until recent times, and most unfortunately, been over-
shadowed by it, is a collection of one hundred *Meditations on
the Love of God* which, if not always dealing with the mystical
life, at least breathes in every chapter the mystic's spirit.   A
Franciscan like Juan de los Ángeles, he dwells no less upon
man's love to God than upon God's love toward man.   He
takes us back to the simple but ardent language of the Carmelites,
far away from theories and learning, quoting few authorities for
his words.   If he repeats himself from time to time it is to
emphasise truths which will bear eternal repetition ; for his
book is avowedly a series of short meditations and not a con-
nected treatise.   This, too, is no doubt the reason that we find
no formal account of the mystic life, but only isolated passages
which often might well be unintelligible to those who already

know nothing of it. Such are the meditations on the unitive life and the transformation of the Lover in the Beloved, which in no uncertain way speak of the writer's experience and prove that he could have written, if not like San Juan de la Cruz, at least like Fray Juan de los Ángeles.

We have no wish, in what is but an introductory survey, to trace the course of Spanish mysticism through its period of decadence and decline in the seventeenth century to a point well-nigh of extinction in the eighteenth. In a study which for reasons of space has dismissed the Carmelite and Franciscan mystics in a few paragraphs and has omitted entirely some twenty or thirty writers who have a claim on us at least as strong as that of many whom we have mentioned, it would be an ill-advised anti-climax to say much of Francisco Ribera or Alonso Rodríguez, still more so to write of Molinos and the quietist school or of such works as find an echo in the life of a Sor María de Ágreda. It is enough to note that, under influences which cannot now be detailed, not Spain alone but many another country was brought under the influence of a pseudo-mysticism which described the aspirant's " progress "— for the term is hardly consonant with the reality—in words like these :

The soul that seeks to be perfect begins to mortify its passions ; and when it is advanced in that exercise, it denies itself; then, with the divine aid, it passes to the state of nothingness, wherein it despises, abhors and immerses itself ; knowing itself to be nothing, that it can do nothing, and that it is worth nothing. From hence follows a dying to itself, and to its senses, in many ways, and at all times ; and finally, from this spiritual death proceeds the true and perfect annihilation ; insomuch, that when the soul is once dead to its own will and understanding, it may properly be said to have reached the perfect and happy state of annihilation, which is the last dis- position for its transformation and union, though the soul itself doth not understand or comprehend it ; because if it could it would not be annihilated : And altho' it has got to the entrance of this happy state of annihilation, yet it must know, that it must still walk on, and must be further and further purified and annihilated.[1]

That such ideas, with others favoured by the exponents of quietism, impeccability and "illumination," should have developed naturally from those set forth by the mystics of the Golden Age is hardly possible. As we turn the pages of the *Spiritual Guide*, and mark its insistence upon "passive contemplation," "spiritual martyrdom," "perfect annihilation," and "nothingness" we are far from the mystics of conquered Granada and the spiritual "progress," "strife" and "warfare" of Carmelite and Franciscan. We therefore leave the degradations of pseudo-mysticism on one side and close our survey with an account of one who, in spirit at least, closes the great age of mysticism both in verse and in prose. This is the Augustinian scholar and poet, Fray Luis de León.

He closes it in more ways than one. During the whole of the sixteenth century the greatest mystics were consciously or unconsciously men of letters : the Golden Ages of mysticism and literature are, as has been said, inextricably interwoven with each other. Luis de León is the last great mystic to find a place—and that place a high one—in the story of Spanish literature. Again, he is the last of the mystics (within a few years at least) to preserve the sane, practical, realistic attitude towards the things of this world which marks Spanish mysticism as a whole. Another reason is allied to this. With Fray Luis we come nearer earth. Through his work there breathes a wind from a quarter unknown to his mystical contemporaries : the breath of the humanistic spirit. "It was humanism," says the greatest of living Salamancans, "which tempered the pure mysticism of Spain, reasonable as it was even when boldest, ever respecting reason's rights and laws. The principal worker of this partnership was Luis de León. . . . Classicist and hebraizer, he combined the spirit of Greek humanism with that of Hebrew prophecy ; he held, in the sixteenth century, what a modern thinker would call the faith of the twentieth." [2]

[1] Molinos : *Spiritual Guide*, II, 19. For interest the translation is taken from an English edition dated 1775.

[2] Miguel de Unamuno : *En torno al casticismo*, p. 173.

Fray Luis is indeed a mystic with a difference, and we must
read him as such.   He has nothing of the ascetic's spirit ; on
the contrary, he is a faithful disciple of Horace, and an upholder
of comfort and moderation.   In this as in other respects he
forms a striking contrast to Fray Luis de Granada, just as the
calm and placid style of the one may be contrasted with the
torrents of the other's eloquence.   In their love of nature, however, the two are not unlike.   It was a happy day for the
Salamancan friar when he learned to realise that "Christ
dwells in the fields." [1]   And thenceforward he found Him in
the woods and gardens where he walked, in the placid river
which flowed through his native city, in the songs of the birds,
in the sunshine and the starlight : especially in the starlight,
of which he writes in lines that in their original are famous
throughout Spain :

> When I behold the sky
> With stars innumerable spangled bright,
> And then the Earth descry
> Encompassèd with night,
> Buried in sleep, oblivion infinite,
>
> Sorrow and love arise
> And with a burning fever fill my breast,
> And ever from my eyes
> The tears flow without rest
> Till my tongue speaks at last, with grief oppressed :
>
> O dwelling of great might,
> Temple of lovely light incomparable,
> My soul that to thy height
> At birth aspired, what spell
> Doth in this dark, low prison-house compel ? [2]

All this is to him most wonderful ; "Nature's vast ever-acting
energy" indeed appals him, but Nature's face is also a mirror
in which his spiritual life and his innermost self are reflected.
Here we touch the true mystic, and in thoughts like these lies

[1] *Nombres de Cristo:* ' Pastor.'
[2] " Noche Serena " (see pp. 169-72 below).

much of the attraction both of the hardly surpassable poems and of the *Names of Christ*.

The origin of this series of conversations upon the subject of its title we have already discussed,[1] and of its theme it is enough to say that Fray Luis develops it with fervency and devotion as well as with literary skill. It will always be a classic in Spain. But a few words must be added upon the peculiar type of mysticism which it reveals, and which is found also in the poems. While, on the one hand, there is but seldom in Luis de León's aspirations any desire for absorption, transformation or annihilation of his personality in that of Another, there is a continual, insatiable, and overwhelming desire for peace. It is when he thinks of Christ as the Prince of Peace that his longings are most deeply stirred, and his noble conception of that desired haven as a state in which the soul is in perfect harmony with God inspires his finest passages. Towards the attainment of that goal the friar whose own temperament was ever restless and unquiet like his life on earth, directs all his energies and cares.

Indubitably he has no thought of reaching a state of union so lofty as that described by San Juan de la Cruz, before the final consummation of bliss in the life to come. Yet his ideal is a high one, and he traces the steps which lead to it with the full consciousness of its greatness. A beautiful passage on "the birth of Christ in the soul" describes the mystical gifts of prayer, the "glories of contemplation" and the "ecstasies of the spirit," while more than once we have glimpses of Fray Luis' ideal state, in words which recall the language of his greatest mystical contemporaries.

For all his kinship with the Renaissance, he has much in common with these; and as one reads his work, its diversity and comprehensiveness become more amazing. On no more striking a personage, on none with a richer storehouse of treasure could we close a survey intended merely to give an idea of the vastness of a scarcely navigated ocean. We may

---

[1] See pp. 12-13 above.

say of Spanish Mysticism, as Luis de León says of the mystic life itself:

The tale is endless; for as I let out the sails, even then do I catch fresh vistas to be explored; and the farther I journey, the wider are the seas which come into my view.[1]

[1] *Nombres de Cristo :* ' Faces de Dios.'

CHAPTER V

THE BASIS OF SPANISH MYSTICISM

HOW deeply mysticism is implanted in the soul of Spain the foregoing pages testify. It is but natural that the blooms of so intensely native a plant should not only be of singular profusion and beauty, but also bear a character of their own. Of their beauty, those who read must judge. To their profusion, the three hundred mystical writers and the three thousand or more of their works will bear witness. Their individual character, however, is scarcely less noticeable than their number, and it is not hard to discover the traits which are most representative of the mysticism of Spain and at the same time distinguish it recognisably from that of other lands.

First and most strikingly of all,[1] Spanish mysticism has little to do with metaphysics. To some extent, this is to its loss. The Spaniard has ever abhorred abstractions and subtleties; he has even disliked systems in general; and he has never been at home with the professor of philosophy.[2] To say this, of course, is not necessarily to endorse the oft-quoted dictum of Rousselot that mysticism " was for long the true philosophy of Spain," [3] much less to deny to Spain her philosophers or to depreciate the part played by Neo-Platonism in the Spanish

---

[1] If we except, as a somewhat negative characteristic, the striking fact that these writers formed no school, certain of them even appearing ignorant of the existence of contemporary mystical writers in Spain at all. Let it be noted here that no one of the traits cited below is claimed as characteristic exclusively of Spanish mysticism. It is the combination of all the characteristics in nearly every Spanish mystic that gives the movement its individuality.

[2] La ciencia cuyo mayor título de nobleza está en *no servir para nada* (según la opinión del vulgo). Menéndez y Pelayo, *Ciencia Española*, I, 96, *n.*

[3] *Op. cit.*, p. 3.

Renaissance.[1]   But it is essential to realise the Spanish love for
the concrete and substantial,—even for action rather than for
speculation, though the casual observer may find this difficult
to believe.   More than one keen thinker and student, nevertheless, has given expression to so extreme a view.   " It is a
mystery of our race—this dislike of the abstract—" says
Menéndez Pelayo.   " The propensities of the Spanish people
are all for action." [2]   " The soul of Spain," is Angel Ganivet's
view, " speaks through its deeds, for thoughts can be expressed
in many ways, and the best way is not always by speech."
So he draws a picture of Spain leaving subtleties to the school-
men and expressing truth in the language of war.   " Our
theological and philosophical *Summa*," he ends, " was in our
Romancero." [3]

This aversion to abstractions is nowhere better reflected
than in the Spanish mystics.   They are skilled practical
psychologists, superb " directors " of the consciences of individual souls, and well able to throw their experiences into
works which appeal no less to the many than to the few.
Commonplaces for them simply do not exist : St. Teresa's
' Entre los pucheros anda el Señor ' is unforgettable.[4]   They
owe little to their predecessors, save to the Bible and the
Fathers, whom they quote and adapt continually.   Yet their
mysticism is not derived from the Fathers [5] but from their own
experience.   Their writings and their lives alike are simple,
their faith is spontaneous, the conception which they hold of
the " infused science " is devoid of subtleties and somewhat shy
even of generalisation.

[1] *Cf*. Rousselot, *op. cit*., p. 55.

[2] *Op. cit*., I, 94.   " I speak of Spain as she is," he adds, " and not of the
fantastic and chivalrous country pictured by the foreigner."

[3] *Cf*. J. E. Rodó : *El mirador de Prospero* (essay entitled ' El Cristo a la
Jineta '), and Azorín's essay : ' El Genio Castellano.'

[4] Even more so than the well-known lines, inspired by a similar thought :

> Who sweeps a room as for Thy laws
> Makes that and th' action fine.

[5] Occasional important exceptions have been noted here and there in this
book.

"Castilian mysticism has its starting-point neither in the abstract idea of the One, nor in the world of representations whence it may rise to know the *invisibilia Dei per ea quæ facta sunt.* . . . It proceeds from the introspective knowledge of the self, the eyes being closed to the sensible and even to the intelligible in order to reach the bare essence and centre of the soul, which is God, and to be united in "substantial experience" with Divine Wisdom and Love."[1]

All this is but another way of saying that Spanish mysticism is intensely fervid, realistic and personal. Nothing could be less like pantheism, nothing farther from self-annihilation. St. Teresa's first mystical work is a Book of her own Life. Luis de León writes *On Self-knowledge.* "The soul's first step," says San Juan de la Cruz, "towards a knowledge of God is a knowledge of itself."[2] In truth, the Spanish mystic's primary care is to know himself, and this to him is an inseparable part of his great ideal—to know and to be one with God. In the mysticism of any Christian there is much of this: it is almost inherent in any true definition of the word. But in Spain it has unparalleled force and intensity: we are never far away from it. Long ago in the Middle Ages Ramón Lull had preached on the theme of God and the Soul:

Said the Lover to his Beloved: 'Thou art all, and through all, and in all, and with all. I would give Thee all of myself that I may have all of Thee, and Thou all of me.'[3]

The Lover said to the people: 'He who truly remembers my Beloved, in remembering Him forgets all things around.'[4]

They said to the Lover: 'Whither goest thou?' He answered, 'I come from my Beloved.' 'Whence comest thou?' 'I go to my Beloved.' 'When wilt thou return?' 'I shall be with my Beloved.'[5]

But even the *Book of the Lover and the Beloved* must yield in this respect to the sixteenth-century mystics. "I for God and

---

[1] Miguel de Unamuno: *En torno al casticismo,* p. 153. *Cf.* Azorín's essay 'El Genio Castellano,' in *Lecturas españolas,* pp. 29-30.

[2] *Avisos y sentencias espirituales* (ed. B.A.E., XXVII), 300.

[3] *Libre d'Amich e Amat,* 67.   [4] *Ibid.,* 132.   [5] *Ibid.,* 24.

God for me, and no world beside!" cries Juan de los Angeles.[1]
"Nought is needful, save only God."[2]   "For He is the centre of
our soul, the resting-place of our desires, and the sphere of our
love."[3]   The hammer-strokes of the *Maxims* of San Juan de la
Cruz beat out again and again the same message:

Keep the image of God alone and clearly in thy soul.

By this may be known the soul which in truth loves God,
if it is content with nothing save only with God.

To find all delight in God, the soul must find its only
delight in Him.

Enter within thyself and work in the presence of the Spouse
of thy soul, which is God.

Live in the world as if there were in it but God and thy
soul.[4]

"God and the soul"—"myself and God."   This is the only
world of the typical Spanish mystic:

> Wenn ich ihn nur habe,
> Wenn er mein nur ist,
> Wenn mein Herz bis hin zum Grabe
> Seine Treue nie vergisst:
> Weiss ich nichts von Leide,
> Fühle nichts als Andacht, Lieb' und Freude.
>
> Wenn ich ihn nur habe,
> Lass' ich alles gern,
> Folg' an meinem Wanderstabe
> Treugesinnt nur meinem Herrn,
> Lasse still die Andern
> Breite, lichte, volle Strassen wandern.[5]

Hardly less important, and in greater need of emphasis, is
the active character of the mystic's faith.   Even if an impersonal
creed were possible to men so robust as those we have to deal
with, their introspective habits would save them from it.   A
pseudo-mysticism, quietistic to a degree, was later to develop in
Spain: an ideal of complete passivity—of self-annihilation—on

[1] *Lucha Espiritual*, I, xi. : " Yo para Dios y Dios para mí, y no más mundo."
[2] *Ibid.*, I, x.   [3] *Ibid.*, Proemio.
[4] *Avisos y sentencias espirituales* (ed. B.A.E., Vol. XXVII), 26, 60, 84, 206,
345.
[5] Novalis: *Geistliche Lieder.*

the one hand, and a rude, sensual *alumbrismo* on the other,
were to supersede the pure aspiration of the Lover for the
Beloved.   But the mysticism of the Golden Age is active,
ardent, militant, as befitted an ardent and militant race.   It
aims at affirming, not denying, the power of the human will.[1]
Its bowmen bear the "arrows of desire," and press upon
Heaven with no "lazy breath" but with a "sharp dart of longing love."   St. Teresa's Christian presses on—progresses—from
mansion to mansion.   Juan de los Ángeles describes the mystical
strife of man with God, or the storming of the gateways of His
mystic Kingdom.   The pilgrim of the *Dark Night of the Soul*
descends his staircase, leaves the house at dead of night, and
journeys to his Goal.   The traveller makes the steep ascent of
Mount Carmel, or of Mount Zion.   The betrothed seeks her
Loved One, travelling from one land to another with tireless
zeal.   Even Orozco and Luis de León, for all their insistence
on the joys of peace, write much of the road which leads to it.
"But I would warn thee, my brother," says the former, even
while writing of the highest degree of contemplation, "that he
who would see the face of that most powerful Wrestler, our
boundless God, must first have wrestled with himself, and be a
man that is perfect in the active life."[2]   There is no passivity
here,—rather (as has been well said) a "divine knight errantry."[3]
Only in the state of Union can true rest be found : till then, all
is energy, activity, strife.

A few critics, it is true, have thought to find "traces," here
of pantheism, there of quietism, in stray passages.   Vaughan,
whose chapters on the Spanish mystics—or rather on two of
them—are all but a caricature, actually considers St. Teresa a

---

[1] Oliveira Martins, a Portuguese writer, goes so far as to say in an interesting,
though little known book (*O mysticismo, principio de energia do caracter peninsular*,
Lisboa, 1879. *Cf.* pp. 178-84) :—

O mysticismo hespanhol tem este caracter proprio, unico, e verdadeiramente
novo na Europa : é a affirmação da Vontade humana.

[2] See pp. 58-9 below.

[3] A "caballería a lo divino" : the phrase is hardly translateable (Oliveira
Martins, *op. cit.*, p. 182).

truer quietist than Molinos.[1] Lea finds both quietism and pantheism in San Juan de la Cruz, and suggests that the errors for which the quietists were condemned passed unnoticed in his writings.[2] Some of the passages cited describe those seasons of refreshing which the mystic like everyone, needs,—times at which his strength is to lie still. May he never "sit meek now and expect the light?" Others speak of the life of Union, the "transformation" of the soul, under images which, in truth, may easily enough be misunderstood. Yet even in these descriptions of the highest mystic state attainable by man, the "possession" of the Beloved is at least as prominent an idea as the "losing of oneself" in Him. The supreme joy of possession informs them all. As we read the *Spiritual Canticle*, the *Alphabet* or the *Ascent of Mount Zion* we think of such verses as Traherne's, every line of which throbs with an unbounded longing to attain:

> For giving me Desire,
> An eager thirst, a burning ardent fire,
> A virgin infant flame,
> A Love with which into the world I came,
> An inward hidden Heavenly love,
> Which in my soul did work and move,
> And ever ever me inflame
> With restless longing, Heavenly avarice,
> That never could be satisfied,
> That did incessantly a Paradise
> Unknown suggest, and something undescried
> Discern, and bear me to it : be
> Thy Name for ever praised by me.

There is the spirit of Spanish Mysticism. The saint who told her sisters in religion to "be as strong men" is not likely to preach Nirvana. Her 'quiet,' and the quiet of those for whom she stands, can only be "a rest most busy."

---

[1] " Who then is the Quietist—Molinos or Theresa? Both write books to mark out the mystic's pathway. Theresa adds the caution 'Sit still.' Manifestly, then, the excess of passivity lies with her." (*Hours with the Mystics*, II, 172.) This is only one instance of the author's many perversities.

[2] *Chapters in the Religious History of Spain*, pp. 225 ff.

If these are the traits the union of which particularly distinguishes Mysticism in Spain, it has also, and often in an intensified degree, all the characteristics common to Christian Mysticism in other lands. One has but to reflect once more upon the tremendous spiritual force behind the mystic ages, or upon the immensity of their output and the stores of mystic energy which this presupposes, to see that such must needs be the case. In Spain, if anywhere, we should have the finest qualities of mysticism in a deepened as well as a widened form. Can anything else explain why prejudice has been again and again set aside, and Catholic and Protestant have united in honouring and revering the two saints of Carmel? And does not that explain, too, the alleged " exaggerations " of the Spanish mystics which both parties have attacked: an ardent and consistent asceticism on the one hand, a frequent indifference to forms and ceremonies on the other? At least, it is possible.

Let us consider but one trait of brotherhood: the mystics' praise of love. In Spain, as emphatically as elsewhere, they have one and all pointed men from the paths of intellect and reason to the path of love. However earnestly they have desired the spiritual gifts—even the mystic's especial gifts—they have first followed after love. If the Spanish mystics have delighted in the *Song of Songs*—translated it, commented it, glossed it, preached upon it, suffered for it—the reason is surely in its centre and heart: that great pæan of earthly love, which they have ennobled and spiritualised in themselves:

> For love is strong as death ;
> Jealousy is cruel as the grave :
> The coals thereof are coals of fire,
> Which hath a most vehement flame.

> Many waters cannot quench love,
> Neither can the floods drown it :
> If a man would give all the substance of his house for love,
> It would utterly be contemned.

Here is their theme:

> Love, thou art absolute sole lord
> Of life and death.

Not Jacopone da Todi, not Richard Rolle, to whom love was life, not even St. Francis of Assisi himself, wrote more eloquently of love than the Fool of Love, Ramón Lull. The eloquent company of Spanish Franciscans in the Golden Age take up their master's theme. Yet the wonderful post-resurrection scenes in the *Conversion of the Magdalene* thrill with love as intense as the passionate words of any. The very titles of the works we have studied,—the mere headlines of our survey—bear the same testimony : *The Art of Loving God and our Neighbour*, *Conceptions of the Love of God*, *Treatise of the Love of God*, *Devout Meditations of the Love of God*, *Triumphs of the Love of God*. The greatest of the mystics are those who sang best of love : St. Teresa, as Crashaw felt when he penned his noble *Hymn*—San Juan de la Cruz, who knew that Living Flame of Love

> He gave us from His fire of fires, and bade
> Remember whence it sprang, nor be afraid
> While that burns on, though all the rest grows dark,

and defined "mystic theology" itself as "that infused contemplation in which God secretly instructs the soul, and instructs it in perfection of love."

Nor may we conclude without making remembrance of one whose very name is unknown to us, yet whose few simple lines are the greatest of Spanish hymns,—among the noblest, indeed, ever penned,—the hymn of the true Lover :

> No me mueve, mi Dios, para quererte,
> El cielo que me tienes prometido,
> Ni me mueve el infierno tan temido
> Para dejar por eso de ofenderte.
> ¡ Tú me mueves, Señor !
>
> .   .   .   .
>
> Muéveme, en fin, tu amor en tal manera,
> Que aunque no hubiera cielo yo te amara,
> Y aunque no hubiera infierno te temiera.

PART II

PAGES FROM THE SPANISH MYSTICS

I. ENGLISH TRANSLATIONS

HERNANDO DE ZÁRATE

(? - ?)

Fray Hernando de Zárate was an Augustinian who lived in the second half of the sixteenth century. Beyond the facts of his birth in Madrid, his residence in Córdoba, and his having professed theology in the University of Osuna, nothing is known of his life.

THE GLORY OF HEAVEN

NO human tongue can say how great is the glory of the Heaven which God has prepared for His lovers ; for, as St. Paul says, "Eye hath not seen, nor ear heard, neither have entered into the thought of man, the things which God hath prepared for those that fear him."[1] But from that which we know of the faith and the sacred writings we can discover a few traces, from which the rest may be conjectured.

Our imagination cannot conceive what glory it will be to see God face to face, in whom our happiness essentially consists, since we neither know what is the face of God, what is His essence and substance, nor can we all grasp how and with what light we shall see Him. And therefore we shall content ourselves with making conjectures ; as did a painter—according to Pliny—who was ordered to portray a great and tall person upon a small canvas, and painted on it the form of a man as small as the canvas, and at his feet a satyr measuring his thumb with a foot-rule. Whence the prudent beholder might deduce, by proportionate multiplying, how many feet his body would

---

[1] An inexact quotation from 1 Cor. 2⁹ : Quod oculus non vidit, nec auris audivit, nec in cor hominis ascendit, quæ præparavit Deus iis qui diligunt illum.

measure, by the measure of his thumb, and would find that
he was a mighty giant.

Even so did the Lord when He wished to grant the Apostles
a glimpse of His glory, that they might know what their own
glory would be, and showed them a semblance of it on Mount
Tabor.   For He showed them but the glory of the body, and
of this but the brightness only, and of that but a small part,
as much as was sufficient for that mountain ; for otherwise, being
Himself as bright as the sun, that brightness had not been as
secret a thing as He willed it to be and as in very truth it was ;
indeed, there are those who say that this mystery took place by
night.   Thus will it be with this discourse, in which we cannot
pretend to give more than a glimpse of the glory of Heaven,
since we describe it not expressly, but rather describe what
we conjecture its greatness to be, so far as this can be comprehended by those in this mortal body, to the end that we may
see the excellence and worth of those works by which it may
be merited.

To this end, then, let us consider that any one of the
angels, be he the least of all, is a better and more perfect work
of creation in his nature than any mortal.   Secondly, that of
all the multitude of angels created by God, each one is greater
than his fellow in perfection, since no two are of the same kind
and nature, as are men.   For as no two numbers are equal,
but each one, though it be infinite, exceeds another, and the
farther they are from unity, the greater, even so are the angels,
and the less they diverge from their Sovereign Good and
Perfection, which is God, the nearer to perfection are they,
though none, even by travelling an infinite distance, can attain
to Him ; hence their perfection is measured by the shortness
of their distance from Him, and not by their nearness to Him.

In this regard, therefore, if in corporeal things there is so
much that is good to be seen and comprehended, what will it
be to see the most perfect angel, and the nearest to (or least
distant from) God?   And if from such an angel to the infinite
Nature and Perfection of God there is infinite distance of perfection, what will it be to see the very Essence of God?

Truly it is not without cause that we shall need a new and a higher light, and new and sovereign strength, since even to imagine this Essence we need them. The Baptist is so great a saint, that some place him immediately after the Mother of God; yet Christ, after spending a long time in his praises, ended by saying that he who was least among the blessed was greater than he. How happy, then, will be one of those who in that blessed kingdom are the greatest! Thou hast but to weigh the words of the Evangelist, who says that we shall be like to God, for we shall see Him as He is. In this respect, therefore, the glory of the soul cannot be too much esteemed, since through it we shall become by participation gods, for this is to be like God.

ALONSO DE OROZCO

(1500-1591)

One of the most fertile writers of all those with whom we have to deal, Alonso de Orozco was also among the longest-lived. He was born, of noble parentage, at Oropesa, in the province of Toledo, studied at Toledo and Salamanca, and at the age of twenty-three made his profession in the Augustinian convent where St. Tomás Villanueva was prior. The greater part of his early life was passed in the government of various religious houses; his activity as a writer dates from 1542, in which year he was visited in his dreams by Our Lady, who commanded him to take up the pen. "Being asleep in our monastery at Sevilla," he himself relates, "I saw in my dreams our Mother most pure, the Virgin Mary, who spake to me this one word: *Write*. So great was the joy which I felt in my heart that I could not express it in words. . . . And when I awoke I said, 'O Queen of the Angels, I pray thee, if this vision be true, that thou wilt assure me of it and command me again to write.' And when I lay down to sleep that same night, I saw her once more, and she said to me: '*Write*.'" [1]

He gave himself so vigorously to this work that he left over fifty treatises of various kinds. Nor did he confine himself to writing. In 1554 he became preacher to Charles V, and on Philip II's removal of the Court to Madrid, in 1560, Fray Alonso, who was equally in favour with this monarch,

---

[1] *Confesiones suyas*, Bk. III, Chap. 9.

accompanied him and remained in Madrid until his death. For all his intimacy with the royal house, Orozco lived the simplest and most austere of lives, refusing many posts of honour including the Archbishopric of Toledo, and gaining the popular title of 'el Santo de San Felipe.' He was not, however, beatified until 1881.

Of the Great Sweetness which God Imparts in Prayer and Contemplation

"And when the Queen of Sheba had seen all Solomon's wisdom, there was no more spirit in her." [1] . . . Having considered in the last chapter that devotion which is a great gift of God, and how it disposes and prepares the soul for all spiritual things, so that it runs with joy along the heavenward road, doing with sweetness and delight what he that hath it not finds hard and dry, we may now see what great delights and riches our boundless God communicates to souls that practise prayer and contemplation in things divine.

This sweetness represents to us the wonder of the Queen of Sheba, who, hearing Solomon speak of things so exquisite and of such great wisdom, was as it were enraptured, without spirit and carried out of herself. And here is to be considered this: if the words of a wise man who was but a sinful mortal sufficed to cause wonder in so learned a queen, how much more should the words of our Redeemer move and transport us, raising our souls above all created things! Well knew the Bride what she said and well did she savour the Divine word when she said: My soul lost itself in love and delight when the Beloved spake.[2] So the Christian is moved within him as he hears the voice of God, and the Divine fire which is stirred within his heart none can describe in words, for the tongue can only stammer when it would fain declare the deep things of the spirit. For such things are high and lofty, passing all understanding; were they capable of expression, indeed, they were less excellent. The soul is glad

---

[1] 1 Kgs. 10⁵.

[2] *Cf.* Cant. 5⁶: Anima mea liquefacta est, ut locutus est, and Cant. 2⁵: Quia amore langueo. The reference is no doubt to the former passage, though there are probably reminiscences in it of others.

when she hears the voice of God, and her spirit fails her utterly :
for the heart is softened, and upon it, as upon melted wax, is
imprinted the understanding of the Lord Who speaks.   The
soul expands, her affections grow, and as love grows and expands
all the other virtues increase with it.

Blessed indeed is the soul to whom God thus speaks, neither
by angels, nor by preachers alone, nor by books, nor by creatures,
but by His Very Self.   The holy king David in a psalm says
thus : I will hearken what the Lord shall say in me.[1]   So He
takes up His abode in our heart as in His rightful seat, whence
He gives us wonderful communications, rebuking our negligences,
and inspiring us to progress in spiritual life and practice.   For
as a captain inspires his soldiers to give battle, even so does our
Saviour exhort us when He speaks to us inwardly.   And here it
is needful that our ears be deaf to all the noise of the world, that
we close the door to everything and silence our very thoughts,
for, as His Voice is low and sweet, so it demands great attention
and care.   ' I will hearken what the Lord shall say in me.'

And whereof, O holy king David, does He hold converse
with the soul?   He tells us that the Lord shall speak peace
unto His people.[1]   What can He speak that is called Prince of
Peace—in the words of Isaiah—but peace?   His lips drop as
the honeycomb,[2] as the Bride saw, for He speaks to us of peace
which is very gentle and sweet to all.   St. Augustine, in the
book of the City of God, says that all things desire peace, and
St. Dionysius affirms the same, since peace is an attribute of
heaven.   This peace is quietness and rest to the soul, a fore-
taste of that perfect peace which we have in glory.   O divine
peace, may our hearts repose in thee, may our souls rest in thee
as in their centre, and all noise and tumult of worldly thoughts
be stilled.   O, haven of rest whither our desires journey, receive
us, that in thee we may find repose.

It would seem that this heavenly peace is the fruit of that
precious tree of love, since it has so wonderful a savour.   The

---

[1] Ps. 84[8] Vulg. : Audiam quid loquatur in me Dominus Deus, quoniam loque-
tur pacem in plebem suam. Cf. Ps. 85[8], A.V.   Note change of tense.

[2] Cant. 4[11] : Thy lips, O my spouse, drop as the honeycomb.

fruit of love, says the Apostle, is peace and joy in the Holy Spirit. How unhappy are they that flee from such a treasure, following after vice and wickedness, making war against their own consciences, and knowing nought of this peace. For it is written : There is no peace unto the wicked.[1] But the friends of God,—they who learn to pray and contemplate, and to pray to God inwardly, hearing the sweetness of His music,—shall enjoy great peace and quietness, lost in wonder, as we read here was the Queen of Sheba, who hearing the great wisdom of Solomon, was lost in wonder and as it were without strength. . . .

A great thing is it that the soul which has scaled the heights of contemplation, being still in mortal flesh, may be caught up so as to behold God in His Essence, without use of the senses, as St. Paul affirms of himself. And this, as St. Thomas says, is a state midway between that of the blessed in Heaven and of those who live here below on earth. But although this be so, let us hear the counsel of Solomon. ' Hast thou found honey, brother ? Eat so much as is sufficient for thee, lest thou be filled therewith and vomit it.[2] ' Honey is contemplation and prayer ; let each one take with prudence and discretion that which is sufficient for him. Let him not exceed his state and his strength ; let him not desire raptures and new visions, for into such things the devil is wont to enter, as in our own times we have seen. Let the Christian humble himself, let him see to it that he help the poor and comfort the afflicted, let him pray and contemplate the greatness of God, and let him covet no more feelings than those which God is pleased to grant him. With David let him say before his prayers : Lord, I have become as a beast before Thee.[3] Here I present myself before my Lord and King ; and I would taste no enjoyment but that which Thou willest, to Thy glory and to mine own profit.

[1] Isa. 48[22] (cf. 57[21]). There is no peace, saith the Lord, unto the wicked.
[2] Prov. 25[16] : Mel invenisti : comede quod sufficit tibi, ne forte satiatus oderit te.
[3] Ps. 72[22], Vulg. : Jumentum factus sum apud te. Cf. Ps. 73[22], A.V.

Our great Father, expounding that verse of a Psalm, 'How
great is the multitude of Thy sweetness, which Thou hast laid
up for them that fear Thee!',[1] says thus : God lays up His
sweetness for them that fear Him that they may humble themselves, and with greater diligence seek God.   Greatly should
this sentence be pondered by those that treat with God in prayer.
Let them wait upon the Lord, and not faint when they receive
fewer favours than they desire.   And let them consider that the
Lord knows better what He does than do they that ask Him.
Aristotle says : The law of friendship is to have one wish to do,
and one not to do, that there should be one will and not two.
Canst thou tell me, then, brother, that thou hast love towards
God, if thou keep not the law of friendship ?   Why dost thou
not submit thy will in all things to the will of thy Friend, Christ
Jesus ?   Wouldst thou know if thou hast profited greatly ?
By this shalt thou know it : if dryness is as sweet to thee
as devotion because thus the Lord wills it, if in sickness thou
dost find the joy of health, and if poverty is as sweet to thee as
riches ; and finally, if in disgrace and dishonour thou dost find
the savour of honour, because therein is the sweetest will of thy
Redeemer and Lord, thine own being mortified even as to spiritual
favours.   All this is a sign that thou hast profited greatly : do
thou prize it, then, and give thanks for it to God.

OF THE LAST DEGREE OF CONTEMPLATION, AND WHICH IS THE CONTEMPLATION OF GOD IN HIMSELF

"This is the generation of them that seek the face of the
God of Jacob." [2]   These are they that ever seek the Lord, desiring to see the glorious face of Christ, the very Jacob.   In this
the last degree, my brother, our intent and desire reach their
end.   For we have to strive thereto, not that we may find our
God in His image (which was the first degree) considering Him

---

[1] Ps. 30[20], Vulg. : Quam magna multitudo dulcedinis tuæ, Domine, quam
abscondisti timentibus te! Cf. Ps. 31[19], A.V. : Oh how great is thy goodness,
which thou hast laid up for them that fear thee.

Ps. 23[6], Vulg. : Ps. 24[6], A.V., marg., and R.V. A.V. has (wrongly) ' O
Jacob.'

in ourselves; nor are we to follow in His footsteps, by contemplating Him in His creatures, which was the second degree. Nor even are we to consider Him made man, and suffering for us upon the Cross, as in the third degree; but after the highest manner are we to contemplate Him in His Essence and most perfect Being, without indirection of any kind.

Here the Eagle, as the prophet Ezekiel saw, must fly above its own sphere.[1] Two flights it must make: the first must be higher than the man, and the lion and the calf, which were the three forms seen together with the eagle. The second is the flight of the soul above itself, casting aside all natural reason. By the form of the man which the prophet saw in that vision might be understood the first degree of contemplation, in which we may each one contemplate God in ourselves. By the form of the lion is denoted the second degree, in which God is contemplated in His creatures. And by the similitude of the calf, which in the Law was an unblemished sacrifice, might be denoted the third degree, in which we contemplate God made man, and offering Himself as a Sacrifice on the Cross for the sins of the world. By the eagle which flies higher yet we must now understand this last degree of contemplation in which are exercised those of whom the holy prophet David said, that they seek not the Lord alone.[2] This contemplation is according to the three degrees aforesaid, but they who practise it by a mighty effort raise their eyes unto the sun, contemplating in that great 'wheel'[3] the wonderful perfection and Being of their Creator, Who is called the Face of Jacob.

But I would warn thee, my brother, that he who would see the face of that most powerful Wrestler, our boundless God,

[1] The translation, if it is meant for such, is inexact. The original (Ezek. 1⁹ Vulg.) has: Non revertebantur cum incederent sed unumquodque *ante faciem suam* gradiebatur. A.V., R.V. have 'they went every one straight forward.'

[2] That is, that they do not merely follow God in the active life, but seek the very "Face of the God of Jacob" (see the first words of this extract) in the life of mystical progress. There is probably no direct reference here to the Wrestling Angel, though the mention of Jacob suggests the following paragraph to the author.

[3] Ezekiel 1¹⁵: Now as I beheld the living creatures, behold one wheel upon the earth by the living creatures, with his four faces.

must first have wrestled with himself, and be a man that is perfect in the active life, and have practised himself for a while in the first three degrees of contemplation. For St. Gregory says: It is better far that he who feels himself unable for contemplation should exercise himself in the active life, with humility, and, if need be, all his days, rather than devote himself presumptuously to contemplation, wherein by some error he may be deceived as his pride would but merit. This is that which our Redeemer said: If thy right eye offend thee, pluck it out, for it is better for thee to enter the kingdom of heaven with one eye, than having two eyes to be cast into hell.[1] Far better will it be for thee to be saved in the active life (which is, as it were, the left eye) than to presume to follow the contemplative life knowing thyself unfitted for it: so shouldst thou lose the merit of both.

FRANCISCO DE OSUNA

(? – c. 1540)

Very little is known of the life of this venerable mystic, whose writings so deeply impressed St. Teresa. He takes his name, after the custom of many of his contemporaries, from the place of his birth. A Franciscan monk, he was elected Commissary General for the Indies, at the general chapter of 1535. He was unable, however, for some reason to take up his duties. He appears to have died about the year 1540. He is known to have lived in France—for some time in Paris, and probably also in Toulouse, where editions of some of his works were printed.

The mystical writings of Osuna are practically all to be found in the *Tercer Abecedario Espiritual*, which first appeared in Toledo in the year 1527. He did as much as any of his compatriots to popularise mystic theology; Juan de Ávila, indeed, fearing lest Osuna's less instructed readers should confound mysticism with religion, recommends "that they read not in general the third *Abecedario*, which will do them harm, for it tends to suppress thought entirely, and this is not meet for all" (*Epistolario espiritual*, XXIX). Nevertheless the book was widely read, and deserves to be better known to-day than it is, both in Spain and elsewhere.

---

[1] Mt. 5[29], Mk. 9[47]. The quotation follows neither version exactly.

Of the Vigilance that He Must Keep upon Himself Who in Purity of Spirit would Attain to God

Before we begin the exposition of this Alphabet, it will be well to set down three considerations which appear essential to every person who would attain to God and are common to every spiritual exercise.

The first is that friendship and communion with God are possible in this our life and exile upon earth ; and that not in small measure, but as straitly and securely as was ever bond between brothers or between mother and son. This friendship and communion between God and man has no less consequence and assurance for being a thing called spiritual, and I speak not of that divine acceptation, nor of that doubt which mortals have when they know not if they are in grace or no, for of this we will speak elsewhere ; but I speak of the communion sought and found by those that study to reach a state of prayer and devotion, which is so certain a thing, that there is nought in the world more certain, nor of greater joy, nor of higher worth or price.

Think not that they who go to the world in sorrow and tears, hungry, ill-clothed, worn by long watchings, persecuted and scorned, with pale face and sunken cheeks, nought but bones, sworn foes of the dissolute,—think not, I say, that such are content with a life so hard, which to thee seems wearisome that hast all things at thy will. Without doubt these persons would soon fall away, did not God our Lord come forth to welcome them in the open arms of His friendship, with greater consolation and joy than when a mother welcomes her little son who comes to her fleeing from things which affright him. The mother stretches out her arms to the child, and not only embraces him, but opens her bosom to him, satisfies his hunger, and lays her face against his, so that his sighs and tears cease, for his fear is stilled.

. . . .

The second consideration is that since God is no respecter of persons, this communion is no less possible,—oh man,

whoever thou art—to thee, than to others.   For thou art made
no less in the image of God than are others, nor do I suppose
thou hast less desire of happiness than others.   Yet, as thou
hast been fashioned, not by God, but by thy desire for freedom,
I think thou wilt say that thy age, or office, or humour, or
infirmity, or temper, excuses and withdraws thee from this.
I know not how I shall reply to thee, save as the wise man
says : He that would separate himself from his friend, seeketh
excuses, and he will ever be to be blamed.[1]   If thy excuses
satisfy thee, I know not; I can but say that me they offend ;
and I say with St. Augustine that in the sum I believe thee
not, for there is no cause that can take from thee a faculty so
wholly thine own.   If thou saidst that thou couldst not fast,
nor take the discipline, nor wear rough clothing, nor labour,
nor journey, we could believe thee ; but if thou sayest that thou
canst not love, we believe thee not.   And if St. Augustine says
this of the love of one's enemies, how much more truly may it
be said of the love of God, for which there are so many more
motives than for the other.

The third consideration is this,—that in order to seek this
communion, by whatsoever means, we need to have a care over
the soul that shall never let it rest, to the end that it may be
directed solely to seeking God : this care or intent cannot well
be understood but by outward similitudes.   We see one who
has lost some possession go seeking it distressfully, looking now
in one place, now in another, imagining it to be in everything
he sees.   He who travels, if he be a good traveller, has the
intent fixed in his heart to finish the day's journey, and orders
all things toward this end.   In his heart he is travelling ever
farther along the road ; his care makes him to rise up early and
dream by night that he has arrived at his goal ; if he grow
weary, the thought of his task gives him strength.   He who
mines gold has such lust of it, that he thinks to find it in every
clod and to discover it with every blow that he gives ; and for

---

[1] Prov. 18[1] (Vulg.) : Occasiones quærit qui vult recedere ab amico; omni
tempore erit exprobrabilis. A.V. and R.V. differ considerably from this rendering.

his great desire he ceases not until fortune fails him everywhere.
He that angles is greatly attentive to his float, that he may see
if the fish bite, and he thinks only of those that he has caught
or will presently catch, and that with great care as to his business. Without such solicitous intent and care I think that none
ever found God, by whatsoever way he travelled; and the man
who would find Him orders his life with the single aim of seeking after Him, without determining in what way or manner.

Of the Recollection of the Soul

For the reason aforesaid of its great excellence, this exercise
has many names, both in the Sacred Scriptures and in the
writings of holy and learned men. Some call it mystic (that
is to say, hidden) theology; because in the secret hiding-
place of the heart it is taught by our good Master Jesus. This
mastership He has willed to reserve for Himself, and to His
servants He has given less talent and faculty to instruct others
in it than in any other science, for as the chiefest of all Masters,
He wills to keep the chiefest of all teaching for Himself. And
Theology is mistress and queen among the sciences, for, as the
wise man says, she calls the other sciences, her handmaidens,
to the castle of faith, that there they may serve their mistress,
Theology.[1] Which science is of two kinds : the one is called
' speculative ' or (which is the same thing) ' enquiring,' and the
other ' hidden,' whereof this Third Alphabet treats and which it
expounds. Let it not be supposed that I presume to teach it
herein, for no mortal has ever taught it : Christ has kept for
Himself the office of teaching it secretly to the hearts in which
it dwells, and thus this hidden theology is by much the more
excellent a divine science than that other theology whereof we
spoke before, which is called speculative. That theology of
which our treatise tells seeks not to search or enquire, knowing
that, as it is written, the searcher into the Divine Majesty shall
be crushed and overwhelmed by the great glory of God. This

---

[1] Prov. 9^1, ^{3} : Sapientia aedificavit sibi domum, excidit columnas septem. . . .
Misit ancillas suas ut vocarent ad arcem, et ad moenia civitatis.

theology is better or more perfect than the first, as Gerson says, for it uses the first as a beginning, and as steps whereby it may climb the ladder of love.

The first theology God teaches in order that we may contemplate Him as the highest Truth, while this of which we speak, presupposing the other, which it takes as proved, passes to the love of Him as the highest Good. The one belongs to the understanding, concerning which even devils are sufficiently enlightened in the faith, since, as it is written, they believe and tremble.[1] But the other belongs to the will when it is filled with love for the highest Good, which is the will of the righteous man who loves God. The one theology will vanish with faith when faith gives place to that Sight which is our reward. But the other theology will be perfected by the addition of love ; no longer will it be hidden, but will be manifest to all, from the least even unto the greatest.

The first theology, which is called 'speculative,' uses reasons and arguments and discourses and probabilities as do other sciences ; and hence it is called scholastic theology, and the science of learned men, for excelling in which great talent is needful, with books and time and constant exercise, and vigil and labour under a skilled master, as in other sciences. But the hidden theology of which we speak is mastered, not in this manner, but by pious affections and exercise in the theological virtues which illumine it, and the gifts of the Holy Spirit, and the evangelical beatitudes which perfect it according to the hierarchical acts, namely purgation, illumination and perfectation. And as often happens, even in animals, and still more in men, where there is less knowledge there is more perfection and love, as we see in boys, who love their parents the more the less they know of them, and in novices who in their first year or years are more devout, with all their simplicity, than afterwards when they are proficients.

From that which has been said, it follows clearly that, to discover this highest theology, there is no need of much science

---

[1] James 2[19] : Tu credis quoniam unus est Deus : bene facis : et dæmones credunt, et contremiscunt.

acquired or laboriously sought,—howbeit infused science must not be lacking, nor is it lacking to those that are prepared to receive it.   For once we have learned by faith that God is to be desired and loved, and is wholly love,—then, if our affections be purged and prepared and exercised, I know not how we shall be hindered from being thus transformed, inflamed and raised to a state which knows all to be but one clod, one fragment, or (to speak better) one fount of love. . . .

Likewise this manner of prayer is called the art of love, since only by love is it attained, and by it more than by any other art or industry is love multiplied, and also because Christ, the God of love, instructs in it those of a loving heart.   Many a time they who cannot be conquered by force are conquered by art, as was so with David, who more by art than by strength conquered Goliath ; just so is it, too, with elephants, which are conquered by the art of hunters who themselves are weak. Wherefore this exercise is called an art by which those of little strength vanquish Him that is most strong, and bring Him captive to their hearts, binding Him with the chains and fetters of love, saying with the Bride : I hold Him and will not let Him go.[1]

This art is called the art of love, which is said to be as strong as death, that conquers all.   Whence it is to be understood that this exercise has in itself both art and strength, which are the two best means to conquer all things.

Furthermore, it is called union, for when man after this way attains to God, he becomes one spirit with Him by an exchange of will, so that the man wills nought but that which God wills, neither does God withdraw Himself from the will of the man, but in all things they are one, like things that are perfectly united, which lose their own natures and are wholly transformed in a third.   And this it is that happens in this business, for if God and man before had diverse wills, now they agree in one without dissatisfaction of either.   And hence it results that the man is at unity with himself, and with his fellows ;

---

[1] Cant. 3[4] : Tenui eum, nec dimittam.

were we all so the multitude of the faithful would be one heart and mind together in the Holy Spirit, the beginning of Whose generation is formed by the Father and the Son. He it is who makes us to be one in love, that He may beget us in grace, and bring us all to be made one together with God, that He may not have to bring us to Him singly.

This exercise is also called profoundness, which thing contains darkness and depth ; for it is based upon the deep and profound heart of man, which is dark indeed,—that is, deprived of human understanding, so that the Spirit of God may come upon its darkness, and the waters of its desires, and say : ' Let there be light '. . . .

Furthermore it is called the coming of the Lord to the soul, for by its means the Lord visits His own who with sighing call upon Him.

And it is called a height which raises the soul, and friendship or the opening of the devout heart to the Heart of Christ.

And it is called spiritual ascension with Christ, and captivity wherein we subject to Him our understanding.

And it is that third heaven whither contemplatives are caught up.

But why should I say more ? This exercise is a refuge whereto we may betake ourselves when storms come near ; a constant resistance against the princes of darkness which in secret make war against us ; a restitution which we make to God in rendering to Him all that of Himself is in us and keeping back nothing. It is a resurrection to spiritual life, wherein to the righteous man is given all power in Heaven over his soul and on earth over his body ; it is an attitude of reverence which we ever have toward God, being hushed in fear before Him ; it is a tree from which virtues blossom like roses ; it is the kingdom of God which we must gain by conquest and by art, since we have it within us, and every day also we pray for it ; it is a royal priesthood, whereby, when we are masters of ourselves, we may offer ourselves to God ; it is a deep hush made in the Heaven of our souls, brief though it be and not lasting as the righteous man desires ; it is a service which we do to God

alone, adoring His Majesty only; it is a seat which we have
made ready for Him that He may abide in the heart of our
being ; it is a tent which the traveller pitches in the desert; it
is our most strong tower of refuge whence we may spy out
heavenly things ; a golden vessel wherein we lay up the manna
in the ark of our inmost selves; it is a valley in which the
richest wheat abounds ; it is a victory which conquers the lesser
world, subjecting it wholly to God ; it is a vineyard to be
tended with vigilance, and the shade that we greatly long for,
where we taste of its fruit ; it is the unction from the Holy One,
which teaches all things; [1] it is a garden enclosed on all sides,
whose key is given to God alone, that He may enter whensoever
He will.

OF THREE WAYS OF PRAYER

The first form or manner of prayer is vocal, according to
which we say that they who recite the Divine office pray, as
also do they that say any prayers whatsoever, pronouncing them
with the lips in praise of the Lord.   Among these the most
blessed prayer of the ' Pater noster ' takes the first place. . . .
He who says this prayer with devotion, prays to the Father in
the Name of the Son Who made it and therefore he is the more
quickly heard of Him ; so much the more quickly than they
who say other prayers as the Author of this was dearer than
the authors of other such to the Eternal Father.

The Lord commanded us that when we prayed we should
not be given to much speaking, but multiply rather our affection
and love than our words : a precept which the Lord Himself
kept in this prayer, which is short and begins with the words
' Pater noster.'   Of these, the first awakens the love of God,
Whom we call Father, and the second the love of our neighbour,
since the word ' Our ' makes him our brother, and a son of God
by grace : we pray for him as well as for ourselves when we
call the Lord Universal Father of all men.   At the end of all
other prayers the Church adds : May this be done through our
Lord Jesus Christ.   But there is no need to add this in the
Lord's Prayer, because by its form of address, as St. Cyprian

---

[1] I John 2[20] : Sed vos unctionem habetis a Sancto, et nostis omnia.

says, the Father knows the words of His Son, and also because the Lord Himself was wont many times to say it when He uttered vocal prayers in His own Person or in the persons of His faithful. For these knew that prayer before any other, since the Apostles taught it to them ; and of none do we read that they made any common prayer to teach others to offer save this prayer alone. . . .

Such are the excellences of this most Christian prayer, that as we find written the Song of Songs, the Day of Days,[1] the holiest of holy things, so we should call this the Prayer of Prayers. . . .

Although, as we have said, this Lord's Prayer is the chiefest among all vocal prayers, man should not for this cause give up the rest, lest weariness be engendered thereby. Besides this we find that some holy persons have made other approved prayers, and often, too, it is an excellent thing for a man to frame vocal prayers with words dictated by his own affection. The Scriptures are full of such prayers . . . and this manner of vocal prayer is most effectual, for it obtains of the Lord quickly that which it demands, and therefore should the devout and faithful use it much in their necessities, making them known to the Lord in few words of their own composing. Not only before they sleep, but before any task, should all pray after this manner, commending to the Lord everything in its turn, speaking familiarly with Him in words prompted by their affections. In this way they may sometimes make known their needs to God, at other times confess their sins, and at others beg for mercy and grace and favour against the perils and fatigues of the world by which they or theirs are assailed.

· · · · · · · · ·

The second manner of prayer is that within the heart, wherein the mouth pronounces no words vocally, but the heart speaks with the Lord, and we ask Him within ourselves for all that of which we have need. Then, as in a secret place, with none hearing us, we speak to the Lord, and are alone with Him ; and here His favours are wont to be greater, for we

[1] Lit. Feast of Feasts,—presumably Easter.

speak as it were in the ear of God. In this manner prayed David, when he said to God : Thy servant hath found his heart to pray to thee. . . .

To this manner of prayer, which the heart makes to God while the tongue is silent, may be assigned all devout and holy thoughts, whether of the Lord's Passion or of the Church, the Judgment, or any other devout thing. For it is manifest that they are praying who think and meditate upon the Sacred Passion, and even they who think upon their sins as they ought, since they think upon them only to beg mercy for them.

For this manner of prayer, which consists in holy thoughts, it is needful that a man should commit to memory the devout stories and mysteries of the Lord, and many good things of those which he hears and reads, which should be as fuel that feeds the fire upon the altar of the Lord. The most fruitful thoughts, nevertheless, of all that a man may have are those of the Sacred Passion. . . . This second manner of prayer, which is the thinking and using of holy thoughts, would not seem to be fitting to beginners nor to the unlettered, yet it is not wholly unsuited to them. For they are obliged at times to think holy thoughts, since they cannot but desire happiness and many other sovereign gifts, such as to love God above all things, which they cannot do without thinking upon Him, one quality of love being to think some time upon the Beloved. They have also obligation to receive the holy sacraments, which presupposes some meditation and holy thoughts whereby a man prepares himself for such great gifts.

I spoke of the desire for felicity, for if we never think upon it we shall never have it ; but nevertheless the religious and the recluse who have left the world to devote themselves to contemplation have obligations in this manner of prayer, and their opportunities are, or should be, far greater, by reason of the sanctuary of their religion, which is established and set apart for the perfecting of prayer. So as vocal prayer is a thing common to devout men and women in the world, this second way of prayer should be common to every good religious in a convent, which must be a house of prayer, and not a den of

thieves.   This last it will be if the alms of others are spent, not
in prayer, but in murmuring and wandering about, against the
will of those that gave them : for this is no other than spoliation
and robbery.   For all those that use the things of others, but
not according to the will and good intention of their owners, of
a certainty usurp that which is not their own and may be called
robbers ; and most evidently the will of those that give alms is
that we may have opportunities of praying to the Lord without
distractions.   So that if we do not this we run contrary to the
prime intention of the benefactor, whose debtors, as I see it, we
are.   Men give us, indeed, their alms, for the love of God, but
with the condition that by means of it we serve the same Lord
God better ; if it were not so, they would not give it us save in
case of extreme necessity, with the object of saving the lives of
those near and dear to them.

.   .   .   .

The third manner of prayer is called mental or spiritual,
whereby the highest part of our soul in the highest purity and
affection is raised to God upon the wings of desire and holy
aspiration strengthened by love.   The greater is this love, the
fewer are the words it has, and the more comprehensive are
those words and the more effective ; for love, if it be true love,
seeks not tedious and subtle reasonings, but works great things
in silence, knowing that if it withdraw itself from the creatures
and take shelter in God, it will be unreservedly received by
Him, the more so according as it is the more completely and
fervently recollected.

Of those that pray thus the Lord says in the Gospel : The
true worshippers shall worship the Father in spirit and in truth,
—for God is a Spirit and they that worship Him must worship
Him in spirit and in truth—for such He seeketh to worship
Him.[1]   The greater is the conformity between him who prays
and the Lord to Whom he prays, the more acceptable will be
the prayer ; so that, as the Father is in Himself pure spirit and

---

[1] Joh. 4²³: Veri adoratores adorabunt Patrem in spiritu et veritate.   Nam et
Pater tales quærit, qui adorent eum.

has nothing that is of the body, our prayer will be the more welcome to Him the farther it is withdrawn from the imagination, and even from the thoughts of the heart. For these cannot be so high as not to be full low by comparison with the Lord, whereas the desires that embrace God in His essence and without the intermediary of bodily parts, and the love that has no care for words, these pray to God with the greatest purity and in the closest and most spiritual way, for the soul says not that it prays save that prayer in the Song of Songs : My Beloved is mine and I am His.[1] No words could be more spiritual, more recollected or more comprehensive than these, nor could they express more of the aim of the prayer to those that experience it.

That which God can do for His Lover beyond this is to give Himself to him, and that which man can do further is to give himself to God ; we cannot, however, do this last without His grace, and therefore said the Bride first of all ' My Beloved is mine ' rather than ' I am my Beloved's.' It is to be observed, moreover, that this self-giving of man to God, and of God to man, is a gift so perfectly given that when it is given God seems to be wholly and entirely in man. I mean that, did faith not enlighten the man who possesses God, he might almost say that within himself is comprehended the whole of God, and that apart from him He is not. At times the righteous soul sees itself so full of God, that the narrowness of its bosom seems to confine His Presence, though in fact He is without limit. The gift which in the giving of themselves recollected souls offer at times to God is likewise so abundant that for themselves they keep nothing ; in this way they lose their free choice and their will, and so entirely are they mindful of God and given up to Him that they are as forgetful of themselves as though they were not.

Of these three manners of prayer the Wise man says : See how in three ways I have declared it to thee.[2] These three

---

[1] Cant. 2[16] : Dilectus meus mihi, et ego illi.

[2] Prov. 22[20] : Ecce descripsi eam tibi tripliciter, in cogitationibus et scientia. A.V. has ' Have not I written to thee excellent things in counsels and knowledge ? '

ways the interlineal gloss explains, saying that they are in word (which is vocal prayer), in thought (which is the prayer of the heart), and in work, which is the spiritual prayer of recollection ; which, if it be real, as far exceeds the other two as work exceeds word and thought.

Of how thou shouldst seek this Love

Now since the devil studies to take away from us this love, which is a fruit of the spirit, a token that God dwells within us, a superabundance of grace, and, as it were, a guerdon given to this servant of ours, the body, that it may serve with joy, it is right that we should study to keep this love. First, we should withdraw ourselves from, all sin, even that which is venial ; for the true lover studies to flee from every offence, looking not at the suffering which is his due but at the Beloved, Whom all evil offends, be it great or small. Secondly, we should practise every virtue, letting no good thing slip which we might do, but being very zealous in works of piety which are of great worth. Thirdly, we should guard our love from provocation in any matter, considering our possessions as things lent to us, that we may not set our love upon them, but upon God. Fourthly, let us see that we stir ourselves up, rousing our hearts from sleep, that they may ever bring forth works of affection and love.

The first of these things will take from us the fear of approaching God. The second will give us boldness to go to Him,—even to embrace Him. The third will give us strength to take by force the Kingdom of Heaven with great violence and power of love. The fourth will make us swift and skilful in this thing to achieve it easily ; if we would do it joyfully, let us use among ourselves such thoughts as awaken love and so pronounce words of love to God, which shall be as if one were to nourish the fire with the fresh breeze of delightful words, pleasing and encouraging our wills, if they are uttered with living faith, withdrawn from all imagination and thoughts of things which we have seen and heard, and carried, together with the whole matter, beyond our human limits. For we must bear in mind that we are speaking in spirit with the most loving God, and not in bodily wise, the soul being not corporeal, nor God, to Whom we must speak, corporeal in His Deity.

OF THREE WAYS OF SILENCE

Three ways of keeping silent are there in recollection, or three ways of silence, leaving aside others which are less to our purpose. The first is when all fantasy and imagination and forms of visible things cease in the soul, and thus it is silent to all created things. The same was described by holy Job, when he said : Now should I have slept and been still, and in my sleep I should have rested with kings and counsellors of the earth which built for themselves desolate places.[1] We sleep to temporal things, and are silent within ourselves, as St. Gregory says, when within the secret place of our soul we take refuge in the contemplation of the Creator. And the saints, who are here called kings and counsellors, build for themselves desolate places, when they desire nought of this world and are oppressed in their heart by no tumult of inordinate desire, but with the right hand of holy contemplation cast out from their bed, which is the heart, all unlawful impulses, despising all transitory things and immoderate cogitations which are born thereof ; and as they desire only the eternal mansions and love nought of this world, they enjoy great tranquillity of soul.

The second way of silence which is in recollection is that when the soul that is most still in itself enjoys a kind of spiritual ease, sitting with Mary at the feet of the Lord, and saying : I will hear what the Lord God shall say in me. And to this says the Lord : Hearken, O daughter, and consider and incline thine ear, forget also thine own people and thy father's house.[2]

This second way of silence may fitly be compared to the act of hearing ,for not alone is the hearer silent to all around,

---

[1] Job 3[13-14] : Nunc enim dormiens silerem, et somno meo requiescerem : cum regibus et consulibus terræ, qui aedificant sibi solitudines.

[2] Ps. 44[11] : Audi filia, et vide, et inclina aurem tuam : et obliviscere populum tuum, et domum patris tui.

but he wills that all should keep silence for him, that he may
the more entirely be turned to Him that is speaking to him,
especially if he knows not where He may be, as in the present
case: for, as is said in the Gospel, we hear the voice of God,—
that is, His inspiration—and we cannot tell whence it cometh
nor whither it goeth; hence it is fitting that we should keep
great silence and listen most intently to Him. So we have two
ways of silence: one is that wherein our imaginings cease, together with the thoughts that revolve in our memory; the other
is a forgetting of our very selves, and a turning of the whole
of our inward man entirely toward God alone.

The first silence is that when outward things no longer speak
to us; the second is of a most calm rest in which we are silent
to our very selves and dispose ourselves to God with a submis-
sion receptive and made ready for Him. This is figured by
the sacred animals of Ezekiel, of which it is said: And there
was a voice above the firmament that was over their heads,
when they stood, and had let down their wings.[1] The voice,
as I said, is the divine inspiration which is received in the ear
of the soul without sound of words, but with the presence of
God only which makes itself felt; and for this reason says Job
that secretly and quietly he heard the hidden word which was
told him, and perceived, as it were, the signs and tracks of his
smallest whisper.[2]

This inspired voice is above the firmament, that is, in the
highest part of the reason, which is closely united with God by
love. The sacred winged animals are contemplatives; and it
is said that they are standing, because when this voice is heard
in the soul it rises to great heights and remains suspended,
almost transported in God, as were the apostles when they saw
Him ascend into Heaven. And in this way Ezekiel was

[1] Ezek. I[25]: Nam cum fieret vox super firmamentum, quod erat super caput
eorum, stabant, et submittebant alas suas.

[2] This rather obscure passage probably refers to Job 26[14], where R.V. has:
' Lo, these are but the outskirts of His ways: and how small a whisper do we
hear of Him!' Vulg., however, reads: Ecce, haec ex parte dicta sunt viarum
eius: et cum vix parvam stillam sermonis eius audierimus, quis poterit tonitruum
magnitudinis illius intueri?

commanded to stand upon his feet that God might speak to him : [1]
to be standing denotes, as St. Gregory says, silent wonder, for
it makes us to be dependent upon God, as Job had elected that
his soul should be, so that the working of the soul's powers all
but ceases, and as this grows less, the soul receives wisdom.

To let down the wings signifies to put forth one's highest
powers and so to receive the Divine influence which is poured
into the soul; in which, as the gloss observes, the contemplative
counts his own strength of no avail.   Nevertheless in silence he
directs it towards God, so that, though of itself it fails, it may find
itself in Him, even as one said : My soul refused consolation.
I thought upon God and rejoiced, I exercised myself and my
spirit failed.

The third silence of our understanding is brought to pass in
God, when the soul is wholly transformed in Him and tastes
abundantly of His sweetness, in which it sleeps as in a wine-
cellar,[2] and keeps silence, desiring no more.   For it has found
satisfaction, and is asleep even to itself, forgetting the weakness
of its state, seeing itself so far deified and united with its pattern,
and clothed in the brightness of God like another Moses who
has entered into the cloud which was above the mountain.
This was that which more truly befell St. John when after the
Last Supper he leaned upon the Lord's breast, and kept silence
for a space concerning that which he felt.

In this third silence it comes to pass that the understanding
is so still and so entirely closed,—or rather, occupied—that it
understands nought of that which is said to it, nor can judge of
aught that passes near it, since it neither hears nor sees.   Concerning this an old man whom I confessed, who had practised
these things for more than fifty years, told me, among other
mysteries, that many times he had listened to sermons and
things of God without understanding a word of them : so hushed
and so busy was his innermost understanding that nothing which
was of creatures could take shape within it.   I told him that he
should withdraw into retirement, to which he replied that voices

---

[1] Ezek. 2[1] : Fili hominis, sta super pedes tuos, et loquar tecum.
[2] *Cf.* Cant. 1[2-4].

were to him as the sound of organs, in which the soul took
delight even though it understood them not : he praised the
Lord as it were in a counterpoint upon them in a way that could
be felt, although he could not make another to understand it.

BERNARDINO DE LAREDO

(1482-1540 [1])

Bernardino de Laredo, a Sevillan, had wished, from childhood, to
enter the religious life, but influential friends dissuaded him from doing
so, and he took up the profession of medicine, graduating as Doctor in
Sevilla University. But, as his biographer tells us, he could not be happy
in the world, and at last he presented himself at the Franciscan Convent
of San Francisco del Monte, near Sevilla, and begged admission as a
humble lay brother (1510). His request was granted, and he became
noted for his exemplary and ascetic life as well as for the success which
attended his ministrations to the sick. Among his patients, even before
his change of life, had been John II of Portugal, whom he attended in a
dangerous illness from which the King eventually recovered.

His great mystical book, *Subida del Monte Sion por la via contemplativa* was first published anonymously, and several succeeding
editions preserved this anonymity. Internal evidence, however, tells us
much about the author which agrees with what is known of Laredo, and
the edition of 1617, published in Alcalá, bears his name, together with
the statement that " for his humility he wished not to declare it."

HOW THE PRACTICE OF QUIET TEACHES THE SOUL TO
RISE ON WINGS OF LOVE

Whenever in this third book we speak of ' infused science '
or ' hidden wisdom ' or ' secret or mystic theology ' or the
' exercise of aspiration,' let it be understood that a sudden and
momentary uplifting of the mind is meant, in which the soul,
by Divine instruction, is raised of a sudden to be united through
the purest love, by the affective way alone, with its most loving
God, without the interposition of any thought or of any intellectual working or of the understanding or of natural reason.
We said before that this operation is above all reason and

[1] Some authorities wrongly give the date of his death as 1545.

human understanding, just as we also said that the mysteries of our pure and holy Catholic Faith are neither built upon natural reason nor admit of comprehension, such as the most high mystery of the Incarnation of the Divine Word, that of the most holy Sacrament of the Altar, and many others. So then this Divine operation surpasses reason and understanding ; and by it the soul is raised in a moment upon the wings of love and is united with its God, so often as it pleases the Divine condescension, without the interposition of any thought of created thing.

Now in this sovereign operation our own part is difficult in the beginning, yet if we persevere with all our might in this raising of our affective nature, we reach that degree of facility at which, as high contemplatives say, the perfectly schooled soul may rise in a moment, as often as it will, to its God, and become united with Him through love. And concerning this St. Dionysius says (and Herp and Henrique de Balma, both high contemplatives, affirm it) that in the practised soul this occurs as often as it pleases, and with such facility, that they cannot predict it.

It is to be observed that the soul in this state of union,—in this rising to its God—gives no more than its own free-will. He who works in it is our God ; and as He works again and again with this free-will which is offered by the soul, and with its raising of the affective nature, by the inspiration of love which God gives, the soul reaches that state of happiness allowed by our Lord—and even in these times there are those who can affirm and show by means of witnesses how great is this truth.

It will be seen with joyful emotion that facility in this blessed uplifting of the soul comes not of its own solicitude and frequent practice, but by continual times of visitation by its most loving God. And thereto it disposes itself with the disposition of a pure intention, for the oftener it is visited by its great Reviver, so much the more reluctant is it to ask and receive this love further. So often does our Lord and loving Physician visit the soul that is faint for His love, that the soul reaches a point at which it cannot and would not escape the arrows of love, never lacking the Physician Who with a glance heals it.   And this He does so completely that the soul has but to cry out of a sudden concerning its grievous sickness, and straightway it has its remedy, and the visit of its Beloved Physician.   No sooner is it afflicted with love, than with the affliction it has the remedy.

Concerning this let it be considered that there cannot be, nor was there ever, a King so powerful that with the strongest batteries and many munitions he could vanquish another King or Lord so happily as the enamoured soul can vanquish, take and hold its most loving Lord with love alone.   And this is the cause thereof.   As it is His own clemency that conquers Him, and as the conflict of the loving soul succeeds the conquest, and the wounds are those of love, it is necessary that he who does battle be taken captive and that the Conquered be imprisoned in his prison, and be ever in our keeping.

How the Sleep of the Soul's Powers Quickens the Flight of Living Love

In the second chapter of the Book of the Canticles, the Bridegroom of the Church, Christ Jesus our Beloved, says these mellifluous words : My dove is one only, etc.[1]   Elsewhere He calls her 'my dove' and entreats her to open to Him.[2]   Now since, as was explained in Chapter 17, the Church is the heritage of Jesus Christ, and every righteous soul is part of this heritage, and since our God calls this His Church a dove, it remains to be said that, when the soul knows Holy Church (of which it is a part), it longs for the wings of living desire which this wondrous dove possesses, desires awakened by her perfect doctrine and with which it can rise in loving flight to its most loving God, in Whom is its true consolation.

And therefore said our authority, the psalmist, in the person

---

[1] This is not Cant. 2 (*cf.* however, Cant. 2¹⁴ : " Columba mea, in foraminibus petræ, . . . " etc.) but Cant. 6⁸ : Una est columba mea, perfecta mea, una est matris suæ, electa genitrici suæ.

[2] Cant. 5² : Aperi mihi, soror mea, amica mea, columba mea, immaculata mea.

of the enamoured soul: Who will give me wings like a dove![1]
which is to say: O that I might be filled with the love and
the desire of Holy Church that I might seek my God in perfect
contemplation! And since, while we continue in this mortal
life, true rest is impossible to the soul without great interruption,
that counsel must be comprehended which in the sixty-seventh
psalm the psalmist gives to the righteous soul, under the figure
of Holy Mother Church, the heritage of our God, spouse of
Jesus Christ, our dove without guile, which desiring that those
who are both her children and God's should inherit her wings,
speaks to them in this manner: Though ye have lien between
two landmarks, or boundaries or inheritances (or, as the gloss
has it, in the authority of two testaments) ye shall be as the
wings of a dove covered with silver,—her wings shall be even
as if she is a dove of silver—and the back of this dove shall be
as finely polished gold.[2]

Sleep as to temporal things signifies little heed for them.
Now from the small heed which the righteous soul gives to all
things beside God proceeds spiritual sleep, in which the powers
of such souls slumber, and are infused and transformed into the
love of their God, in purity of substance. In such a way does
this come to pass that the soul, in this manner of sleeping, in
its inward quietness, receives the operation of none of its powers,
nor has its comprehension to do with any created thing, but all
is spiritual. To this restful slumber, to this sleep of the soul's
powers, to this repose of the soul, to this flight of the spirit in
quiet contemplation, to this path of aspiration it is that the
Prophet invites, and that it may take flight in this aspiration he
desires that the soul may have wings. And he speaks of the
wings as of a dove, because this is a loving bird, which, representing the Church, presents to us the same love in the Most
Holy Spirit.

[1] Ps. 54[7], Vulg.: Quis dabit mihi pennas sicut columbae ? Cf. Ps. 55[6],
A.V.: Oh that I had wings like a dove!

[2] The passage here commented, Ps. 67[14], Vulg., is one of great difficulty.
The Vulgate has: Si dormiatis inter medios cleros, pennæ columbæ deargentatæ,
et posteriora dorsi ejus in pallore auri. Cf. Ps. 68[13], R.V. and the commenta-
tors thereon.

Whence it is seen that this peaceful slumber, this blessed
sleep which unites the soul with God, had been experienced by
David when he said in the fourth Psalm : In the quietness and
peace of his secret hiding-place, in which God is found within
the interior of the soul, ' I will both lay me down in peace and
sleep'—in the peace of this my Lord.[1]

We continue our commentary. ' Between two landmarks'
or ' between two allotments.' From this we observe that the
soul which is skilled in quiet contemplation, sleeps in this way
as touching temporal things, and takes so little heed of them,
because it is coming the nearer to God, that only for love of
Him can it forbear to neglect those things to which it is obliged
by charity and obedience and by the bare necessity of satisfying
its own genuine scanty needs. Now the neglect of these transient
things withdraws the soul from all that is transitory, as far as
its affections are concerned, and the burning desires for eternal
blessings raise it to the level of that world which will endure for
ever. So that neglect of the present and a desire for the future
causes the soul to be as it were mortified, asleep and suspended
midway between two domains, to wit, this present death and the
life which is to come. So sleep means here that suspension and
quiet silence. And the two landmarks are this transient world,
and the world that is everlasting.

How Perfect Contemplation Brings with it Piety, Charity and Love

It is to be understood that when the contemplative approaches perfection he looks but little at his own advantage, or
devotion or gain ; for all his study is to be purely, simply and
entirely in conformity with the will of God. And this conformity has great merit, and is of the greatest profit, were it
but in the desire to suffer whatever thing may befall, with
deliberate determination, for the love of Jesus Christ, Whose

---

[1] The reference is to Ps. 4[9-10], Vulg. : In pace in idipsum dormiam, et
requiescam, etc., with a reminiscence, probably, of Ps. 26[5] : Quoniam abscondit
me in tabernaculo suo ; in die malorum protexit me in abscondito tabernaculi sui.
Cf. Pss. 4[8], 27[5], A.V.

most innocent life he has set in his soul as a mirror of all his
actions in both the inward life and the outward.

Yet it is to be noted that the merit of a good desire can
never reach perfection until it be a living desire. I mean that
if thou dost set before thee patience or any other virtue, it is a
great merit, but when thou dost run a great risk of losing it
and seest that thou hast it and dost persevere in it, then know
well that that is a living desire which thy soul did conceive.
I say not that thou shouldst no longer feel strife within thee,
for when no strife is felt, and this in a natural way, there is but
small merit, and no admonition to virtue is needful for such
resistance. But when thy neighbour or his affairs occasion thee,
rightly or wrongly, inward grief, and make thy heart to suffer
anguish, and thou dost look in the mirror of thy soul and
findest there Christ, thy pattern, Who is meek and lowly,
and dost conform thyself to Him for very love of His great
love, and receive from His hand all that the world offers thee
of prosperity or adversity—this indeed is prosperity and perfection.

And to carry to its highest point this state of perfection,
all feelings of our own advantage must be rooted out, as we
have already set down. It is certain that the soul that will
receive with joy and for love of Christ Jesus any trial or trials
whatsoever, is greatly advantaged over those that will have the
contrary, that is to say, naught but prosperity; for the former
will find his desire wherever he go, while he that seeks prosperity will find it only with much labour, will keep it with
misgiving, and will hold it but for a brief space.

Here we must bear in mind that sentence of the last
chapter, which says: The hidden life of the prudent contemplative will be a life of great repose, and to suffer for the love
of Jesus Christ all such trials as the world may offer him will
be to him consolation. And if at times (since we are all human)
we are tempted to be negligent, touched now and again by
affliction, or attacked by sensuality, the same conformity which
dwells within the soul vanquishes such temptation and puts it
to flight. So that no mischance presents itself which for the

From this may be inferred a well-known precept, which is taught by all masters of the spiritual life (though but ill understood by those that read it): to wit, that as the means are done with when the end is reached, as the boat is still when it comes to its port, even so when man, by means of the labour of meditation, arrives at a state of rest and at the enjoyment of contemplation, he should forthwith cease from that toilsome and pious enquiry. And, content with gazing upon and remembering God,—as though he had Him present—he may enjoy those feelings which are given him, be they of love, or wonder, or joy or other such. The reason for this counsel is that the end of the whole matter consists rather in love, and the emotions of the will, than in speculation of the understanding, when the will is taken and captured by this emotion. Therefore we should dispense with all reasonings and speculations of the understanding, in so far as we may, to the end that our soul, with all its strength, may be occupied in this one thing, and not disperse its strength by acts of the other powers.

For this reason one doctor counsels that when a man feels himself to be on fire with love for God, he should forthwith abandon all reasonings and thoughts, how high soever they seem, —not that they are evil, but because they become in this case hindrances to a greater good, which is none other than the ceasing of all movement when one has reached the goal—and abandon meditation, for love of contemplation. This may be done notably at the end of the whole exercise, that is, after the petition of the love of God, of which we have written above. And this firstly, because it is presumed that, once the fatigue of the exercise is past, there will have resulted some regard and love for God, since, as the wise man says, ' Better is the end of a prayer than the beginning thereof.' [1] And secondly, because after the fatigue of meditation and prayer, it is but right that man should give some small respite to his understanding, and allow it to rest in the arms of contemplation. For at that time a man can put away all the imaginings that present themselves to him, hush the understanding, calm the

---

[1] Eccl. 7^9 : Melior est finis orationis quam principium.

memory, and fix it upon our Lord, considering how he is in
His presence, and making now no speculations upon the secret
things of God.

Let him be content with the knowledge of Him which he
has through faith, and apply his will and his love ; for love
alone embraces these, and in it is the fruit of all meditation.
Scarcely is there anything which the understanding can know
of God,—only the will can greatly love Him.   Let a man im-
prison himself within his own self, in the centre of his soul,
wherein is the image of God, and there let him wait upon Him,
as one listens to another speaking from some high tower, or as
though he had Him within his heart, and as if in all creation
there were no other thing save God and his soul.   Even himself
should he forget, and that which he is doing, for, as one of the
Fathers said, 'that prayer is perfect, in which he who is
praying, remembers not that he is praying.'

And not at the end of the exercise alone, but also in the
course of it, or in whatever part this spiritual slumber should
overtake us, when the understanding of the will is, as it were,
asleep, we should make this pause and enjoy this great benefit,
and then return to our labour, having tasted and digested this
one morsel.   Just so the gardener, watering a patch of ground,
after filling it with water, turns off the flow of the current and
allows the water to soak in and disperse itself over the depths
of the earth ; when all that it has received is drained away, the
gardener turns on the flow from the spring once more, that it
may receive more and more, and be the better watered.   But
what the soul feels at such times as this, and what light, fulness,
love and peace it receives, cannot be expressed in words, for
here is that peace which passes all understanding, and that
felicity which in this life can be attained.

Some few there are, so far captivated by the love of God,
that hardly have they begun to think upon Him when immediately the memory of His dear Name melts all their being.
And these have as small need of reasonings or meditations on
loving Him, as a mother or a bride needs to make her feast
upon the thought of her son or her lover, when men speak to

her of him. And others, not only in the exercise of prayer, but apart from it, are so absorbed and immersed in God, that they forget all things,—yea, even themselves—for Him. And if this effect can often be reached by the terrible dread of a despairing soul, how much the more may it be caused by the love of that infinite beauty, since grace is no less powerful than nature and guilt!

When therefore the soul feels thus, in whatever part of her prayer she feels it, she should in no wise put it aside, even though all the time of the exercise were spent without the performance of the prayer or meditation which had been planned —unless these were of obligation. For, as St. Augustine says, vocal prayer should be abandoned if at any time it were to impede devotion, and just so meditation, if it were to stand in the way of contemplation.

And here also it is to be strictly noted, that as we must leave meditation for emotion, in order to rise from the lower to the higher, so, on the other hand, it will be fitting at times to leave emotion for meditation, if the emotion were so vehement that peril to the health were to be feared, did one persevere in it. This oftentimes occurs with those who devote themselves to these exercises without this counsel, and perform them indiscreetly, attracted by the power of the divine sweetness. And in a case such as this (says a Doctor) a good remedy is to let some emotion of pity fill our minds, by meditating for a space upon the Passion of Christ, or on the sins and miseries of the world, to ease and relieve the heart.

JUAN DE ÁVILA

(1500-1569)

Juan de Ávila, known also as the "Apostle of Andalucia," was born at Almodóvar del Campo, studied jurisprudence at Salamanca and theology at Alcalá. On his ordination, finding himself unable to undertake missionary work in America as he had hoped, he resolved to devote himself to evangelising the south of Spain, where he spent the greater part of his life. Unlike most of the Spanish mystics, he belonged to no religious order.

His relations with such great personalities as Fray Luis de Granada, St. Francisco de Borja (whom, in 1539, he converted), St. Ignacio Loyola, and St. Teresa intensify the interest which his deeply spiritual yet no less markedly individual writings arouse. The first named of these mystics composed the earliest life of Juan de Ávila known.

He suffered at the hands of the Inquisition (1532-4) and spent some months in prison, on account of suspected heresies in his writings. But in general no preacher of the age was more widely respected, nor indeed more worthy of respect. He had not only a love of souls, but an instinctive, as well as experiential, knowledge of the individual soul, which made him a skilled director, and the adviser of no less a saint than St. Teresa. Among the links which bind these two mystics is the significant fact that her *Life* was sent to him for his approval a few years before his death.

Juan de Ávila was beatified in 1894.

LETTER TO A SICK GIRL COMFORTING HER IN HER TRIALS

Lady, I have learned that you are sick ; and this does not grieve me, for, if it comes from some excess of penance that you have done, the chastisement is well worth the pains ; and if it is but that our Lord sends it let the share He gives you in His Cross be ever welcome.   And although on one hand your suffering causes me to suffer also, how much so our Lord knows, on the other hand I am glad, for I see clearly the great gain of one who I wish may gain greatly.   I would not for my spiritual children ought save rods, for the time of consolation is not yet. And now, lady, lift not your eyes from the Cross, nor your heart from Him Who was raised upon it.   Rest not until you have found suffering sweet, for herein appears love.   Have no pity upon yourself, for both in Heaven and on earth you have One Who loves you dearly, and that which comes to you has been closely scanned and sent from the very hand of Him Who most truly loves you.   Let not your faith grow cold in need and danger, nor your love amid trials.

When a fire is strong the wind cannot quench it, but rather makes it stronger.   So when a soul loves God as it were in play, its fire of love is quenched like a tiny candle with the first breath of wind that reaches it.   But true love grows amid trials, for the more there comes to be borne, the greater the strength it gathers

together to bear it; and if it be of God it conquers all trials—
no water is sufficient to quench the fire which has come from
Heaven. God has called such a soul to love Him, and love is
not a thing for a mere pastime: one must hate oneself to love
Christ, and deny oneself to confess Him, and be cruel to oneself
to be gentle and meek with the Lord. If we love Him and
desire to have fruition of Him, let us lose ourselves. If we
would see Him, we must go through fire and water for Him.
If we would make room for Him in our hearts we must cast out
our very selves and all created things, for God will have only an
undivided and an afflicted heart, not from ill-will that He bears
us, but because, since His Blessed Son was afflicted, He would
not have His sons in other guise. This is that which seems lovely
in His sight, that He should see in us the image of His Only-
begotten Son; and even as there is nothing on which a soul so
much loves to look as on Jesus Christ suffering on the Cross,
and as the more afflicted and devoid of beauty He appears the
more lovely He seems, even so the more we suffer, the lovelier
do we appear to God.

And it is no great matter that the soul which would appear
fair to God should deck itself in such a way as to please Him,
since women of the world do many things and are at great ex-
pense to please the sons of men. Lady, our adornments must
be changed to please God.

With burning acid gold is refined, and when the dross is removed it comes from the crucible refulgent. Let us have shame
that we are so cold in an emprise so great as that of pleasing
God. Ah, did we but feel true shame we should take courage
to shed our blood for Him that we might be the lovelier in His
sight. . . . The emprise of love is not of words, but of pain, of
cruel torments, worldly disgrace, abandonment by men, and the
withdrawal of the protection of God. And with all this upon
us we must keep a cheerful countenance, neither complaining
nor letting our heart be sad. Rather we must be like the
martyr, who, when his bowels were torn out and he was tortured
with iron combs, called only on the Name of Jesus and said only
in his heart 'Blessed be God,' and would have suffered more

had it so pleased God.   A gift and a favour is it to suffer for
Christ, given only to those whom He greatly loves.

LETTER TO A RELIGIOUS URGING HIM TO THE PERFECT LOVE OF GOD

Very Reverend Father : *Pax Christi*.   Since it pleases not
our Lord Jesus Christ that I should be now where I may enjoy
the company of your Reverence and of the reverend collegians
as I would, blessed be His Name.   I bear it in patience, and I
think that therein I do no little penance, for it is a hard thing
for a man to endure being separated from one whom he loves ;
and in truth I have never so greatly desired the correction of
your Reverence as now, for I think it would be of great service
to our Lord.   But since to those who love Him all things appear
good, I will say somewhat in absence, until God shall grant me
your presence.   I desire greatly, reverend sir, that we should
seek God, Who is our Good ; and this not in any light manner,
but as one seeking a treasure which he desires, and for love of
which he sells all that he has, thinking himself still rich in
possessing this single thing, in the place of many things which
he had aforetime.

O Lord God, in Whom the innermost being of our heart may
find rest !   When shall we begin, I say not to love Thee, but
even to wish that we may love Thee ?   When shall we have a
desire for Thyself that is worthy of Thee ?   When shall we be
moved by truth, and not by vanity, by beauty and not by
foulness, by quietness and not by restlessness, by the Creator,
so bountiful and all-sufficient, rather than by the creature, which
is so poor and empty ?   Ah, Lord, and who shall open our
eyes to show us that apart from Thee is nothing that can satisfy
or abide ?   Who is he that shall reveal to us something of
Thyself, that we may be filled with love for Thee, and that we
may walk, run—yea, fly—to be for ever with Thee ?   Alas, that
we are so far from God, and that it grieves us so little, scarcely
causing us sorrow !   Where are those sighs of deep affection
which come from souls which once have tasted of God and then

are withdrawn from Him a little? Where is that which David said: Surely I will not give sleep to mine eyes or slumber to my eyelids, until I find out a house for the Lord?[1]

And we ourselves are this house, when we are not lost in distractions among divers things, but recollect ourselves in unity of desire and love; and then we find ourselves and are the creatures of God. I believe that the reason of our lukewarmness is, as one said, that he who has never tasted of God knows neither what it is to hunger, nor yet to be filled. And thus we hunger not for Him, nor yet do we find satisfaction in His creatures, but are cold, indifferent, slothful and faint-hearted, without relish for the things of God and like to be spewn forth by Him Who will have no lukewarm servants. For His servants must be inflamed with fire, which He came to bring to the earth and wills not but that it be kindled. And that it might be kindled He Himself was consumed and, as it were, burned upon the Cross, like unto the red heifer without the camp,[2] that we ourselves might take the wood of the Cross, be warmed and set on fire, returning some manner of love to Him who has so greatly loved us, and considering how just a thing it is that we should be wounded with that sweet wound of love, since we see Him, not only wounded by love, but killed.

It is but meet that we should be made captives by love for One Who for our sakes was delivered as a Captive into the hands of cruel men. Let us enter into the bondage of His love, since He entered into that of ours, and became as a meek lamb before His oppressors. This bondage it was which bound Him to the Cross, for greater and stronger far were the ties and bonds of our love, than the ropes and nails with which men constrained His body as love constrained His heart. Wherefore let our hearts be bound with His love,—the very bond of salvation— and let us desire no freedom which shall loose us from such bondage ; for as he that is not wounded by His love has no true

---

[1] Ps. 131⁴·⁵, Vulg. : Si dedero somnum oculis meis, et palpebris meis dormitationem; et requiem temporibus meis, donec inveniam locum Domino, tabernaculum Deo Jacob. *Cf.* Ps. 132⁴·⁵, A.V.

[2] Numbers 19.

health, so he that is not bound in His bondage has no true freedom.

Let us then no more resist Him, but allow ourselves to be vanquished by His weapons—to wit, His favours—by which He would slay us that we may live with Him.   He would fain consume us, that our old man being destroyed, which is in the likeness of Adam, our new man may be born through love, which is in the image of Christ.   He would fain melt our hard hearts, to the end that, as on metal that is molten by heat the image willed by the artificer may be imprinted, so we, softened by love which causes us to melt as we hear the voice of the Beloved, may be without resistance, and ready for Christ to imprint upon us the image that He wills,—that is, the image of Christ Himself, which is the image of love.   For He commanded us that we should love one another as He loved us.   And St. Paul tells us that we should walk in love, even as Christ loved us and gave Himself for us ; so that if we love not, we are not like Him, we have another countenance, we are other than He is, we are poor, naked, blind, deaf, dumb and dead, because love alone gives light to all things, and He it is who has the spiritual care of our souls, which without Him are as is the body without the soul.

Let us love, then, reverend father, and we shall live ; let us love, and we shall be like to God, and we shall wound our God, who with love alone is wounded ; let us love, and God will be ours, since love alone can possess Him ; let us love, and all things will be ours, for all will serve us, as it is written: All things work together for good to them that love God.* If this love seems good to us, let us lay the axe of diligence to the root of our love of self and let us cast this enemy of ours to the ground.

LUIS DE GRANADA

(1504-1588)

Born in Granada, twelve years after its re-conquest by the Catholic Monarchs, Luis de Sarria is always known by the name of his birthplace. His life was that of a busy Dominican preacher. After long years spent in deep theological studies, in which he showed great brilliancy, he was appointed prior of the convent of Escala Coeli, near Córdoba, in which district he first became noted for his eloquence. After a short time spent as chaplain to the Duke of Medina-Sidonia, he took charge of a newly founded convent at Badajoz, and later became Provincial of his order in Portugal. As confessor of the Queen he found great favour, and was offered indeed an Archbishopric, which, however, he declined. His unambitious nature found its reward and satisfaction in a long and peaceful life, unusually free from persecution and anxiety, until, at a great age, his health and sight both began to fail, and he died on the last day of the year 1588.

Of his non-mystical books, the *Guía de Pecadores* is deservedly the most famous. Besides being one of the chief devotional books in Spain, it won great favour in France, and found its way, in many editions and under various forms, to England.

ON THE SEA

Yet another property has the sea, which is among the chiefest works of creation, and on the one hand reveals the gentleness, on the other the indignation and wrath of the Creator. For what is there more peaceful than the sea when it is still and free from the raging of the winds—'a young ladies' sea' as we call it—or when it is gently stirred by a soft breeze, and its waves, one after the other, ripple quietly in towards the shore, with a gentle murmur, each following the other till it breaks upon the strand? This then represents the tenderness and mercy of the Creator towards the faithful. But now is the sea lashed by mighty winds, and its fearful waves rise up towards the clouds, and the higher they rise, the deeper are the chasms they reveal. The wretched sailors toss up and down, the sides of their great vessels furiously battered by the waves; the men are brought into mortal fear, their strength is exhausted and they despair of their lives. All this pictures to us the fury of the Divine wrath, and the greatness of that power which can raise and calm such tempests when He pleases. And this the Royal Prophet declares to be among the signs of God's greatness, when he says: "Thou, O Lord, rulest the raging of the sea; when the waves thereof arise, Thou stillest them. The heavens are

Thine, the earth also is Thine; as for the world and the fulness thereof, Thou hast founded them. The north and the south, Thou hast created them."[1]

There remains yet to be related another excellence of the sea, and this is so great that the mind and the pen fear to attempt it. For what words suffice—I say not to describe, but even to call by their names (if names they all have) the varieties of fish which this element contains. What Intelligence, what Wisdom was that, which could invent, not only so many species, but so many forms of fish so different in size—some very small, others incredibly great, and between these two extremes, a host of other differences on either side? For if God created the whale, He created also the frog, and to make the one which is so great cost Him no more labour than to form that[2] which is so small. There are artificers who cut silk or paper with scissors in a thousand different forms and fancies as the caprice takes them, the paper or silk obeying the mind and will of its shaper. But what Shaper was the first of all, Who could cut and trace all the various forms which we perceive in the fish of the sea, giving to each its individual property and nature. For he who cuts with the scissors does but shape a form, endowing it with no more than with what it represents. But this Sovereign Shaper gives, together with the form, a soul, a life, senses, movement and skill to seek its own sustenance, offensive and defensive weapons for its preservation, and above all such fertility in the propagation of its kind as, had we not known it, would be totally incredible.

Who will count the eggs of the shad or the merluce or any other fish? And from each of these tiny eggs comes a fish as great as that from which it proceeded, however great that fish may be. And the water, like a kindly mother, by the power of the Creator, receives it into its bosom, and nurtures it till it

---

[1] Apparently a free rendering of Ps. 88[10,12,13], Vulg.: Tu dominaris potestati maris, motum autem fluctuum ejus tu mitigas. Tui sunt caeli, et tua est terra; orbem terræ et plenitudinem ejus tu fundasti; aquilonem et mare tu creasti. Cf. Ps. 89[9,11,12], A.V. which has been partly followed in the translation.

[2] So we may translate; but it is to be feared that Fray Luis considered the frog to be a ' fish,' as also the whale.

comes to maturity. What is there more wonderful than this? For as Divine Providence created this wealth of fish for the sustenance of man, and as those who entrap fish cannot see them in the water as hunters see their game on the ground or in the air, He ordained that the fertility and reproductiveness of the fish should be so great, that the sea would be full of them wheresoever the draw-net was thrown. Many and all but innumerable are the varieties of birds and beasts on the earth, but in the sea there are incomparably more, for this element, as it would seem, is less disposed to receive inhabitants which should people it, and to give them food, such as we see on the earth, to sustain them.

What shall I say, too, of the varieties of shell-fish which the sea affords? What of the variety of forms with which many of them imitate the beasts of the earth? For there are fish which have the shape of a horse, others of a dog, others of a wolf, others of a calf, others of a lamb. And, that there might be nothing left for them to imitate, others have our own form and are called 'men of the sea.' And besides this, what shall I say of the shells which yield that fine scarlet that is the adornment of kings? What of the other shells, of scallops, of snail-shells great and small, wrought in a thousand ways, some whiter than snow, some spangled all over with divers colours. O wonderful wisdom of the Creator! How marvellous, O Lord, are thy works! With infinite wisdom hast Thou made them all, and not the earth only, but also the sea, is full of Thy marvels!

ON THE BEAUTY OF THE HEAVENS

And the loveliness of the heavens, who shall declare it? How pleasant on a calm midsummer night to gaze on the full moon, which is so bright that all the stars are extinguished by its glory! How much more do travellers on summer nights take pleasure in this light, than in the sun, although the sun is the greater! And when the moon is invisible, what is there lovelier, what that tells more eloquently of the Creator's omnipotence and beauty, than the sky, spangled with so vast and various an array of glorious stars,—some great and resplendent, others small, others again in magnitude between them—which can be numbered by none save by their Creator alone? Only the custom of seeing all this destroys our wonder at such great beauty, and the cause it gives us to praise that Sovereign Painter, who knew so well how to adorn the spacious vault of heaven.

Imagine a child to have been born and grown up in a prison, and reached the age of five-and-twenty years having seen no more than what was within its four walls. If he came out of that darkness a man of understanding, the first time that he saw the star-spangled sky on a calm night, he could not of a certainty fail to be awed by the beauty of its adornment and the vast array of stars to be seen in whichever direction he turned his eyes : to east or west, to the north side or the south. Nor could he but exclaim : "Who can have adorned such great heavens with so many precious stones and such brilliant diamonds? Who can have made so many lights and lamps to illumine the world? Who can have decked out a land of such beauteous meadows with such variety of flowers, save some most glorious and powerful Creator? A pagan philosopher, amazed at this work of God, once wrote : *Intuere coelum et philosophare*, which signifies : Look up at the sky, and begin to philosophise. That is to say : by that great variety and beauty which here you see, know and consider the wisdom and omnipotence of its Author. And the Prophet, too, could philosophise equally well upon this matter, when he exclaimed : "I shall see, O Lord, Thy heavens which are the work of Thy hands, the moon and the stars which Thou hast founded." [1]

And if the beauty of the stars is wonderful, no less so is their efficacy in influencing, or even engendering all things in this lower world. Especially is this true of the sun, for as it goes farther from us, in the time of autumn, all the fields and groves lose their beauty, together with their leaves, until they are bare, sterile and to appearance dead. And when the sun

---

[1] Ps. 8³, Vulg. : Quoniam videbo caelos tuos, opera digitorum tuorum, lunam et stellas quæ tu fundasti. *Cf.* Ps. 8³, A.V.

turns and approaches us again, then the fields are clothed in a new dress, the trees take on leaf and flower, and the birds which before were dumb, begin to chirp and sing; vine and rose-tree put forth shoot and bud, and make ready to reveal the beauty which is enclosed within them. So great, indeed, is the dependence of this world upon the influences of the heavens, that if some part of them be hindered in its functions for never so short a space (as happens in the eclipses of sun and moon and at interlunary seasons), we at once feel changes and disturbances even in our human bodies, the more so if we are weak and infirm.

On the Unitive Life

Accordingly, when a man in this mortal life reaches so high a degree of love that he despises all things which perish, taking unlawful content or pleasure in none, but fixing all his pleasure, love, care, desire and thought upon God, and this so constantly that always, or well-nigh always, his heart is set on Him (for in Him alone he finds rest, and apart from Him none); when in this way a man is dead to all things, and alive only to God, the greatness of his love triumphing over all other affections, then he will have entered the vaults of precious wine of the true Solomon, in which, inebriated with the wine of this love, he will forget all things,—even himself—for His sake.

I see well that few can arrive at this degree,—that the necessities of life, the requirements of justice, and even of charity, call us many a time to leave God (if we may speak thus) for God Himself. But still I write of this that we may see the end towards which we have to journey, in so far as we are able, for, even though none can reach it, those who press forward with soul and intent towards higher things will come nearer than those who set a limit to their desires at a lower level.

Of this matter a wise man says: In everything good we must desire the utmost possible, that at least we may arrive half way. And with this will and desire St. Bernard said: May my soul, O Lord, die not alone the death of the righteous, but the death of angels—that is to say, may it be as dead to worldly things, and as far removed from them, as not only the righteous but the angels are, if that be possible.   For the most ardent and burning desire has not to reckon with its own strength, nor to know bounds, nor to measure itself with reason, nor to desire only what is possible, for it looks not at what it can but at what it wills to do.

This is the love which in mystic theology is called ' unitive,' because its nature is to unite the lover with the object of his love so that apart from it he finds no repose, and on it therefore has his heart ever set.

A Prayer

Then who, O Lord, is all my well-being and my final goal, but Thyself?   Thou, O Lord, art the goal of all my journeys, the safe harbour of my voyages, the crown of all my desires. How then shall I not love thee with this love?   The fire and the air rend the mountains, and cause the earth to tremble when they are beneath it, and would rise to their rightful place.   Then how shall not I break through all creatures, how shall not I make a way through steel and through fire, till I come to Thyself, Who art the place of my rest?   Into a receptacle made for some vessel naught but that vessel will go.   Then how shall my soul, a receptacle which Thou hast fashioned for Thyself, be content with aught but with Thyself alone?   Remember then, O my God, that as I am for Thee, Thou also art for me.   Flee not from me, O Lord, lest I attain not to Thy Presence.   Slow, slow are my steps, oft times I halt by the way, and oft turn back : be not weary, O Lord, of waiting for one who follows Thee not with equal step.

O my God and my Salvation, why do I so often halt?   Why do I not run with exceeding lightness to my Exceeding Good, in Whom all good is contained?   What can man desire, that is not found in that ocean of goodness rather than in the wretched and muddy pools of creatures?   Men love riches, love honours, long life, tranquillity, wisdom, virtue, joys and such like things, and with so great a love do they love them, that many a time for their sakes they are ruined. O foolish and base lovers, that love the shadow and despise the substance, that go to fish in dirty pools and forget the sea! If each of these things deserves to be loved for itself, how much more should He be loved Who is of greater worth than they all! If the father of the prophet Samuel could say with truth to his wife, who was weeping because she had no sons, that he alone was worth more to her than ten sons, with how much more truth wilt Thou, O Lord, say to the soul of the just man, that Thou art worth more to him than all the creatures? For what rest, what riches, what joys can be found in the creatures that are not infinitely more abundant in the Creator? The joys of the world are carnal, vile, deceptive, brief and transitory. They are won with labour, held with anxiety, and lost with grief. They endure but a little, yet the harm they do is great. They inflate the soul and feed it not, deceive it and sustain it not; and therefore they make it not happier but more wretched, more athirst, more removed from God and itself, and more like to the condition of the beasts. For this reason, said St. Augustine, wretched is the soul whose affections are entwined round things below, for when he loses them he is torn to pieces. And then he comes to know his wretched state through experience of the ill which he suffers by reason of these affections,—though he was miserable, too, before he suffered it. But Thyself, O Lord, none can lose, save he who leaves Thee of his own free will: he that loves Thee enters into the joy of his Lord, and he will have naught to fear, but rather will be at peace in Him Who is Peace Eternal. . . .

May I love thee, then, O Lord, with the straitest and most fervent love. May I stretch out mine arms—yea, all my affections and desires, to embrace Thee, sweetest Spouse of my soul, from Whom I hope for all good. The ivy clings to its tree in every place, so that the whole of it seems to be throwing out arms to grasp the tree more closely, for by means of this support it mounts on high and attains what to it is perfection. And to what other tree but to Thyself must I cling, that I may grow and attain what I lack? The ivy-plant clinging to the tree grows not more nor throws more widely its lovely branches than

the soul grows in virtues and graces when it clings to Thee.
Then how shall I not love Thee with all my soul, and strength,
and powers? Help me, my God and my Saviour, and raise me
on high in quest of Thyself, for the grievous weight of this mortal
life drags me downward. Thou, O Lord, Who didst mount the
Tree—even the Cross—to draw all men unto Thyself; Thou
Who with so vast a love didst unite two such contrary natures
in one Person, to make Thyself one with us, do Thou grant that
our hearts may be united to Thee with so strong a band of love,
that they may at last become one with Thee, since Thou didst
unite Thyself with us, that we might be united with Thyself.

SANTA TERESA DE JESÚS

(1515-1582)

St. Teresa's life may be read in her own words in the *Libro de su
Vida :* it is a long and arresting story, whether the reader regard its
active or its contemplative side as the more important. For, both as
mystic and foundress, St. Teresa was one of the few pre-eminent women
that Spain has bred, and when it is borne in mind that her works, written
under obedience and not as conscious art, have found their way to a high
position in Spanish literature, the full extent of her greatness begins to be
realised.

Teresa de Cepeda y Ahumada was a daughter of Ávila by character
as by birth. Attracted to the religious life from her childhood, she
entered the Carmelite Convent of the Incarnation in her native city in
1535. For thirty years she remained there, her spiritual life developing
as she grew older, until she received a call from Heaven to restore the
rule of her order in the primitive strictness from which it had long since
degenerated.

In 1562 the first convent of the Reformed (or Discalced) Carmelite
nuns was founded in Ávila and dedicated to St. Joseph. For the next
twenty years Teresa's life is a record of journeys, foundations, opposition,
persecutions, ill-health, failures and triumphs. "Nothing is impossible
if Our Lord wills it," is a phrase (from her Letters) typical of the spirit
of calmness and confidence in which she worked. These same Letters,
which cover the period of her active life as a foundress (1561-1582), reveal also the woman of affairs,—busy, methodical and practical,—a woman,
too, with an intimate knowledge of the human heart, its weakness and its

strength. She is bound by some link or other to most of the great ascetics and mystics of her age. The works of Francisco de Osuna, San Pedro de Alcántara, Luis de Granada and many others formed a large part of her reading ; Juan de Ávila was among her correspondents and friends, San Juan de la Cruz was one of her first two male recruits for the reform ; while to Luis de León fell the task of examining her manuscript works. And just as in this way she is the centre of the greatest mystics of the time, and her life a connecting link or a thread which runs through their own, so the mysticism which finds expression in the *Camino de Perfección* and the *Moradas* has something in common with mysticism of every type. It is neither for the beginner alone nor for the proficient ; it neither despises asceticism nor enforces it ; it avoids the extremes of quietism while extolling the fundamental truths from which that doctrine springs. Thus the works of St. Teresa are a legacy to all who call themselves or would fain be called mystics in spirit and in truth, and as such they have never lacked a multitude of readers.

AUTOBIOGRAPHICAL

We were three sisters and nine brothers : all of us, by God's grace, like our parents in virtue, I myself excepted, though I was my father's favourite, and before I began to offend God I think I had some reason to be ; for I grieve, when I remember the good inclinations which the Lord had given me, and how badly I made use of them. And my brothers and sisters in no way hindered me from serving God.

One favourite brother I had, of about my own age,—though I loved them all dearly and they me. We used to read together the Lives of the Saints, and as I read of the martyrdoms of the Saints for God's sake it came to me that they bought their fruition of God very cheaply. And I wished very much that I might die thus, not for any love that I bore Him, but to enjoy without delay the great riches in Heaven which I read of. With this brother I used to discuss how it might be accomplished. We decided to go to the country of the Moors, begging our way 'for the love of God,' and to be beheaded there. And I think the Lord had given us courage enough even at so tender an age, if we had seen any way of accomplishing this. Only the greatest obstacle seemed to us to be our parents. It impressed us greatly when we read that the

pain and the glory were for ever.   Again and again we talked
of this, and we liked to repeat many times 'for ever—ever—
ever.'   It pleased the Lord that by these many repetitions the
way of truth should be impressed on my mind in childhood.

When I saw the impossibility of going where I should be
put to death for the faith of God, we set about becoming
hermits, and in a garden which we had at home we contrived
to build hermitages as best we could by piling up small stones
which soon fell down ; and so we found no way of satisfying
our wishes.   It fills me with devotion even now to think how
early God gave me what I forfeited by my own fault.   I gave
alms as I could,—and that was but little.   I contrived to be
alone in order to perform my devotions, which were long, and
especially the Rosary, to which my mother was very much
devoted, and taught us to be so too.   When I played with
other little girls I loved to build convents and play at being
nuns ; and I think I wanted to be one, though less so than the
other things I have mentioned.

I remember when my mother died I was about twelve years
old or a little less.   When I began to realise my loss I went in
my grief to an image of Our Lady, and I begged her with many
tears to take my mother's place.   I think that, although I did
it in my simplicity, it has stood me in good stead ; for I have
found the Virgin by experience to be my Sovereign indeed
whenever I have recommended myself to her, and at last she
has brought me back to herself.   It distresses me now to see
and reflect on that which has prevented me from being faithful
to the good desires in which I began.

Ah, my Lord! since it seems Thou art resolved upon my
salvation, may it please Thy Majesty to bring it to pass, and to
grant me as many graces as in the past.   Has it not been Thy
pleasure,—not for my advantage but for Thy greater honour,—
that this abode wherein Thou hast so continually to dwell be
not so defiled?   It grieves me, O Lord, even to say this, for
well I know that the fault has been mine alone ; for nothing
more can I think of that Thou couldst have done to make me
from that early age entirely Thine.   Nor can I complain of my

parents, for I saw in them nothing but what was good and concerned for my welfare.   And when I outgrew my childhood, I began to understand the natural gifts which the Lord had given me (and they were said to be many); and instead of giving thanks for them, I made use of them all only to offend Him.

SIMILITUDE OF THE WATERS

The beginner must think of himself as of one setting out to make from a barren piece of ground, full of weeds, a garden in which the Lord may take His delight.   His Majesty uproots the weeds, and will set good plants in their place.   Let us then suppose that this has already happened,—that a soul has determined to live the life of prayer, and has already begun it.   With God's help, we have, like good gardeners, to make these plants grow, and water them with care so that they die not, but rather produce flowers which shall give out great fragrance and so afford refreshment to our Lord.   So may He come often to this garden to delight Himself therein and take His pleasure among these virtues.

Let us now consider how this garden can be watered, that we may know what we have to do, what labour it will cost us, if the gain outweigh the labour, and for how long this labour must be borne.   It seems to me that the garden can be watered in four ways : by taking water from a well, which costs us much labour ; or by a water-wheel and buckets, when the water is drawn by a windlass—I have drawn it thus at times : it is less laborious than the other way and gives more water ; or by a stream or a brook, which waters the ground much better, for it becomes more thoroughly saturated, and there is less need to water it often, and the gardener's labour is much less ; or by showers of rain, when the Lord Himself waters it without any labour of ours, and this way is incomparably better than any of those which have been described.

And now I come to my point, which is the application of these four manners of watering by which the garden is to be kept in fertility, for without water it must fail.   I think I shall be able to give some explanation of the four degrees of prayer

which our Lord, of His goodness, has at times applied to my
soul.   May He also of His goodness grant that I may so speak
as to be of some profit to one of the persons who commanded
me to write this book, whom our Lord has brought in four
months to a point far beyond that which I have reached in
seventeen years.   He prepared himself better than I, and thus
his garden, without labour on his part, is watered by all these
four means,—though the last watering he receives only drop by
drop; but his garden is making such progress that soon, by the
help of the Lord, it will be submerged.   I shall be glad for him
to laugh at my explanation, if he finds it foolish.

Of those who are beginning the life of prayer, we may say
that they are those who draw up the water from the well.   This,
as I have said, is very laborious, for they have to weary themselves in keeping recollected the senses which hitherto have been
accustomed to a life of distraction.   To do this is a great labour.
Beginners must gradually accustom themselves to disregard what
they see or hear, and to practise this recollection, during their
hours of prayer.   They must be alone, and in solitude must
think over their past lives.   All, in fact, must do this, and often,
beginners and proficients alike.   Some, however, will do it more,
and some less, as I shall show hereafter.   Beginners at first advance very painfully, because they have not completely convinced
themselves that they are sorry for their sins; and yet they are
sorry for them, just because they are resolved so truly to serve
God.   They must strive to ponder much upon the life of Christ,
and that, again, is wearisome to the understanding.   Thus much
we can accomplish of ourselves,—of course with the grace of God
helping us, for without that, as all know, we cannot have so
much as one good thought.

All this is denoted by beginning to draw up water from the
well.   God grant that there may be water in it to draw!   That,
however, is not our business; we are concerned to draw it, and
to do what we can towards the watering of the flowers.   And
God is so gracious that when, for reasons which His Majesty knows
—perhaps for our great good—He wills that the well should be
dry, then if we, like good gardeners, are doing that which in us

lies, He Himself preserves the flowers without water, and makes our virtues grow. By water I here mean tears, and if there be no tears, I mean tenderness and an inward feeling of devotion.

What, then, will he do here who sees that, for many days, there is nought but drought, distaste, dislike, and so little desire to go and draw water that he would give it up entirely if he did not remember that it is pleasing and serving the Lord of the garden; if he were not anxious that his service should not be lost, as well as the gain which he hopes for from the great labour of lowering the bucket into the well so often, and drawing it up without water? It will often happen that even for that purpose he is unable to move his arms—unable (that is) to think a single good thought; for working with the understanding is the same as drawing water out of the well.

What then, as I have said, will the gardener do here? He will be glad and take heart, and consider it the greatest favour to work in the garden of so great a Sovereign; and as he knows that he is pleasing Him by so working—and his purpose must be to please not himself, but Him—let him praise Him greatly for placing such confidence in him, for He sees that without receiving any recompense, he is taking very great care of that which was entrusted to him; let him help Him to bear the Cross, and let him consider how He lived with it all His life long; let him not seek his kingdom here, nor ever cease from prayer; and so let him resolve if this spiritual drought should persist his whole life long, never to let Christ fall beneath the Cross.

THE FIFTH MANSIONS

Similitude of the Silkworm

You will think that all there is to see in this Mansion has been described, but much remains yet, for, as I said, some receive more than others. As far as the meaning of Union is concerned, I think I can say no more. But when the soul to which God grants these favours is prepared for them, there is much to say of what the Lord works in it. I will speak somewhat thereof, and in such manner as I am able.

To explain it better, I will make use of a suitable comparison, which will also show how in this work, which is the Lord's, we are powerless, yet how much we can do in preparing ourselves to be granted these favours by the Lord. You will have heard of God's wonderful way of making silk, which only He could invent, and how it comes from a seed or egg which resembles a little peppercorn. (I have only heard of this, and never seen it, so, if it is incorrect in any way, the fault is not mine.) The heat when the mulberry trees begin to put forth leaf gives life to this little egg, which, until its food and sustenance were ready, was dead. It feeds on the mulberry leaves, until, when it is full-grown, one puts out twigs, upon which, with its own tiny mouth, the insect begins to weave the silk, and prepares a small cocoon in which it buries itself. Then finally, the worm, which was large and ugly, comes out of the cocoon a lovely white butterfly.

If this could not be seen and were related to us as a story of past ages, who would believe it? For what reasons could we find to explain why a creature so irrational as a worm or a bee should work so diligently and industriously for our advantage, or why the poor little worm should lose its life in the attempt? This alone, my sisters, is matter enough for a short meditation, even if I say no more, for in it you may consider the wonders and the wisdom of our God. And what would it be if we knew the properties of everything? Greatly do we gain in thinking diligently of these great things, and in delighting to be the brides of so wise and powerful a King.

To return to what I was saying. This silkworm is like the soul which takes life when, kindled by the Holy Spirit, it begins to use the general aids which God gives us all, the remedies which He left in His Church (as confessions, sermons, holy reading) to all of which a soul dead in negligence or sin, and subject to temptations, may have recourse. Then it is that the soul begins to live, and feeds on these and on devout meditations, until it is full-grown, which is what concerns me now—the rest matters little. When the silkworm is full-grown (as was said at the opening of this chapter) it begins to spin the silk and build the house wherein it must die. This house, I should like to explain here, is Christ. I think I have read somewhere, or heard, that our life is hidden in Christ, or in God (which is the same thing) or that Christ is our life. However, whether this be so or not, it matters little to my present purpose.

You see, then, by this, my daughters, what we can do through the grace of God, if His Majesty Himself be our dwelling, as in the Prayer of Union He is, and this dwelling we build for ourselves. It almost seems as if we can, as it were, take away from God or add to Him, when I say that He is the dwelling, and that we can make it ourselves, and in it dwell. This we can indeed do, though we do not take from God or add to Him, but like the silkworm we take from and add to ourselves. And ere we have finished doing all that we can in this matter God will take this insignificant little work of ours, and join it with His greatness, and give it such worth that the Lord Himself will be its reward. And as it is He who has paid the greatest price, so His Majesty will join our poor trials with the great sufferings which He has endured, that both may be as one.

To work, then, my daughters! Let us hasten to perform our work, and spin this cocoon, setting aside self-love and self-will, being bound to nothing on earth, practising penance, prayer, mortification, obedience, and all the other good works which are known to you. Let us do as we have learned—and we are taught all that is needful for us. Die! die like the silkworm when it has accomplished that for which it was created, and you will see God and be buried in His greatness, as the silkworm is in the cocoon. Notice that I speak of 'seeing' God, for, as I have said, He manifests Himself to the perceptions in this kind of union.

Let us now see what becomes of the silkworm. For why have I said all this? Why but because, when the soul is in this state of prayer, and quite dead to the world, there comes out the white butterfly. Ah, greatness of God! How does a soul come out from this state—that of having been buried for a time in God's greatness, and so near Him that the state never lasts—as I think—half an hour? I tell you in truth, the very soul does not know itself: look at the difference between an ugly worm and a white butterfly—it is the same here. It knows not how it has deserved so great good (or rather, how the good has come, for it knows well that it deserves it not at all). It finds itself anxious to praise the Lord, to throw off this mortal life, to die a thousand deaths for God. Then of necessity it begins to suffer great trials, without the possibility of doing otherwise. It has burning desires for penance, for solitude, for all to know God; and to see how He is offended troubles it greatly. And although in the next Mansion we shall speak of these things in greater detail, for this Mansion and the next are almost one, the effects are of very different power; for, as I have said, if, after God visits a soul in this Mansion, it endeavours to progress farther, it will see great things. To see, then, the restlessness of this little butterfly! (Yet it has never been quieter or more at rest in its life.) God is to be praised for that it knows not where to settle and make its abode; such an abode has it had that all it sees on earth leaves it discontented, especially when God gives it often of these graces, for then almost every time it gains something new.

It sets no store by the things it did when still a worm,—to wit, the gradual weaving of the cocoon. It has wings now: how then can it be content with crawling slowly along since it can fly? All that it can do for God seems little, by comparison with its desires. It sets little store by the sufferings of the saints, having learned by experience how the Lord helps and transforms a soul, so that it seems no longer itself, nor even its own likeness. For the weakness which it seemed to have before in doing penances is now turned to strength; no longer has it the ties of relationship, friendship or property which neither acts nor determinations sufficed to loosen but seemed only to bind the more firmly: now it is grieved at having to do what is necessary in order not to sin against God. It is fatigued by all this, for it has found that there is no true rest in the creatures.

VERSE

I.

Since Thou dost give us habits new,
  Great King, we urge
Thou may'st from evil gentry free
  These robes of serge.

Take courage, daughters, since the cross
  Ye do embrace,
And beg of Jesus Christ, your Light,
  To grant you grace,
And He will be your sure defence
  In conflict base.

  O Lord! from evil gentry free
    These robes of serge!

To earn disquiet by our prayer
  Doth ill requite,
The while devotion from our soul
  Swift wings its flight;
But rest your heart in God, with His
  Your will unite.

  Do Thou from evil gentry free
    These robes of serge!

Since you have come that you may die,
  Be not afraid
Nor by this gentry's courtesy
  Be you dismayed,
For in this combat sore, your God
  Will be your aid.

  Do Thou from evil gentry free
    These robes of serge!

Set Thou from evil gentry free
  These robes of serge,
Since Thou hast given us habits new,
  Great King, we urge
That Thou from evil gentry free
  These robes of serge.   [Trans. Anon.]

2.

O Beauty, that doth far transcend
All other beauty! Thou dost deign,
Without a wound, our hearts to pain—
Without a pang our wills to bend,
To hold all love for creatures vain.

O mystic love-knot, that dost bind
Two beings of such diverse kind!
How canst thou, then, e'er sever'd be?
For bound, such strength we gain from Thee
We take for joys the griefs we find.

Things void of being, linked unite
With that great Beauty infinite.
Thou fill'st my soul which hungers still:
Thou lov'st where men can find but ill:
Our naught grows precious by Thy might!

[Translation by the Benedictines of Stanbrook.]

SAN JUAN DE LA CRUZ
(1542-1591)

"Small in stature indeed, but great, I know, in the sight of God:" so St. Teresa described the young friar, Juan de Yepes, when he enlisted in her army of the Reform and became founder of the first house for men. The life of San Juan de la Cruz is, like that of the "seraphic mother" St. Teresa, an example of the triumph of an indomitable spirit over the weaknesses of the flesh. Frail by nature and rendered more so by a life of extreme asceticism, he championed the Reform, preached, journeyed and founded monasteries all over Spain, besides writing books which by common consent reach the utmost heights of mystical experience and a number of poems which, apart from their deep spirituality, are among the finest, regarded purely as literature, ever written in Spanish.

San Juan de la Cruz bore the brunt of the fierce opposition which came, as might indeed have been expected in those days, from the followers of the mitigated rule. In 1577, some ten years after he had embarked upon his life work, he was imprisoned in a dark and narrow cell in Toledo, and subjected periodically to severe and degrading punishment. Escaping—miraculously, so his biographers say—from this dungeon, he spent a long period in Andalucia, never staying for long in one place, though in Granada he served a monastery for some time as prior. Before long, he was again involved, against his will, in strife—this time of an internal nature, disunion in the Reform having followed St. Teresa's death, and culminated in open revolt against the rule of the Provincial. These years proved to be the last of San Juan's life. Yet he was not allowed to spend even his closing days in peace, for, suspected of being in league with disloyal members of the order, he was judged guilty and deprived of his office. Some six months after this blow, he died, worn out by his austerities, at the early age of forty-nine.

THE DARK NIGHT

(i) *Of the Night of Sense*

This night,—which is the name we give to contemplation,—causes in spiritual persons two kinds of darkness or purgation, corresponding to the two parts of man, namely, sense and spirit. Thus the first night, or sensual purgation, wherein the soul is purged or laid bare, will be according to the senses, subjecting them to the spirit. The other is the night, or purgation, of the spirit, wherein the soul is purged and laid bare according to the spirit, and this night subdues and prepares it for the union of love with God. The night of sense is a common experience, and the lot of many : these are the beginners, of whom we shall speak first. The night of the spirit is the lot of very few : these are the advanced and the proficient, of whom we shall speak hereafter.

The first night or purgation is bitter and terrible to sense. The second, being of the spirit, is incomparably more awful, as we shall presently show. But since the night of sense is the first in order, and comes before the other, we shall say something briefly of it now : briefly, because being the commoner experience, it has been written of more fully. Of the night of the spirit we shall treat at greater length, little having been either said or written about it, because it is so little known.

The conduct of beginners in their progress towards God is not greatly to be praised, as we have said above ; it is very largely ruled by their own love of self and their inclinations. God longs to advance them, and lead them from this low condition of loving to a higher stage of love for Him, to free them from the low exercise of the senses and the reasoning whereby so unworthily and with so many hindrances, as we have said, they seek after Him.   He would fain lead them into the way of the spirit, that they may commune with God more abundantly and with greater freedom from imperfections, now that for some time they have walked in the way of virtue, persevering in meditation and prayer, and withdrawing their affections from worldly things by reason of the sweetness and love which they have gained, together with some measure of spiritual strength in God.   So in a certain degree they have bridled their love of creatures, and for God's sake are capable of bearing a little heaviness and dryness, without going back to that more pleasant time when they found spiritual exercises more to their taste and liking.   When the sun of divine favour shines, as they think, more brightly upon them, God shuts off from them that light, closing the door, or the fountain, of the sweet spiritual water, which they were wont to enjoy in God as often and for as long as they wished.   For then, while they were weak and tender, no door was closed to them, as St. John says in the Apocalypse : Behold, I have set before thee an open door, and no man can shut it : for thou hast a little strength, and hast kept my word, and hast not denied my name.[1]

And now God leaves them in such darkness that with their sense of imagination and their reasonings they know not which way to turn.   They cannot take a step in meditation, as they were wont, their inward sense being overwhelmed in this night, and left in such dryness that they find no pleasure and sweetness in spiritual things and sacred exercises which formerly gave them delight and joy, but instead find only insipidity and bitterness. And now, as I said before, God feels that they have begun to grow, and seeking to strengthen them and bring them out of swaddling-clothes, takes them from His gentle breast, and set-ting them down from His arms, shows them how they may walk alone.   And this they feel to be very new and strange, for everything is the contrary of what it was.

This experience commonly comes to recollected persons more shortly after their beginning than to others, because they are freer from occasions of backsliding, and more quickly wean

<hr>

[1] Rev. 3[8] (A.V.).

their appetites from things of the world, which is the essential for entrance into this blessed night of sense. In general, little time elapses after their beginning before they enter the night of sense; and the greater number of them enter it, in fact, for they will generally be seen to suffer from dryness. For this manner of sensual purgation, which is very common, we might allege much authority from Holy Scripture, where it continually occurs, especially in the Psalms and Prophets; but to avoid prolixity, we will leave them, though some few of them will be cited hereafter.

(ii) *Of the most Intimate Purgation which is the Second Night of the Spirit*

This (second) dark night is an inflowing of God into the soul, which purges it of its ignorances and imperfections, habitual, natural and spiritual. Contemplatives call this ' infused contemplation,' or 'mystical theology,' whereby God secretly teaches the soul and instructs it in the perfection of love, the soul itself doing nought but wait lovingly upon God, hearing Him and receiving His light, without understanding that this is infused contemplation. And since this is the loving wisdom of God, it makes special effects in the soul, preparing it, by purifying and illumination, for the union of love with God. It is the same loving wisdom that by illumination purifies the spirits of the blessed which here purifies and illumines the soul.

But there may be raised this doubt : Why should the soul call ' dark night' that divine light which, as we say, illumines it and purges it of its ignorances ? To this the reply is that for two reasons the divine wisdom is not only night and darkness to the soul but also pain and torment. The first is the height of divine wisdom, which exceeds all the capacity of the soul, and to it is therefore darkness. The second is the meanness and impurity of the soul, for which cause the wisdom of God is painful and afflictive to it, besides being dark.

To prove the first of these reasons we must assume a certain doctrine of philosophers which says that the clearer and more manifest are divine things in themselves, the darker and more secret are they, naturally, to the soul. Just so, the brighter is a light, the more it darkens and blinds the pupil of the owl, and the more directly the sun is gazed at, the greater the darkness caused to the visual organs, for it deprives them of power, so greatly does its strength exceed their weakness. So, when this divine light of contemplation strikes the soul, which is not yet perfectly enlightened, it plunges it into spiritual darkness, because it not only transcends it, but also blinds it and deprives it of the operation of its natural intelligence.

For this cause St. Dionysius and other mystical theologians call this infused contemplation a 'ray of darkness,'—that is, to the soul not yet enlightened and purified,—for by its great supernatural light it conquers the natural power of the reason, and deprives it of its natural means of understanding. For which cause David also said: Nubes, et caligo in circuitu eius; that is, clouds and darkness are round about him[1]—not that this is actually so, but that so it seems to our feeble understanding, which is blinded and dazzled, because it cannot attain to such heights. Wherefore David himself said: Prae fulgore in conspectu eius nubes transierunt: At the brightness that was before him his thick clouds passed[2]—that is the clouds between God and our understanding. And this is the cause why, when God descends from Himself to the soul not yet transformed, this illuminating ray of His secret wisdom causes thick darkness in the understanding.

And that this dim contemplation in its beginnings is also painful to the soul is clear. For since this infused divine contemplation has many qualities of exceeding goodness, and the soul which receives them, being not as yet purified, has many miseries, hence it follows, since two contraries cannot co-exist in one subject, the soul must of necessity suffer and be in pain, since in it these two contraries are found, working the one against the other, by reason of the purgation of the soul's imperfections, which is being wrought by means of this contemplation.

This we will show in the following way inductively. First, since the light and wisdom of contemplation is most pure and

---

[1] Ps. 96², Vulg.; 97², A.V.   [2] Ps. 17¹³, Vulg.; 18¹³, A.V.

bright, and the soul upon which it strikes is dark and impure, hence the reception causes the soul much pain, just as when the eyes are weak and affected by evil humours the invasion of bright light causes them pain.   This pain in the soul, caused by its impurity, is exceedingly great when the divine light strikes upon it.   For when the pure light strikes the soul, in order to expel its impurities, the soul perceives itself to be so unclean and wretched that it seems as if God is fighting against it—that it has become the adversary of God. . . .

The second manner of the soul's sufferings arises from its natural and spiritual weakness; for, when this divine contemplation strikes it with a certain force, in order to strengthen and subdue it, it suffers so greatly in its weakness that it all but faints. This is particularly so at times when the divine contemplation strikes it with rather greater force; for sense and spirit, as if they were beneath some great and gloomy burden, are in such torment and agony that they would find death itself a welcome relief. . . .

A wonderful and a piteous thing it is that the soul's impurity and weakness should be so great that the hand of God, in reality so soft and so gentle, is felt by the soul in this state to be severe and heavy, even though it neither presses nor even rests upon it but only touches it—and that most mercifully, for He would fain grant the soul His graces, not chastise it.

O, LAMPS OF FIRE!

Let it first be supposed that lamps have two properties— to give light and to burn.   To understand this verse, it must be remembered that God, in His one and single Essence, contains all the virtues and powers of His attributes; He is omnipotent, wise, good, merciful, just, strong, loving; and other attributes and virtues are His of which we know nothing here below.   And since He is all this, it follows that, when He is in union with the soul and is pleased to reveal Himself to her in a very secret knowledge, she begins to see in Him this greatness and all these virtues perfectly and profoundly comprehended in

8

His one and single Essence, so far as is consistent with faith. And since each of these virtues is the very Essence of God, Who is Father, Son and Holy Spirit, each attribute being God Himself, and God being infinite Light and the infinite Divine Fire, as has been said above, thus it is that each one of these attributes gives light and burns as God Himself.

And thus, according to these signs of God which the soul has known in unity, God Himself is to the soul as many lamps, because she has the knowledge of each of them, and each in its own way gives out heat of love; all of them unite to form one simple essence, and all of them are as one lamp, which lamp is all the lamps, because it gives light and burns in all ways.

When the soul sees this, the one lamp is to her as many lamps; for, although it is but one, it is all-powerful, contains all virtues and comprehends every spirit, and thus we may say that the one lamp burns and shines in many ways in one,—that is, as omnipotent, as wise, as good, and the like. It endows the soul with knowledge and love, and reveals itself to her according to the measure of her power for the reception of all. The brightness which the lamp sheds upon her as omnipotent endows her with the light and warmth of the love of God with respect to His omnipotence, and in this way God is to her a lamp of omnipotence, shining and burning according to this attribute. And the brightness shed by the lamp with respect to its wisdom, endows her with the warmth of the love of God the all-wise. And so of the other attributes; for the light shed by each of the aforesaid attributes of God, and by the rest, endows the soul with the warmth of God according to such attribute. Thus is God to the soul as innumerable lamps, shedding light and love, in these secret communications and signs, which, as I see it, is one of the highest possible in this life.

These are the lamps in which God revealed Himself to Moses on Mount Sinai, when He passed before him, and immediately he fell on his face to the ground, and declared some of the wondrous attributes of God which then he saw: he loved Him according to the things which he had seen, and which he declared distinctly in these words: *Dominator Domine Deus, misericors, et clemens, patiens, et multae miserationis, ac verax, qui custodis misericor-*

diam in millia : qui aufers iniquitatem, et scelera, atque peccata,
nullusque apud te per se innocens est;[1] O Lord, O Lord God,
merciful and gracious, longsuffering, and of great compassion and
true, keeping mercy for thousands, Thou forgivest iniquity and
transgression and sin, Who art so just that none is innocent before
Thee.   From which it appears that the principal attributes and
virtues which Moses then saw and loved were the omnipotence,
dominion, mercy, justice and truth of God, which is the highest
of all knowledge and the deepest delight of love.

Whence it follows how admirable is the joy and rapture of
love which the soul receives in the fire of the light of these lamps
—how immeasurable it is, how abundant, as though it were of
many lamps each burning with love, the heat of the one feeding
the heat of the other, as the flame of the one feeds the flame of
the other, and the light of the one the light of the other.   All
form but one light and one fire, and yet each is a fire.   And the
soul is profoundly absorbed in delicious flames, subtilely wounded
in each of them, and in the whole more subtilely wounded in love
of life.   She begins to see more clearly that this love is eternal
life, which is the union of all blessings.   In this state the soul
knows well the truth of the Bridegroom's saying in the *Song of
Songs*, where he says '*Lampades eius, lampades ignis, atque
flammarum,*'—that is, that the lamps of love were lamps of fire
and of flames.[2]

If a single one of these lamps passing before Abraham caused
him great terror, when God passed in a knowledge of rigorous
justice which was to be wrought upon the Canaanites,[3] how
much more light and joy of love will be shed by all these lamps
of the knowledge of God, which shine tenderly and lovingly here,
than that single lamp caused of darkness and terror in Abraham?
And how much and how greatly advantaged, and how manifold

[1] Ex. 34[6-7] (Vulgate). The Vulgate, however, prefixes the words: 'Stetit
Moyses cum eo, invocans nomen Domini,' whereas A.V. and R.V. have 'The
Lord passed by before him and proclaimed.' The variation affects the translation
following.

[2] Cant. 8[6] (Vulgate). *Cf.* A.V.: The coals thereof are coals of fire, which hath
a most vehement flame, and R.V.: The flashes thereof are flashes of fire, a very
flame of the Lord.

[3] Presumably an inexact reference to the "burning lamp" (A.V.) of Gen. 15[17].
(*Cf.* 15[12], 15[18].)

will be thy light and thy joy, seeing that in all and by all of
these thou perceivest that He gives thee the fruition of His love,
loving thee according to His virtues, attributes and properties!
For he who loves and does good to another honours him and
does him good according to his attributes and properties. And
thus, thy Bridegroom, being within thee in His omnipotence,
grants Himself to thee and loves thee with omnipotence; and,
since He is wise, thou perceivest that He loves thee with His
wisdom; being good, thou perceivest that He loves thee in His
goodness; being holy, with holiness; and in like manner of the
rest. And as He is liberal thou perceivest too that He loves
thee with liberality, without self-interest, but only to do thee
good, revealing to thee gladly this His countenance full of grace,
and saying to thee: I am thine and I am for thee; and I love
to be even as I am that I may give Myself to thee and be thine.

The Obscure Night of the Soul

Upon an obscure night
Fevered with love in love's anxiety,
(O hapless, happy plight!)
I went, none seeing me,
Forth from my house where all things quiet be.

By night, secure from sight,
And by the secret stair disguisedly,
(O hapless, happy plight!)
By night and privily,
Forth from my house where all things quiet be.

Blest night of wandering,
In secret, where by none might I be spied,
Nor I see anything;
Without a light or guide,
Save that which in my heart burnt in my side.

That light did lead me on,
More surely than the shining of noontide,
Where well I knew that One
Did for my coming bide;
Where he abode might none but he abide.

O night that didst lead thus,
O night more lovely than the dawn of light,
O night that broughtest us,
Lover to lover's sight,
Lover with loved in marriage of delight.

Upon my flowery breast,
Wholly for him, and save himself for none,
There did I give sweet rest
To my beloved one ;
The fanning of the cedars breathed thereon.

When the first moving air
Blew from his tower, and waved his locks aside,
His hand, with gentle care,
Did wound me in the side,
And in my body all my senses died.

All things I then forgot,
My cheek on him who for my coming came ;
All ceased, and I was not,
Leaving my cares and shame
Among the lilies and forgetting them.

> [Translation by Arthur Symons],
> (*Cities and Sea-Coasts and Islands*, p. 67).

LIVING FLAME OF LOVE

O flame of living love
That dost eternally
Pierce through my soul with so consuming heat,
Since there's no help above,
Make thou an end of me,
And break the bond of this encounter sweet.

O burn that burns to heal !
O more than pleasant wound !
And O soft hand, O touch most delicate,
That dost new life reveal,
That dost in grace abound,
And slaying, dost from death to life translate.

O lamps of fire that shined
With so intense a light
That those dark caverns where the senses live,
Which were obscure and blind,
Now with strange glories bright,
Both heat and light to his belovèd give.

With how benign intent
Rememberest thou my breast
Where thou alone abidest secretly,
And in thy sweet ascent,
With glory and good possessed,
How delicately thou teachest love to me.

[Translation by Arthur Symons],
(*Cities and Sea-Coasts and Islands*, p. 69).

PEDRO MALÓN DE CHAIDE

(c. 1530-1589)

Malón de Chaide was an Augustinian friar born in Navarre and an
alumnus of Zaragoza. In 1557 he made his profession at Salamanca,
where he was later a pupil of Luis de León. For some time he held
Chairs of theology in Zaragoza and Huesca. He is best known as an
ascetic and mystic, but there seems no doubt that he also wrote a considerable amount of verse, though none of it has survived but what is
intercalated in the *Conversión de la Magdalena*, his one extant work.
Of a *Tratado de San Pedro*, of which he speaks in the preface to this
treatise, as a sequel to it, nothing is known—not even if it was ever
written. Three years after its author's death in Barcelona only did the
Conversión de la Magdalena see the light. The first edition, published
in Alcalá (1592) was followed by two further editions from that city (1598,
1603) and an edition from Barcelona in 1598.

THE CONVERSION OF THE MAGDALEN

(i)

Ecce Mulier

These four things made the sins of the Magdalen very
grave, and thus, it was no great matter that the Evangelist

should say: Behold a woman in the city which was a sinner.
Now it seems to me that we have not yet penetrated to the
depth of all that there is in these words. I find the word
'Behold' twice in the Sacred Scriptures, and one of these
appears to be contrasted with the other. The one is this
phrase 'Behold a woman'; the other is 'Behold the Man,'
which was said of the Son of God.

The Evangelist St. John relates that when Pilate wished
to deliver the Redeemer out of the hands of the Jews, knowing
that for envy they sought His death, he commanded Him to be
scourged that he might move them to pity. Then he brought
Him out stripped, and wearing a crown of thorns on His sacred
Head, and covered with an old purple robe. And as He came
forth again to the Jews, who with great instancy were clamouring
for His death, Pilate said to them: Behold the Man, as if he
had said: You accuse this Man of being a rioter and a perverter
of the people, you say that He boasts Himself to be a King;
now you see Him here, with nought but the form of a man,—
yet how much the more princely is He!

On the one side then, place Christ, wounded and bound, His
Head pierced by thorns, His Face spit upon by men and
bearing marks of the lash, His Body covered with blood from
the scourging, His Divine Eyes filled with tears. And on the
other side place the Magdalen,—wanton, profane, full of sins,
notorious, nameless, an enticement of the devil, a snare to souls.
Hear Pilate saying Behold the Man, and turn to St. Luke
who replies to him Behold the woman. Then consider the
wondrous mystery which is here: Behold the Man and Behold
the woman. That there may be a Behold the woman, there
must needs be a Behold the Man; without the one, there cannot
be the other. Behold the Man: for He became Man by divine
grace. Behold the woman: woman in the weakness of her
nature. Behold the Man,—the just Man. Behold the woman,
—a sinner. Behold the woman who sins. Behold the Man, who
pays the price. Behold the woman, condemned. Behold the
Man, who bears the penalty. Behold the woman who merits
the punishment. Behold the Man, who is scourged. Behold

the woman, free ; [1] Behold the Man, bound. This is the Man Who, being God, became Man; this is the woman who, being a sinner, has become a saint. The Man, Who dies that this woman may live ; the woman, who lives because this Man has died. This Man is brought out by such as this woman before Pilate ; this woman is brought by this Man before the Father. Pilate delivers this Man to man as his ransom ; Christ presents this woman to the Father as a precious gift.

O sovereign exchange ! O sweet Jesu, our Treasure, Who dost give Thyself as the price for a sinful woman at Thy Father's command and through the strength of Thy love. See, sons of men, the great love of your God, Who says : Take God and give Me a man ; take My Son, and give Me a woman that is a sinner. Tell me, then, great Lord, is this an exchange that can be borne? Seest Thou not that Thou art cheated in more than half its value? To give God for a man—who has heard the like? The Just for a murderer, the Innocent for the guilty, the Lord for a servant, the Son for a slave, the Maker of all things for a piece of His own handiwork? Who has heard of glory being exchanged for dust? The greatest riches for the greatest poverty? The Divine heights for the depths of humanity? Behold the Man! The cure for all my ills, the Ransomer who pays my debts, whose blood laves my sins, whose price redeems my offences.

Pilate presents Thee to me, O Redeemer of my soul. Thy Father gives Thee to me. Thou dost die for me. Thou sayest : This is My Blood, which is shed for you. Thy Father says : So did I love the world, that I gave it My only-begotten Son. Pilate says to me: Thou seest then the Man Who does all this : Behold the Man. But I reply : Behold my God. They show me a Man, but I know Thee for God. Behold the Man, Who dies for me. Behold my God, Who of Himself rises again. Behold the Man, who shows my weakness by His sufferings. Behold my God, Who by His victory gives me His strength.

[1] *Suelta* also means 'light,' 'wanton,' and the play upon the two meanings is intentional. *Cf.* p. 119, l. 24, above.

Sweet picture of my salvation! How I needed Thee to be such that Thou shouldst lose Thyself to find me.

(ii)

Reflections of the Magdalen

"Tell me then, O Magdalen, will it not be well for thee to wait till the Lord come out from the feast? For it is unseasonable to shed tears among the baked meats, it is ill done to water content with thy tears." "Alas!" says Mary, "every moment's delay is to me as a thousand years of hell! I know that I have to do with God, and not with any man. He who has borne with my wickedness, will not be wearied by my penitence. This my Beloved, to Whom I go, has meat more savoury than that which the Pharisee gives Him, for His meat is to do His Father's will. For He Himself says thus: My meat is to do the will of My Father. And the will of His Father, as He says, is that of them which He gave Him He should lose none:[1] He will not then lose me."

"But if I am His meat, at what more fitting time can I go than when He is at table? I would reach Him ere He rises from the feast; for the dish arrives out of season when the covers have been removed." "But seest thou not, Magdalen, that He is in the house of the scornful Pharisee, who prides himself on his devoutness, and will murmur at your penitence." "Ah, I see myself, and am shamed by none. My God and the angels see me: what matters it to me that men see me also? Already they know me for an enemy of God and a sinner; let them know me now for a mourner and a penitent." "But at least, if thou goest, wilt thou not go as a rich and noble maiden? Dress that hair, confine it with a fillet of rich gold, entwine it with eastern pearls, make for thyself ear-rings with two fine emeralds. Wear a golden necklace of finely-wrought enamel, place a rope of pearls six times round thy neck with an eagle of sovereign workmanship depending from it, and bearing in its talons a resplendent diamond that shall fall upon thy breast.

---

[1] Joh. 18⁹: Quia quos dedisti mihi, non perdidi ex eis quemquam.

Wear a gown of brocaded satin with ornaments of gold, a satin and lace dress which shall be resplendent at a hundred paces' distance, much lace with pearls and precious stones, a girdle that has no price, and a smelling bottle of ambergris which is fragrant afar off.   Don more rings than thou hast fingers ; make thyself a jeweller's counter for the number of thy trinkets."   For thus do women of our day deck themselves when they go to hear Mass, with more colours on their faces than in the rainbow, and thus they go to adore Him who was spat upon, scourged, stripped, crowned with thorns and nailed to a cross, Jesus Christ, the only Son of God.

Do such as these hold themselves Christians? Ah, how deceptive is this elegance, grace and beauty! "Favour is deceitful, and beauty is vain; but a woman that feareth the Lord, she shall be praised."[1]   Ah, unhappy is our age, perdition and punishment shall come upon the name of a Christian.   Who has seen such great misfortune as that which comes to pass in our commonwealths?   Enter our churches and sacred temples, you will see the altar-pieces depicting the stories of the saints. On one side you will see the picture of St. Lawrence, bound and stretched upon a gridiron, the flames issuing from beneath and swathing his body ; the coals are red-hot, the flames so bright that they make one shudder to behold them.   The tormentors are feeding them with iron-pronged forks, one is blowing with a bellows to quicken them.   You may see the flesh of that noble man burnt and scorched by the fire; already it has torn him asunder and the flames are consuming him even to that invincible breast. . . . On another panel you will see the picture of St. Bartholomew, stripped and bound and stretched upon a table where they are flaying him alive.   On another side is the stoning of St. Stephen : the stones fly thick on the road, the face of the martyr is bleeding, his head cut open so that it moves the beholder to compassion, while he himself is kneeling and praying for the murderers who are slaying him.   Elsewhere you will see St. Peter hanging from a cross, St. John Baptist

---

[1] Prov. 31[30] : Fallax gratia, et vana est pulchritudo, mulier timens Dominum, ipsa laudabitur.

beheaded, and the deaths of many other saints; and finally, above all, the Christ on the Cross, all naked, covered with blood, His Body cut with the scourges, His Face swollen, His Eyes lifeless, His Mouth blackened, His Side pierced,—a very picture of death.

Tell me, then, Christians, why are such figures painted above our altars? Why do they not show us Christ in His glory, seated above the heads of the angels, and the saints in their splendour, full of joy? Why do they present them to us dying and suffering great trials? I think it is that we may understand how by the torments which they suffered upon earth they attained to the glory of the heavens, and how we must follow them in their trials if we would be partakers of their rest.

Since this is so, is it not unfitting that you should kneel to pray before one that is crucified, another that is flayed alive, another stoned, another torn asunder by the teeth of lions, while you yourself appear before them bedizened and decked with jewels as though you were going to some wedding? How are you not ashamed to kneel before them in such raiment? And how will you look upon those whom you see thus shamefully entreated? How beg them to be your advocates with God, when they would turn their eyes upon you with loathing? No other adornment or trappings would the Magdalen have with which to appear before God, save the adornment of her soul: with this she is on fire and as it were a furnace of love.

Ah, that one could have seen this holy woman in the street, so self-forgetful that she took not so much as a towel wherewith to wipe the feet of the Lord of Glory! With none of her former display does she go, nor has she the train of attendants she was wont to have, nor does she tarry in the streets to be gazed upon. Rather, with her eyes cast down to the ground, and her heart fixed upon her Lord and her great Good, shedding tears so that she scarcely sees the street through which she is passing, she goes in haste with great anxiety, saying within herself thus:

O new and heavenly Bridegroom of my soul! Divine Physician of my infirmities, stay but for a moment, wait for

this most unhappy sinner, who comes to fling herself at Thy
sacred Feet! Oh, Beauty ever-ancient, ever-new, how late
have I known Thee, how late have I loved Thee! Oh feet
that art so slow to arrive where my heart desires! Why do ye
tarry longer in bearing me to my Healer than in carrying me,
as of old, to my perdition? Make haste, my feet, and bear me
to the Spring of my glory, which may temper the fire that
consumes my heart! See, O my feet, that if ye tarry, the
Healer will depart, and nought but the fire of hell that is await-
ing ye will remain. O splendour of glory, how my heart desires
thee!

(iii)

'One Thing is Needful'

Then Mary, although she was forgiven, determined after the
Ascension of the Lord into Heaven to withdraw into a desert
place, where she might be alone and enjoy the contemplation
of her Beloved. Ah, what sweet moments she would spend
in that rugged land, among those crags! Carried away in
spirit, as though she were already a citizen of Heaven and had
thrown off that mortal vesture in which she was clothed, she
quitted the earth, and rose unfettered to the home of her Beloved.

There she gazed upon those celestial mansions of the royal
city of Jerusalem,—a city filled with infinite light, its streets
and squares thronged with citizens, which are the blessed
company of heaven. Through its gorgeous palaces thrilled
music of ravishing sweetness, born of soft angelic voices which
praise the great Prince of the World, without for a moment
ceasing. When she considered the buildings made by no
human hand, but only by the will of that most wondrous God,
she had no eyes for so great beauty. She beheld the city,
which was four square and of great immensity. Its foundations
were of all the precious stones which we know here on earth,
as St. John relates in the Apocalypse,[1] for they were of jasper

---

[1] See Rev. 21, *passim*.

and sapphire, chalcedony and emerald, jacinth and topaz, and many more which are named in that book. The walls shone like the sun, so that no human eyes could look upon them. On each of the four sides were three gates, so that together they made twelve, and each gate was a precious stone. The towers and battlements were crowned with clearest crystal and as touching the emeralds and rubies set in the purest gold and illumined by the light and splendour of the true Sun which shines there, no human thought can describe their unspeakable beauty. The ground, the streets and the squares of this blessed city are of the finest gold.

Herein dwells for ever springtime most fair, for the bleakness of winter has been driven from it. The fury of the winds cannot strive with the lofty trees, nor the snow break down the tender branches with its weight. No sickly autumn strips the verdant groves of their leaves, for there is fulfilled that word of David : 'Their leaf shall not wither.'[1] For ever there dwells a mildness and a calm which keeps in its state of perfection all the freshness that Heaven holds. The flowers in the Heavenly meadows—white, blue, golden, of manifold and varied colours, —surpass in their splendour the emeralds, rubies, bright pearls and Eastern stones. Here the rose is more beautiful and fragrant than in the gardens of Jericho, the springs are lovelier than liquid crystal, the water is sweeter, the fruit more mellow to the taste.

O life that art life indeed! O glory that art glory alone! O royal city, whose citizens have great delight! None know the meaning of pain or sickness. Death comes not to thee, for all is life. There is no pain, for all is delight ; no sickness, for God is their health indeed. Blessed city, whose laws are of love, whose citizens are ruled by love, in which all love, whose office is love, where they know naught but to love ! One wish have they, one will, one counsel. They love one thing, desire one thing, contemplate one thing, and are united with one thing : yea, that one thing,—that is the one thing needful.

[1] Ps. i⁴.

SONNET

O patience, that dost wait eternally!
O heart of mine so hard, that cannot love!
How am I wearied as from Thee I rove!
How dost Thou, never wearying, pardon me!

O Face Divine, how often did I see
Thy grieving gaze toward me sadly turned,
While I, my Lord, Thy laws have basely spurned,
And Thou hast loved and suffered silently.

Guardian of all men, turn Thy wrath away
From this Thy child of earth, oh turn again!
See, Thine own child am I: raise me, I pray,
For 'tis not pleasure now that makes me stray,
But habits fought and striven against in vain:
I hate the sin, and yet I sin alway.

JUAN DE LOS ÁNGELES

(1536-1609)

Juan Martínez has often been spoken of as a native of Extremadura, but it would appear that he actually came from Ávila. No details of his childhood are known, nor can it even be stated when and where it was that he entered the Franciscan order, at some time before 1562, taking the name Juan de los Ángeles Before any of his prose works were published we know him to have written verse. He became celebrated, however, when still quite young, as a conventual preacher and as a lecturer in theology in one of the Chairs or *cátedras* of his order. In the monastery of St. John Baptist at Zamora he began his first great book, the *Triumphs of the Love of God*, which however did not meet with the success that might have been anticipated.

Meanwhile, after filling for four years a provincial post, he was sent to Sevilla with some others to found a monastery, a task which proved no easy one. In Sevilla he wrote his dialogues entitled the *Conquest of the Kingdom of God*. These were to have been published in Lisbon, where he retired for a short time from active service in 1592, but he was recalled to Madrid in the following year, and it was then only that the book appeared. It had a far better reception than the *Triumphs*, and went into several editions in four or five years.

In 1596 Fray Juan was sent as Superior to Guadalajara, and, in the years which followed, made first long tours in Extremadura and Andalucia, and afterwards visits to France and Italy. The year 1601 saw him elected Provincial Minister, and from that time his fame grew steadily until his death eight years later. It is pleasant to find the provincial chronicler recording of this preacher before King and Empress an anecdote like the following : " He was preaching one day to a noble and intellectual audience . . . when his father entered the church in the garments of a poor labourer. So he said from the pulpit : 'Brethren, this old man who has entered is my father ; of your goodness make a place for him : he has come to hear me.' And such was the admiration of that noble company at the humility of the preacher's action, that they gave him the first seat of all."

PRELUDE TO THE "CONSIDERATIONS ON THE SONG OF SONGS"

And if any book needed the spirit of prophecy it was this ; and not that alone, but also a knowledge of an infinitude of natural things and their properties, because at every step these are found as the symbols of things spiritual. In the first chapter alone, which has occupied me for more than two years, I have met so many difficulties, that often I have wished to turn back from the task, and much weariness and discouragement has assailed me because I have entered so vast a maze. When I began to think, as touching God, as of One having a mouth, and breasts, like those of women,—a name, like ointment poured forth, —robes more fragrant than precious spikenard [1]—a bed that is green,[2]—houses of cedar-wood and cypress [3]—cells and retreats [4] —the kiss of a bride [5]—blackness and comeliness [6]—tents and shepherds [7]—kids and sheep,[8] and the like, then I was carried out of myself, and lost all courage, and all desire to write.

And the virtue of this is that in saying it I reprove myself, and compel myself to give a reason for my persistence,—nay, my daring—in endeavouring to undertake a task so arduous and

---

[1] Cant. 1³, Vulg. : Oleum effusum nomen tuum.
[2] Cant. 1¹⁵, Vulg. : Lectulus noster floridus (cf. A.V. 1¹⁶, ' Our bed is green ').
[3] Cant. 1¹⁷ (Vulg. : 1¹⁶).   [4] Probably Cant. 1³ (Vulg. : cellaria sua).
[5] Cant. 1¹, Vulg. : 1², A.V.   [6] Cant. 1⁴, Vulg. : 1⁵, A.V.
[7] Cant. 1⁷ (Vulg. : juxta tabernacula pastorum).
[8] Cant. 1⁷, Vulg. : 1⁸, A.V.

difficult, so utterly beyond my powers. I know that I am not excused from blame by speaking of my four-and-twenty years as a preacher, and constant exercise in the Scriptures ; nor the zeal which, through the mercy of God, I have ever had for the profit of souls ; nor would it suffice to be learned and versed in many tongues, if such I were ; nor to be pious and learned as St. Thomas, were I both. For that Saint feared to essay this task—yea, even one so great as he—and all the Saints feared it, though they were full of the knowledge of the Lord and of heavenly riches. What, then, has committed me to this task ?

First, the entreaties of a friend, a weighty man, and notable in learning, both human and divine. Knowing my mind, and how it is inclined to things of affection and love, both from his reading of the *Triumphs* and *Dialogues*, and from his acquaintance with me and hearing of my sermons, he judged that great service would be done to God, and no small benefit to the Christian commonwealth, if I devoted myself to writing upon this book, in which everything breathes forth and is fragrant with love. For as we said elsewhere, and as we shall in a more fitting place repeat, there is described here the chaste and pure love which is between Christ and the Church, or between Christ and the soul that has merited the name of Spouse and can say as in the opening verse : Let him kiss me with the kisses of his mouth.[1]

The second consideration that urged me was an inclination and a love for this book, since the day that I was granted license to read in it by virtue of my office,—a love so great that, even when I understood not what I read, I felt a particular delight and consolation of spirit as long as I was occupied in it. And this love grew with the years and was but strengthened by readings in the saints who wrote of this book. . . .

It is a spiritual garden for the delight of Christian souls, who may gather the most fragrant posies of divers flowers for their consolation and pleasure. Here they will see all that is signified by the love of God, its power and its obligations, the heights that it can reach, and the things from which it withdraws

---

[1] Cant. 1¹, Vulg. : 1², A.V.

us.   Here they will see the varying accidents of its nature, and the studies which it inspires,—so different from those which in our days we see in persons called spiritual,—and many will be disillusioned thereby and return to the truth.

I trust and am assured that I shall carry to an end this enterprise which for the glory of God and the edification of His Church I have begun; not that I am governed therein by my own meditations or my powers (for I am neither a prophet nor have in myself the grace of interpreting the Scriptures) but because of all that the saints, and divers persons well approved, and men that are learned and versed in tongues have left in their writings.   For, though I cannot have seen them all, I have seen the most part and the best, so that of myself I write but little, and this little is as a dwarf on the shoulders of a giant, upon which he mounts and which are to him as a watchtower.   Even so is it: for I am a dwarf and a pigmy in comparison with those who have preceded me in writing of this book, and if I should discover and spy out more than they, it will be not because of my greater stature, but through the help of God and of themselves, who have given me light, and opened the way to everything.

My greatest care has been to seek after clearness, and to remove offences and occasions of stumbling from the simple, and thus it will be seen in the whole work, that besides being clear the language is honest, chaste, sober, religious, giving occasion of evil to none.   As touching the exposition of difficult passages, I give the opinions of all, when they are partially or wholly different, and I choose that which I judge to be the best, which is ever that which most nearly touches the soul and ministers to good living.   Especially as regards prayer and contemplation I extend myself most when occasion offers, for I desire that this book may come into the possession of spiritual persons whom I set often in right ways, and give admirable documentary aids to their desire, if such they have, to make progress in mystic theology and communion with their God, through the exercises of free, fruitive and seraphic love, which is the foundation of these Songs.

9

The Doorways to the Kingdom of the Soul

Door of the East

Master. As the beginning and foundation of all, thou must know that there are four entrances or doorways to the centre and depth of the soul, which is the true Kingdom of God : on the east side is one, on the west another, a third is on the south and the last on the Septentrion or north. The eastern door is humility, which is the beginning and foundation of the entire spiritual edifice. At the west is the Passion and Death of Christ, as St. Gregory observed in writing on that verse in the Psalms : *Iter facite ei, qui ascendit in Occasum.* Which declares that the setting of the sun was the death of Christ. The southern door is the abnegation of the will, for never is the soul so bright and resplendent as when it denies and forsakes itself, and when nought remains to it of its own will. On the north side is the fourth door—namely tribulation—which at times seems to close to us the door of Heaven and of all comfort. From the bitter regions of the north break forth and arise all evils and all troubles,[1] and although from each of these things I could make a long treatise of much substance and volume, as do many writers, and at times with small satisfaction and profit to the soul, I will write touching each of these doors only so much as may not be omitted, since my first aim was to teach with brevity that which is most necessary to the spiritual life.

. . . .

Let us, then, come to the contemplation of the eastern door of Humility, through which entered Christ, our Sovereign Pontiff, and great High Priest, into His Kingdom, with so wondrous a prize and such glory as thou hast heard ; when all the creatures of Heaven, Earth and Hell acknowledged Him as Lord, bowing

---

[1] The reference is to Jer. $r^{14\text{-}16}$: "Out of the north an evil shall break forth upon all the inhabitants of the land. For lo, I will call all the families of the kingdoms of the north, saith the Lord. . . . And I will utter my judgments against them touching all their wickedness.

their knees at the sound of that Divine Name JESUS, which His
Father gave to Him Who humbled Himself even to the death of
the Cross.[1] The royal road leading to God is found nowhere save
in a true mortification of the vices and in a true exercise of the
virtues, in which exercise thou must be constant and persevering,
turning aside from it at no time by so much as a hair's breadth
either to the right hand or to the left, keeping thine eyes fixed
upon Beth-shemesh [2]—that is to say, City of the Sun—journeying like those kine which bore the ark straight forward, lowing
as they went, the lowing of their calves which were shut up
being unable to hinder their journey, or to make them turn to
either hand.   Doing otherwise than this thou shalt surely err, and
the higher thou dost fly and make thy nest, even though it be
among the stars, by the highest and profoundest speculations,
the greater and the more terrible will be thy fall.   But if thou
wilt go far in a little time, establish in thy heart the noblest and
firmest foundation of humility, and study to keep it tenaciously
till death, for without this it is impossible that the work of the
spiritual edifice can remain.   This, the crown of all virtues,
Christ made particularly His Own, and in His Life and Death,
by word and by living example, He willed to be the Master and
Teacher of it.

EJACULATORY PRAYER

Pupil. A great thing must freedom of spirit be for this
manner of prayer.

Master. I can affirm to thee in all truth that without it
neither the Kingdom of God, nor God Himself, can be within
us.   He who loses this freedom loses more than the value of
earth and heaven, or of any other creature, or of all created
things.   For what do they all profit me, if my heart is bound
to them, or to the very least of them, so that I cannot turn it
and raise it freely to the Creator.

---

[1] Phil. 2⁸ : Humiliavit semetipsum, factus obediens usque ad mortem, mortem
autem crucis (*cf.* R.V.).

[2] See Josh. 15¹⁰, 1 Sam. 6.

Pupil.   What then are the conditions of this prayer?

Master.   The first and chiefest is purity of heart, without which we are neither apt nor disposed to receive the influences of Divine Grace, by which means our heart is made fast in God, and there is worked in us perfect abnegation and mortification of the passions and affections of man.   And here I add that perfect abnegation and total resignation of ourselves in God, by which means we rise above ourselves, and are emptied of all our properties, conforming ourselves in all things to the will of God, is the secret of the highest perfection, of grace and glory.   Ah, love of self, how much harm to souls dost thou occasion!   So long as this dwells in us it is for ever causing vice to spring up, and bringing forth evil thoughts, and exciting wrong inclinations and vain desires: which things part us from God, stain our souls and harm our inward peace, so that love of self is the greatest impediment that can be found to spiritual progress.   But since much is said of this in the third dialogue, no more will be set down here concerning self-love or self-will.

Two or three counsels I will give thee as to freedom of aspiration.   The first, that thou labour as much as thou canst to have thy heart free from conceits or images of creatures, representations and forms, and most chiefly, from all inordinate affections; which end is greatly served by fleeing from gossip and buffoonery, and all occasions of curiosity and idleness, fair shows and vanities, and useless business and occupations, and from all that which the heart is fain to go after and cleave to. Restrain thyself from superfluity of meat and drink, of dress and outward show; and thus thou wilt immediately and often and continually awaken the strength of desire in thy heart, multiplying thy desires of most pure and fervent love to the Lord.

But take note that here there may be spiritual gluttony, and great harm may be done to the intellect if these prayers be made too impetuously and without moderation; in which thing many have committed adultery, taking more delight in these gifts of God than in God Himself.   For which cause have thou ever care that thy intention be chaste, pure and godlike, that is, in conformity with the good pleasure and will of God, Whose glory only and alone is ever to be sought without respect to our own, as well in prosperity as in adversity.

Take note, thirdly, of the capacity and nobility of our soul, which, though it cannot operate with infinite power, since its virtue is finite, can at least carry to infinity its desires.   God will not demand of thee that thou love Him with infinite love, for this thou canst not ; yet since thy desire may be extended to things unattainable, God will have it extended to infinity, that is, unlimited in its honour, love and desire of Him.   So then in prayers of affection thou hast not to consider the impossibility of that which thou desirest, nor its infinite excess over the virtue of thy soul and its powers of operation, but only whether that which thou desirest be lawful, and tend to the honour and glory of God.

And when impotence on our part alone impedes the effecting of our desires, the desire will be crowned by God as the operation would be crowned if we were sufficient for it, and this belongs to one of the degrees of ' violent love,' which Richard called insatiable, which caused St. Augustine to say, that if he were God, as the true God is, he would cease from being so, that He might so become : this was the desire for a thing impossible, yet it was of great merit before God.   This is that excess of love of the Bride, who says that her virgins love the Beloved exceeding greatly.[1]   And of the man that feareth the Lord said the Prophet that he delighteth exceeding greatly in His commandments.[2]

DIVINE LOVE

God is as it were the centre of love, and to Him the weight of this same love draws every creature.   So greatly is He to be loved that all creatures, both sensible and insensible, love Him in their several ways.   What are the natural inclinations of

[1] Presumably Cant. 1² (A.V. : Therefore do the virgins love thee ; Vulg. : Ideo adolescentulæ dilexerunt te), but the adverb is not to be found here.
[2] Ps. 111¹, Vulg. : Beatus vir qui timet Dominum, in mandatis ejus volet *nimis*. (*Cf.* A.V., R.V., Ps. 112¹), ' delighteth *greatly*.' . . .

things but love by which they are drawn to God? Only through their imperfection do they fail to attain to the highest uncreated Good, and thus they stay and rest in created good, in that which is but a part of the Highest Good. What is gravity in a stone, but love for the centre? What is lightness in fire, but love for the heavens? That which all things desire is called Sovereign Good, and thus the natural desire which is in them may in some sort be called love, although, as we said before, insensible Nature, because of its imperfection, cannot reach, as man and the angels can, that incommutable good, which is God.

St. Augustine said eloquently that love was the gravity of his soul, and that he was drawn whithersoever it drew him. So that the stone finds its true place in the centre, and the centre of our soul is God. Ah, if we who are endowed with reason did but copy the irrational and senseless stones! A thing of wonder is it indeed to see a rock dislodged from a high mountain: with what fury and noise, with how great swiftness does it fall to the place that is furnished for its rest. All that meets it in its path it shatters and breaks, and without once staying in its course it passes to its centre. A rock most powerful indeed was that which sped toward God so that its progress was retarded or impeded neither by distress, nor famine, nor nakedness, nor persecution, nor sword, nor death, nor life, nor angels, nor principalities, nor powers, nor things present, nor things to come, nor strength, nor height, nor depth, nor any other creature.[1] Wondrous the gravitation, worthy of so pure and holy a soul as the Apostle's, that attracts it with such force, shattering all obstacles, till it reaches its centre, which is God. Here, O my soul, here shalt thou rest, as the fire rests in its heavens, as the stone at its centre. For otherwhere than here is no rest; therefore seek it not, for thou shalt not find it. The arm that is disjointed from its place and articulation cannot be without pain and disquiet; neither so can the soul apart from God.

[1] Rom. 8$^{38-9}$. The words 'virtudes' and 'fortaleza' represent the 'virtutes' and 'fortitudo' of the Vulgate. *Cf*. also R.V.

If upon this matter we took the witness of lovers of the world and of the things that are in it, what tragedies, what bitterness would they not recount to us? And, in truth, all creatures as it were do buffet us, and with great outrage do cast us from them, so that it seems as if they are crying to us aloud : " Ye puny men, wherefore do ye draw near to us, for we are not the Good that ye seek or ought to seek. Go upon your way, seek your centre and place of rest, for in us there is none, nor can there be." And yet we are so blind, so mad, so foolish, that though the creatures resist us we embrace them,— yea, we embrace them though they affront us, and even as they affront us we caress them and hold them against their will. If they flee, we pursue them ; and, since they are appointed each one for our service, we clasp them to us, and make them our masters and ourselves their slaves. So great is our blindness and our folly.

A great and a dreadful miracle—yea, a miracle of the devil —is it that men should cease from loving their God and not journey ever towards Him with power and swiftness, as to their very Centre, being stayed at times by obstacles no greater than straws, at other times by obstacles that are none. Who would not wonder at seeing an immense rock suspended and hanging in the air with nothing impeding its course? And how much greater a wonder is it to see a soul created by God suspended in the air of vanity, its course stayed by so slight a straw as a question of 'honour' or some such worldly interest, being for this deprived of its highest Good.

Oh, divine Centre ! Oh, infinite Good that art of infinite attraction ! What is it that restrains me from seeking Thee ? What is it that stays my path ? What that delays my course ? Ah, how great is the attraction of sin, which weighs down our souls so that they may not rise to seek their true sphere, which is God ! Ah, how intolerable is the burden of our flesh ! How thick a veil it is, since it hides from us the face of God ! What hinders me from tearing it down with my own hands, that I may see and may rest in Him Whom my soul loveth ? Oh, Thou Preserver of men ! Why hast Thou set me as a mark against Thee, so that I am a burden to myself?[1] Why dost Thou not take away my transgression and remove from me my iniquity? Alas that I go wandering so gladly among the creatures, seeking a few drops of muddy water, which cannot quench my thirst, but rather excite and inflame it the more, while I leave that most clear and eternal source of all Good, where alone my thirst may be quenched, and where the hunger of my soul may be satisfied for its true Good that shall abide for ever and ever!

The Soul's Intimacy

Pupil. It seems that thou art about to expound to me that which I desire exceedingly to know.

Master. In truth thou canst not have failed to comprehend it from what I have already said; and since we have arrived at this point (I must say first that it is the highest of all in the spiritual life and that to remember it will serve thee greatly hereafter) know that the intimacy of the soul is its simplest essence, stamped with the image of God. Certain of the saints have called it the ' centre,' others ' intimacy,' others the ' apex of the spirit,' others ' mind.' St. Augustine the Great and the most modern writers speak of it as the soul's ' depth,' because it is the most interior and secret place of all, where no images of created things may enter, but only (as has been said) that of the Creator. The deepest hush and the deepest silence are here, for no form of created thing can reach this centre, and in respect of it we are godlike or divine,—so like, indeed, to God Himself that wisdom calls us gods. This empty, void, and formless state of intimacy is raised above all created things, above all feelings and powers of the soul; it transcends all time and place, and the soul remains in perpetual union and unity with God, Who is its beginning.

This intimate union is for ever enlightened and illuminated

---

[1] Job 7[20], A.V. The Spanish ' contrario ' is from the Vulgate ' contrarium ' : Quid faciam tibi, o custos hominum ? Quare posuisti me contrarium tibi, et factus sum mihimetipsi gravis ?

by the eternal uncreate light. So soon as it is revealed and discovered to man, it fills him in wondrous wise with tenderness and love, like unto the man who found the treasure, and for the exceeding joy thereof went and sold all that he had and bought the field. Oh noble and divine temple, which God never leaves, in which dwells the Most Holy Trinity and man tastes eternal life. . . . Here indeed is a well of water springing up into life everlasting ; so great is its efficacy and virtue, and its sweetness, that it conquers and drives out all the bitterness of vice, and exceeds and surpasses all the rebelliousness, controversy and vice in a nature that is vicious and inclined to evil. For when a man drinks of this water of life, it flows through every region, both of the body and of the soul, giving and communicating to body and soul a marvellous purity and fecundity.

Pupil. A great thing indeed is this, and a man should never slacken nor cease from prayer until God grant him to drink of this water, be it but a single draught.

Master. Didst thou drink but one drop thou wouldst no longer thirst after vain things nor after creatures which pass away, but rather after God alone and His love, in which the more thou dost grow the greater will be thy progress in divine union ; and the closer thy union with God and the deeper thy absorption in Him, the more clearly wilt thou know Him, and knowing Him, with the greater ardour love Him. This is the aim of all our exercises and labours ; by this they are ordered, and in this come to an end, for if thou have not love, all thy toils, though they exceed all that men and devils have suffered and do suffer, are vain and fruitless, as thou wilt find set forth at length in our *Triumphs*. In brief, thou wilt be as holy as thou art loving, and no more. And if thou think that I prolong this matter unduly, hear the great father Augustine, who says thus : If thou wilt perfectly fulfil all that explicitly or implicitly is contained in the Divine Scriptures, keep true love in thy soul, for this is the end of the law and of the prophets.

DIEGO DE ESTELLA

(1524-1578)

Born in the Navarran town of Estella, Diego de Ballestero changed his name, and took that of his birthplace, on professing as a Franciscan. Very little is known of his life beyond the fact that he was in great demand as a preacher, that he worked principally in Galicia and that Philip II appointed him a consulting theologian.

His works had a great vogue both in Spain and abroad in the sixteenth and seventeenth centuries, especially the treatise *De la Vanidad del Mundo*, of which four editions and six translations (into Latin, French, and Italian) are known to have been published before 1600. (⸶ into English by Bl. Robert Southwell S.J.)

How Love Bears us to God as to our Centre

Most true it is, O Lord, and by experience most clearly proved, that even as Thou art the Good of men, even so the force of love by its nature inclines man himself to Thee, and bears him to Thyself, as to his source and centre, though oft-times against his nature he is borne towards other things, that are contrary to his true welfare and honour.   For as our nature inclines us to one thing, so also does our whole will bear us to one thing, though by our power of free choice it is capable of following after many, and of itself can turn whithersoever it desires.   For in the will there is no constraint as there is in nature,—and would that there were, O my God, would that we were constrained to union with Thee, so that even against our will we might be capable of nought beside, and might be joined with Thee, even as after this life by Thy great mercy we shall be joined with Thee.

Alas, that I see among men a great miracle, a woeful miracle, and one greatly to be lamented! Wouldst thou not perchance hold it to be a very great miracle if thou shouldst see a great rock suspended in the air, or supported by a feather, or shouldst see that a scrap of paper were sufficient to impede the flow of a mighty river rushing onward with great force? Who that saw such a thing would not cross himself for fear? Who would not marvel and be astounded? Then how shall I not marvel at seeing men whom trivial things suffice to hinder, so that they attain not, O my Lord, to Thee? Strange indeed it is that one who in his nature has so great a force of gravity which bears him to Thee, my God, should be weighted down by such frivolities as those of earth.

We are pilgrims in this world, and so the Holy Scriptures call us,[1] and we journey towards Thee, O Lord, as to our own country, and to the true native land of our souls, wherein, as the Apostle says, we live and move and have our being.[2] And whensoever we sin, we are hindered and halt in the way; the great marvel, and that which excites so great wonder, is that things so trivial can hinder us. My love is the force which moves me. By love I am borne whithersoever I go. Wheresoever my love rests, thither goes my soul; and even as thou, O Lord, hast given a force to the rock that as it falls it may go towards its centre and natural place, even so to our souls hast Thou given the same force, which is a desire for the highest Good, to the end that by this attraction it may the more easily be drawn to Thee. If this, then, O my good God, be so, how can it be that every soul created by Thee doth not with great haste go toward Thee? But we see souls hanging and suspended from a breath of wind, deprived thereby of all good, yet laughing and merry and at rest.

How is it possible that any creature capable of union with Thee should not go with all its strength toward Thee, infinite Centre of infinite good, and hence of infinite attraction? What thing can detain a creature capable of reaching so great a Good? O great weight of sin, which laid upon the neck of mankind weighs it down and causes it to sink to the ground, that it may not rise to its rightful sphere, for which it was created!

In truth, it is a greater miracle that souls should not mount up to their God by love, than that rocks should be raised up and suspended by a breath of wind that they may not fall to their Centre; or than that a thin slip of paper should impede the

---

[1] Heb. 11[13]: Peregrini et hospites sunt super terram.
[2] Acts 17[28]: In ipso enim vivimus, et movemur, et sumus.

course of a swift and rushing torrent towards the sea. Who could ever bear his life with patience if he knew distinctly and clearly of how great good he is deprived and how much good he loses? O most ungrateful veil of my flesh, of how much joy dost thou deprive me! Who is he that may hinder me from tearing and rending thee with mine own hands, that I may go and behold my God, and enjoy Him, and in Him find my rest? Oh, of how many pleasures and of how great happiness am I deprived because of thee! And, what is worse, how do I suffer thee and am at ease, knowing well all this and seeing and perceiving it, and do not rather weep and groan, as would be just, for days and nights over this exile and blindness and pitiable plight of mine!

Whence comes to me an endurance so evil and so ungrateful, but from the veil which is set betwixt myself and God, from this cloud of the flesh which so obstructs me that the brightness of the sun may not shine in my soul? Take away this veil which impedes me, and thou shalt see with what great force my soul will travel toward its centre. Consider the souls of the saints, that are already loosed from this veil and free: with what swiftness and lightness do they go toward their God. Who can impede them? Who can keep them back? Who can deprive them of their rightful place? For therein is full and perfect rest, therein is eternal satisfaction for all the restless desires of the soul.

Truly the Lord is great and highly to be praised, and no less to be loved, but as greatly to be loved as to be praised. When my soul is in the city of the Lord, and in His holy hill, there the power of love is kindled, for there no veil shall intervene to obstruct it. And even now, the thinner is this veil and the more transparent, the nearer shall the soul move to its God, and the greater shall be the strength in it of the impulse of love. On the other hand it happens to many, in whom the veil of this flesh is very thick, because of the great abundance of their riches and other temporal goods, that they travel but little, and that slowly and in dilatory wise towards their Centre. Such as these love not God, or love Him but little. But those that with fast and vigil and other abstinence make thinner this veil of flesh and break its power, to some degree know this blessed light which because of the transparency of the veil shines in the eyes of their souls, even as the Apostle says: Now we see through a glass, darkly.[1]

In this way such as these run after the odour of Thy oint-ments,[2] and at times it even befalls them that through some chinks and holes these rays of divine light shine, if only but for a little space, in the eyes of their souls. Then they are at once melted in love and with a mighty impulse are borne away, at-tracted not by odour but by an exceeding beauty. Yet, alas! for how short a time this radiance of light endures, and how soon such delectable rays are past and gone. They strike the soul, and immediately pass away, and as Job says: " He hideth the light in His hands and commandeth it to come again; and to His friend He saith of it that it is His possession and that he may rise to it." [3] But as soon as He kindles it in His hands, it flashes between His fingers but for a moment.

For if He chose to shine forth in all the fulness of His splendour, even through the hinges of the gates of Heaven,[4] it is evident that with His brightness He would rather blind than illumine the Heavenly spirits, for they would be overcome by such an exceeding great light. For who could endure the Divine Majesty, were it not tempered?

In this way spiritual men are nourished in this life, for so long as they may not see Thee, my God, in that other life, face to face, where they will be in perfection, and at the centre of happiness, having the fruition of Thy Divine Essence.

---

[1] 1 Cor. 13[12]: Videmus nunc per speculum in ænigmate.

[2] Cant. 1[3]: Trahe me: post te curremus in odorem unguentorum tuorum.

[3] Job 36[32,3]: In manibus abscondit lucem, et præcipit ei ut rursus adveniat. Annuntiat de ea amico suo, quod possessio eius sit, et ad eam possit ascendere. A.V. varies in each verse.

[4] This strangely vivid phrase seems to have been inspired by St. Gregory. For a commentary on the underlying idea, see Butler: *Western Mysticism*, Con-stable, 1922, pp. 109-11.

How the Soul is never Stilled, but in God as in its
Centre

As my soul of its nature inclines toward Thee, my God,
because of its love, hence is it that were our nature not corrupted
and deformed by sin, it would need not that Thou shouldst
command it to love Thee, even as now Thou commandest us
not to love ourselves; for being by our nature fully, nay
excessively, inclined thereto, we need not that Thou shouldst
command and admonish us to do that for which we are naturally
fitted and inclined.[1]

And since man of his nature inclines to love Thee,—yea, to
love Thee more than Himself,—why is Thy holy love commanded to us, as is most natural, and not the love of ourselves?
Surely sin is the cause, for thereby did the soul withdraw its
gaze from God, turned and fixed it upon itself, impeding and
stemming that current of love which else would rush with so
great force unto Thee, my God.

Let us say then at once that there were no need of such
commandment had our nature preserved itself in that purity in
which it was created; and hence is it that at its first creation
we read not that Thou didst give such commandment either to
angels or men when Thou didst create them, since they were by
nature inclined thereto and they needed not to be spurred to
fulfil that commandment who by a law of great and inward love
had been formed by their Creator.   But we have forgotten that
natural law and are alienated from our own nature, so that
neither for commands, nor promises, nor threats, nor great and
daily benefits, do we love Thee as we justly ought.   But as a
ball of lead, which by force is kept upon a lofty plane, falls, as
soon as it is released, to the ground, so our soul, if for a while
it be carried away and raised to heavenly things, at once, by its
weight, falls down to earthly and transient things and disperses
all its powers among things of sense.

[1] Or: "comes to us by nature,—yea, and *becomes* us."   The repetition of
viene is intentional.

Tell me then, O my soul,—answer me, O miserable one,—
and declare to me the reason why thou goest so gladly among
the creatures, with such hunger and thirst for them, and so
greatly to thy dishonour ?   Why goest thou begging from them
a poor drop of troubled water, so flat and brackish to the taste,
which rather inflames than quenches thy thirst, forsaking the
pure, delectable and eternal fountain of all blessings, in which
alone thou couldst quench all thy thirst and satisfy all ,thy desire and thy will.

Tell me, thou puny soul, what thing canst thou desire which
thou findest not far more completely in thy God ?   If wisdom
delights thee, He is most wise ; if power and might, He is most
powerful and mighty ; if thou wilt have glory and riches, both
glory and riches in abundance are in His house ; [1] if delights
and pleasures, at His right hand are pleasures for evermore ; [2]
if fulness and abundance of desires, those that possess Him are
inebriated with the abundance of His house.

Then how, knowing this and much more than I can tell thee,
O miserable one, dost thou of set purpose leave this vast storehouse of all that is good, and go, wearied, sad and afflicted, in
search of comforts and pleasures in petty man-made channels.
Thou despisest the waters of the fountain which are given thee
freely, and with great labour dost dig for thyself turbid wells.
O intolerable madness, greatest of follies, stupendous blindness !
Hence comes it that the Lord in His indignation exclaims by
the word of the Prophet, saying : " Be astonished, ye heavens
and let her gates be destroyed, saith the Lord.   For My people
have committed two evils.   They have forsaken Me, the fountain
of living waters, and hewn them out cisterns, broken cisterns,
that can hold no water." [3]

Leave then, my soul, leave, I entreat thee, these dried up,

---

[1] Ps. iii[3] : Gloria, et divitiæ in domo eius.

[2] Ps. 15[11] : Delectationes in dextera tua usque in finem.

[3] Jer. 2[12.13] : Obstupescite, cæli, super hoc, et portæ eius desolamini
vehementer, dicit Dominus.   Duo enim mala fecit populus meus : me dereli-
querunt fontem aquæ vivæ, et foderunt sibi cisternas, cisternas dissipatas, quæ
continere non valent aquas.

pierced and broken cisterns, that with so great pains thou hast
hewn for thyself, and run and betake thyself with great haste to
the fountain of living water, which is thy God and thy Spouse
Jesus Christ, wherein thou canst at thy will entirely quench thy
thirst.   Here shalt thou be filled with delights, yea, true delights
and pleasures, according to thy whole heart and thy whole will,
and as thou desirest.

Only in the Lord shalt thou find quietness and rest and in
no other thing whatsoever of all that is in the world.   He alone
is thy centre and thy true and natural sphere ; out of Him shalt
thou find no contentment, but in Him all good, all rest and all
glory.

How the Love of God Enkindles the Soul in Celestial Desires

Suffer me, O Lord, my happiness, that I may declare unto
Thee the desire to behold Thee which Thy Divine love enkindles
in my soul ; not that Thou shouldst learn aught which Thou
knewest not, since Thou dost look clearly into the secret places
of the heart, but rather because I find none in Heaven or earth
to whom I may make my complaints save only unto Thee.
For as God Thou seest all things, as Father Thou hast compassion, and as Almighty Thou canst heal.   And furthermore, the
affliction which is born of Thy pure and holy love brings with
it consolation when it is taken to Thee, and when he that endures
it considers how blessed is the consummation which he is wont
to receive at Thy hands.

What shall I do, O Lord, but declare that which I feel concerning Thee ?   I know not how the understanding, guided by
Thy light, brought me to Thee and left the will enkindled, so
that, when it would declare that which it finds in Thee, or rather
that which in Thee it hopes to find, neither thought can conceive
it, nor tongue or pen give it expression.

Little does he love and desire Thee who can expound all
that he feels, for as the measure of Thy love is to have no measure,

so the desire for Thy Presence can be expressed but by tears
and not by words.   Wherefore if by a similitude I would declare myself, any one that I find is so unlike that which I need
to express its measure that I had rather say my desire is to
portray it to the life.   I desire Thee not only as the Bride desires the sight of her Beloved Bridegroom, how often soever she
count the days and the hours, since no love of corporeal beauty
or delight could equal the desire for the beauty of Him that
painted the stars, in comparison with Whom, as says Job, the
heavens are not clean, and the angels in His presence are put
to shame.[1]   Nor is my desire like to that of the son who cannot
endure the absence of his most loving father, from whose coming
he expects great honour and advancement.   For Thou art more
than father, and with Thee are all good things, according to
that which Thou saidst to Thy servant Moses : I will show thee
all good.[2]   And to describe these good things in their turn is a
harder task than to count the raindrops.

A small thing in comparison with the desire of Thee is
that of the prisoner and captive, who is in continual peril of
death, for the arrival of a true friend by whose diligence he may
escape so great an affliction and return to his country and
native soil.   For he that loves Thee and attains to Thee will of
a certainty see the redemption of his body and be safe from the
tyranny of this world, and his soul will quickly gain its freedom
in order to submit itself entirely to Thee, and that slavery of apparent freedom wherein Thou mayest be lost will entirely cease,
for he will be no longer in his own hands but in Thine, and
Thou wilt give him freedom, not immediately to part from Thee,
but to enjoy Thee for ever.   So then, O Lord, Thy Divine
love sets so great a desire in me that my soul desires Thee, not
with the desire of this life, but as one desires God.   For such
desire alone is worthy of Thee, and if I should compare it with
any other, this is but to say that between them there is some

---

[1] Job 15[15] : Ecce inter sanctos eius nemo immutabilis, et cæli non sunt mundi
in conspectu eius.   A.V.: Behold he putteth no trust in his saints (R.V. ' holy
ones ').

[2] Ex. 33[19] : Ego ostendam omne bonum tibi.

resemblance, and not that the one is an image of the other. Because to measure with a thing of earth aught that touches Thee is greatly to affront Thee.

With such reservation I will dare to say with the Psalmist : " As the hart panteth after the water brooks, so panteth my soul after Thee, O God." [1] As this beast, tortured by an inward thirst, and pursued by dogs and beaters, hastens to the springs wherein it thinks to relieve its distress, to heal its wounds and refresh itself from its excessive heat, so my soul, enkindled by the inward fire of Thy sacred love, and outwardly assailed by many foes, seeing itself bleeding in all its members, desires Thee, that Thy merciful hand may heal it, and Thy strong right arm defend it, and that Thou mayst guide it to the water brooks, where with the cool water that gushes forth its thirst may be quenched.

He that comes to Thee will have no thirst, O Thou fountain of living waters. He will have but the desire to reach Thy Presence, as says Isaiah : " They shall not hunger nor thirst, neither shall the heat nor sun smite them, for He that hath mercy on them shall lead them, even by the springs of water shall He guide them." [2] Then shall my soul have no more to long for, nor my will more to desire, for when Thy glory appears I shall be satisfied.

This was the desire that moved that prodigal son, so that, forsaking and abandoning the vile employment in which he ministered to base delights, he sought Thee with diligence and returned to his first love, and thus, when he reached Thy presence, the hunger which he suffered came to an end, with all the other trials which he endured in the service of the world. When the waters of Thy Divine consolation fail, O Lord, as they failed when Hagar was far from the house of Abraham, my soul must needs return to Thee, my God, consumed by the flames of the living fire of love, that by virtue of its desires

---

[1] Ps. 41[2] : Quemadmodum desiderat cervus ad fontes aquarum : ita desider a anima mea ad te Deus.

[2] Isa. 49[10] : Non esurient, neque sitient, et non percutiet eos aestus et so quia miserator eorum reget eos, et ad fontes aquarum potabit eos.

enkindled by love it may seek Thee earnestly and move toward Thee with all diligence, O Lord, and there may find life and rest. He who in very deed loves and desires Thee abhors all this present life; all that the world holds is a straitness that oppresses and afflicts my heart, when I think upon Thy heavenly palaces and the inestimable riches of Thy glory. To him who by the favour of Thy Spirit, O Lord, has been raised on high to behold the boundless expanse of Thy Omnipotence and the spacious mansions of Thy holy city, how narrow will appear whatsoever is of the creature! How the eye will find then a fitting object for its gaze when it compares that sight with the sight of aught else!

I wonder not at the word of Thy prophet Isaiah, when after contemplating Thy greatnesses he looked once more upon the things of this world below : " Behold the nations are as a drop of water that oozes out of a bucket. He counted them as a grain, and the smallest of all in weight, and all the isles as fine dust." [1] It even seemed to him that with this comparison he had said but little, and therefore he gives another judgment which is more to the purpose, saying that all is as nothing, and as emptiness, and that as such it must be counted. Which judgment is of greater worth than that of the vain sons of this world, our neighbours on this earth, who consume themselves to extend their boundaries, as if by making their prison house a little wider they increased their freedom of spirit, for which all temporal things are too small. So then, my soul, having seen and known by experience how its desires increase not the things of earth, is moved with the impulse of Thy sacred love. It longs for Thee, O Lord, it burns with celestial desire and is tortured with the delay, sustaining itself in this life only by trusting in that which is written: He shall give the righteous their desire. [2]

Thou didst hear, O Lord, the desire of the poor, and Thine

---

[1] An inexact reference to Isa. 40^{15} (Vulg.) : Ecce gentes quasi stilla situlae et quasi momentum stateræ reputatæ sunt : ecce insulæ quasi pulvis exiguus (Cf. A.V. and R.V. ' are counted as the small dust of the balance.')

[2] Prov. 10^{24} : Desiderium suum justis dabitur.

ear was attentive to the preparation of their heart. All my desire is before Thee, which is none other than to love Thee and see Thee, in whom is fulness of desire, so that desire is no more, as the heart, being full of Thy sacred love, is sure and certain that it will never cease to love Thee, being strengthened in Thy grace and love. Delay not, O Lord, to have mercy on me and grant me happiness, the fulfilment of my desire, since love incites and impels me that I should journey to Thee and love Thee for ever.

OF THE DEGREES OF DIVINE LOVE

We have not, O Lord, this Thy Divine love so completely within our power that we can at once ascend to it, but rather little by little; although in truth, were our nature not exhausted by sins, our love would have its beginnings on high. But since by sin it is corrupted and depraved, it has lost its spiritual light and finds the beginnings of love elsewhere, even as a spring, issuing clearly and abundantly from its source, will find another place of issue if it be closed up with stones and wood and mud, and will come forth, not clear, as at first, but turbid and defiled, its former source being corrupted. So it is with the spring of love, which has made for itself a turbid, foul, corrupt and muddied source; for we begin with the love of ourselves, where we should begin with the love of God, which in very truth is the more natural. But the nature of our love has become depraved, and love has changed its source, so that whereas we should love Thee, our Lord and God, first of all, for Thine own sake, and all things else in Thee and through Thee, now we begin by loving ourselves more than any beside, and all things else through love of our own selves. From this point it is that we begin to progress in Thy holy love, setting in ourselves its beginning and foundation, and loving Thee less for Thyself than for our own sakes, because we know that without Thee we cannot live, since the continual need which we know that we have of Thy Divine Majesty compels and constrains us to seek Thee as our helper and to call upon Thee for Thy graces and all things that are necessary to this life. And hence is it that since without Thee we cannot have that which we love, we love Thee of necessity for our own sakes, for indeed we can do no other.

And so, O Lord, as we continue loving Thee for the need which we have of Thee, we experience and know Thy graciousness towards us, and Thy bounty, benevolence, sweetness and goodness, with many other Divine perfections. Hence comes it that we begin to be forgetful of ourselves, and Thy goodness of itself attracts us, though at first we sought it for our own sakes as a possession for our use and advantage. This is the third degree of love: for the first is our love for our own selves, the second our love of Thee for ourselves, and the third our love of Thee, of ourselves, and of all things beside, for Thine own sake alone.

When Jacob left his parents' home and went to Mesopotamia, and slept with a stone for his pillow, he saw in a vision a ladder with one end upon earth and the other in Heaven, and Thou, our Lord and God, wert reclining thereon. We are not birds, nor may we fly from earth to heaven, and hence it is needful that we mount step by step as on a ladder, by the stages and degrees of love. This love has its beginnings upon earth and in the earthly foundations of self-love, and rises by stages and degrees even to the excellence and perfection of Thy holy love, which is celestial, spotless, throughly refined and pure.

So, rising by these degrees of love, we reach even to heaven; our imperfect love becomes ever more purified, purged and refined, till it attains to the height and summit of that which is love indeed. And then, without regard whatsoever to ourselves, we love Thee for Whom Thou art and as One most worthy of love, since Thou art Sovereign Good and Infinite Goodness. And since our weak, corrupt and imperfect nature has need of Thy help and grace, Thou dost recline, O Lord, upon that ladder, for it is by Thy Divine grace and by the help of Thy hand that we shall mount to Thy excellent and sovereign love. Every good gift and every perfect boon is from above, coming down

from the Father of lights.[1]   How much more so, then, is love,
which is the most perfect boon of all?   Love is a fire, and is
like the fire in its beginnings, for when it comes near to the
substance of the wood, it is impure and full of smoke, but after
it has begun to rise to its own sphere it becomes ever purer,
lighter, clearer and more refined.   So is it with love, which,
though in its beginnings it is imperfect, defiled and earthly,
rises ever towards its rightful sphere, which is God, perfecting
itself until it reach Him and gaining ever somewhat until it
arrive at the point of perfection.

Then at last it has risen as high as it may, and reached that
state which befits it and in which it shall abide.   He who
possesses it has entirely forgotten himself and all things else ; he
is transported and transformed in his God, desiring no other
wealth in heaven or on earth save only the Creator and the Lord
of all things.   This is the true lover, who desires nought for
himself, nor aspires to interests of his own, nor will have any
good thing to be his in heaven or on earth, nor seeks in that
which he thinks and says and does, aught save that God may
be honoured and glorified and His will be done in all things.
Who shall attain to this degree of love ?   Blessed is he who has
come to so high a degree, and forgetting himself and all things
that are his, is entirely carried out of himself and given up to
Thee, my God, so that in Thee he is transformed.

Such felicity and blessedness as this belong not to the present
life but rather to that which is to come.   For this life is full of
cares and necessities which lay hold on the soul, and bend and
incline it to the love of this world, in which it lives captive
against its will.   If at times we attain to this degree of pure and excellent love, we must hold it fast.   For, by reason of our corruptible body, the soul is burdened and oppressed, and weighed down
when it was about to take its upward wing ; the importunity of
the flesh harasses even those who would fain be unmindful of it,
depriving them of repose, and molesting them with many a moil
and tumult, and other such vain thing, when they had for a short

---

[1] James I[17] (R.V., which follows Vulg. most nearly).

space been granted the rest and fruition of their Beloved, Jesus Christ.

Never is there lack of importunate vexations of vain thoughts and cares of the world, which disturbed even the holy patriarch Abraham, when he offered sacrifice and prayed with love to God, as the Lord Himself had commanded him. To this perfect degree of love that soul had attained which said to the Beloved: "My heart hath burned with Thy love, O my Lord, and this flame that is so great hath quenched in me all the fire of evil concupiscence." For no fire will burn beside that sacred fire, wherefore I have no more great concupiscence, but all is the pureness and cleanness of chastity. The fire from heaven has consumed and destroyed in me all other heat, and I am wholly changed, for the most potent force of love has destroyed me and changed me into nothing. So hast Thou fulfilled in me, O my Lord, that which of old through the prophet Thou hadst told us in the guise of a salutary admonition: I will turn my hand upon thee, and throughly purge away thy dross, and will take away all thy tin.[1]

This I see fulfilled in myself, for all that in me was mine own is consumed and melted away. I am turned into nought, for I live, and yet not I, but Christ liveth in me, and I knew it not. I knew not so great a sacrament; I knew not in truth the mystery of so great a change, in that I was to be annihilated and made nought that I might find true being, and that I might wholly fail in my God, as it was written: "My heart and flesh have failed in the living God,"[2] and again "My soul hath failed in your Saviour." Oh, how good is it thus to faint when the soul fails in its God and passes from itself into God, and attains to God and is made one spirit with Him. Most true to our nature would it be, and most truly in conformity with it, that all things should be loved for the sake of Him by whom they were created.

---

[1] Isa. 1²⁵, R.V. The Vulgate has: Et convertam manum meam ad te, et excoquam ad purum scoriam tuam, et auferam omne stannum tuum.

[2] Probably Ps. 84², but this and the next quotation may have various sources.

And this love must be held to be meet and right, being according to nature, and were our souls less fickle and less light, this last grade of love would be the first. Thus ought it to be, and thus would it be, had sin not come between. I can love Thee, O Lord, after three manners, to wit: together with other things, and more than other things, and without other things. He who loves Thee together with other things, placing Thee on a level with them in love, divides the affections and fulfils not the commandment of love. He who loves Thee more than other things, loving these things lawfully together with Thyself, divides not his heart, though in some manner he turns and withdraws it towards other things. This man fulfils the commandment of love, though he has not attained to perfection. But he who loves Thee alone, O Lord, and together with nought beside, this man has reached the summit of perfection and can say with the Bride: "My Beloved is mine and I am his: he feedeth among the lilies." [1] The first manner of love fashions a man for hell. The second builds upon the foundation of the faith wood, hay and stubble. The third builds gold, silver and precious stones, according to the word of the Apostle. [2]

How Love Transforms the Lover into the Beloved

So great and so rare is the power of love, that I must needs be even as is the object of my love, and according to that at which I arrive by love. There is nought that joins or adheres in as lasting a fashion as love, which joins and unites us with the Beloved in such a way as to transform the lover into the object of his love. Love is nought but a mutual and unitive virtue. As iron, when it is greatly heated in the forge, becomes fire, so my heart, as it burns, O my God, in Thy Divine and sacred fire, is wholly transformed in Thyself by love; it is

[1] Cant. 2^{16}, Vulg.: Dilectus meus mihi, et ego illi, qui pascitur inter lilia.
[2] 1 Cor. 3^{12}, Vulg.: Si quis autem superædificat super fundamentum hoc, aurum, argentum, lapides pretiosos, ligna, foenum, stipulam, uniuscujusque opus manifestum erit.

deified, and becomes as God. The iron, cold and dark, black
and hard as it is, becomes converted into fire, and grows soft,
warm, bright and shining, with all the properties of fire, doing
all its offices and everything that is done by fire, since it can
burn, shed light and enkindle.

The Scriptures call Thee fire, O our God and Lord, and
even such do we become when we attain to Thee through love,
for whereas we were once sinners, hard like iron, obstinate, cold,
dark and rude, now that we have attained through love to Thyself and love has thrust us into this forge of living flames, like
to that in which Moses saw Thee in the Bush, we are converted
into Thyself and made as fire, so that we work Divine works and
are spiritual men, and no longer carnal and worldly as we were.
Even so the apostle St. Paul was converted and transformed
into Thee, as he said to the Galatians : " I live, and yet not I,
but Christ liveth in me." [1]

So did the holy Apostle live in Thee, and so was he transformed in Thee, that his life was no longer his own, nor was he
in himself, but in the Beloved. Would, O my God and Lord,
that so my soul might be absorbed in that ocean of infinite love
and goodness, that I might no longer be myself, but rather, by
Divine participation a copy and an image of Thy sovereign
goodness and mercy.

O that it might be granted to my thoughts to turn to One
only, and that the strength of them all might be employed in
burning in reverence before Thy Divine Self! Then might I
say with the Prophet : " The thought of my heart is ever in Thy
Presence." [2] Would, O my God, that I were but a lamp burning on the altar of my soul, kindled with the fire of true love,
and fed by all that I feel and hear of Thy wonderful perfection,
that this perfection might be the most pure oil which of old
Thou didst command to be burned in the Sanctuary. O, that
it might please Thee, Lord, to afflict my soul with that chastisement of love concerning which Thou didst give warning by the

---

[1] Gal. 2[20] : Vivo autem, iam non ego : vivit vero in me Christus.
[2] Probably a reference to Ps. 72[23], Vulg.

prophet Hosea, saying : " I will hedge thy way with thorns, and with walls that thou canst not break down,"[1] that is : I will place difficulties in all things, so that if thou dost seek other lovers thou mayst never find them and so shalt return to Me.[2] O happy plight, that compels the soul to seek only One that deserves to be loved !

Let us then make an end, O my soul, of vain reasonings ; recollect thyself, set all thy purpose and love on thy Spouse Jesus Christ alone.　If in truth thou lovedst God thou wouldst forget all worldly things.　The Apostle counts all these things as dung, for love of Jesus Christ.　So, when our first father was in the state of innocence, God commanded him to eat of the trees of Paradise.　God needed to remind him to eat of them, because the great love that he bore to Him might have caused him to forget to take the sustenance needful to preserve his life. If thou didst love thy God and Lord with great and true love, thou wouldst not have such anxious care for these outward things which so greatly disturb and distract thee.

The more nearly our will attains to God, the farther it is withdrawn from our own selves.　We ought therefore to keep it fixed and intent upon God that we should be forgetful of all that is here below, and transformed, converted, and raised up into God.　If I loved Thee in truth, O Lord, the power of love would make me to be as that which I love, for it would transform me into Thyself, that so I should be like unto that which I love.　And if likeness be a cause of love, this love would be raised up and increased, rising with the homage of my soul and all that is within me,[3] so that nothing should remain but that which is made captive by Thy love.　Look, then, my soul, at thy Beauty and thou shalt understand what is that Beauty that thou must love.　Thou hast a Spouse and knowest Him not,

---

[1] Hosea 2⁶ : Propter hoc ecce ego sepiam viam tuam spinis, et sepiam eam maceria, et semitas suas non inveniet.　R.V. has ' fence,' A.V. ' wall.'

[2] Hosea 2⁷ : Et sequetur amatores suos, et non apprehendet eos : et quæret eos, et non inveniet, et dicet : Vadam, et revertar ad virum meum priorem : quia bene mihi erat tunc magis quam nunc.

[3] Ps. 102¹ : Benedic anima mea Domino, et omnia, quæ intra me sunt, nomini sancto eius.

and though He is the fairest of all things, thou lovest Him not because thou hast not seen His Face. If thou sawest Him thou wouldst not doubt concerning His beauty nor would any keep thee back from loving Him.

So great is the power of love that thou dost truly dwell where thy affections are fixed through contemplation. This is the Kingdom of God which is within thee, and which thou dost put from thee when thou lovest things that are without. If thou lovest this Kingdom of God, my soul, thou art queen in it, and having it within thee thou hast the fruition of the infinite riches that the love of God brings with it. And if the better the things thou lovest, the better thou art, it follows clearly that if thou love heaven thou art heavenly, and if thou set thy love on things of earth thou art earthly. So, as love within my soul produces effects so marvellous, that I am transformed by love and become as that which I love, my heart, O Lord, shall love Thee even to the utmost of its power and strength and virtue, and in so far as it is able. For by this road I am brought to so lofty and noble an estate, and raised to a dignity so wonderful and supreme, that all created things which love Thee not are less than the heart which burns in Thy Divine love.

This passing of the lover into the thing that is loved is neither violent nor painful nor laborious nor enforced, but free and voluntary, sweet and of great delight. And hence the will, that in this way is united through love with the thing it loves, can be by no act of violence withdrawn from it, but by its free will alone. Would, O my God, that my will were deprived of such freedom, and such desire to be free, that when I had once loved Thee, I might never turn back nor change either love or will, but love for ever and ever that highest Goodness and infinite Wealth wherein my heart perpetually burns in living flames of love. But love itself is free, though the will pass into the thing that is loved; and thus the will remains ever will, and has its freedom of power and desire, although by love it be transformed into the Beloved. A marvellous thing it is that in this transformation of the Lover in the Beloved, the love is as the object of its love, and as is the love so is the will whence it is born.

Hence it follows that the thing which is first and chiefly loved gives name, nature and form to the will which loves. Whence it is to be concluded that since the property of love is to absorb, convert and transform the lover into the Beloved or into the thing loved, if the will love chiefly things of the earth, it becomes as earth; earthly it becomes and earthly is its love; and if it love mortal things, mortal and human is its will; if it love angels, it becomes angelic; if it love Thee, our Lord and God, it becomes divine.

Herein is revealed and declared a great dignity in man, namely that through love he may be transformed and changed into anything that he desires, be it higher or lower than he. Of Nebuchadnezzar, who as a beast followed his bestial appetites, being governed by the senses, by which alone irrational creatures act and are guided, the Scriptures say that as a beast he went and did eat the herbs of the field.   And of spiritual men that love God David speaks in the Psalm which says: "I said, Ye are gods, and sons of the Most High." [1]   So then if I may rise to such high dignity by means of love, it is right, my Lord and my God, that my heart should love Thee by night and by day all the days of my life.   And if, O my soul, thou dost say that among all the pains and sorrows of this life thou canst not for sorrow rise to the love of thy God, (as Aaron said, that for sadness of mind he could not make a feast to God) consider that these trials are blows of the steel that God gives to strike from the hard flint of thy heart sparks of fire and love, and that He afflicts thee that thou mayest love Him.   For the most merciful Lord sees that thy heart is not softened by favours, and He wearies thee therefore with trials, that so thou mayest rise to Him through love, and, loving Him thus, acquire new honour and a new being, when thou art transformed through love into God.

---

[1] Ps. 81[6]: Ego dixi : Dii estis, et filii Excelsi omnes.

LUIS DE LEÓN
(1528-1591)

The life of Luis de León is invariably associated with the city of Salamanca, where, when only sixteen, he joined the Augustinian order. He spent most of his later life as Professor in the University of Salamanca : to-day his statue rightly stands in the University court, and the very *cátedra* which he occupied is still shown.

Unlike many of the writers whose lives are outlined in these pages he was somewhat outspoken and even fiery in character, traits which made him enemies and which were partly responsible for the disturbances which marked his career. The details of these events are not over-edifying, and it is sufficient to say that he quarrelled with several of his colleagues, was haled before the Inquisition on charges such as that of having translated the Song of Solomon into the vernacular and spent four years in prison (1572-6). The story goes that, on his release and resumption of his professorial duties, crowds flocked to hear him, expecting, no doubt, eloquent, and perhaps pungent references to his persecutors, as indeed they might. But on taking his accustomed place, he merely began with the words " As we were saying yesterday . . ." and passed on to his subject.

Be this true or no, we have ample information about the last years of Fray Luis' life, which were hardly more peaceful than those which had led to his imprisonment. Passing from the theological Chair which he had occupied to that of Moral Philosophy, he continued to be menaced and admonished by the Inquisition on account of his supposedly heterodox beliefs. Nor did he always keep on good terms with the University : at one time he was in serious danger of being deprived of his Chair. The greatest honour which he received,—by the irony, it would seem, of fate, —came to him but nine days before his death. On August 14, 1591, he was elected by the brethren of his order Provincial of Castile : on August 23 he died.

LOVE AND UNITY

For love, as you were saying just now, Juliano and Sabino, is unity, or its whole office is to bring about unity ; and the greater and better the unity, the greater and more excellent the love ; whence it follows without any doubt that the more the ways in which two persons are as one to each other, the more love for each other will they have.

Now if in us there be both flesh and spirit, and if in so many ways Christ unites His Spirit with ours, stamping it with His likeness, communicating to it His strength, and shedding abroad in it His own Spirit, does it not seem to you undeniable, Juliano, either that His love to us is lacking in something, or that His Body also is united with ours, in so far as it is possible for two bodies to be united? And who will dare to set bounds in this respect to His love, which in all other respects is so exceeding great toward us! Again, I ask: Is it impossible for God to accomplish this union? Or, if accomplished, does it not proclaim and exalt His love? Or does God take no pride in exalting it? Clearly it is possible; most evidently it adds something of perfection; while undeniable and clearest of all is the fact that God prizes perfection in all that He does.

If this, then, is certain, how can it be doubted that God does all that can be done, and all that needs to be done for the end He has in view? Christ Himself says, praying to the Father: "Lord, I will that I and mine own may be one, even as Thou and I are one."[1] The Father and the Son are one, not only because They have love toward each other, nor because They are at one both in will and in judgment, but because They are of one and the same substance, so that the Father lives in the Son, and the Son lives through the Father, and the life and being of both is the same. Then if the similitude is to be as perfect as may be, it is without doubt needful that we, the faithful, both as among ourselves, and as between ourselves and Christ, should not only be knit together and made one by that love which the Spirit sheds abroad in our hearts, but that in our very being, in body as in spirit, we should all be one, in so far as is feasible and possible. It is needful that being many persons, as in fact we are, nevertheless by reason of the same Spirit which dwells in our hearts, and of that same and only Food which sustains us, we should all be one in the Divine Body and Spirit, and closely united with each other both in body and spirit, treated and constituted alike, and that with the treatment and constitu-

[1] Joh. 17[22].

tion proper to the Divine Body and Spirit : and this is the highest degree of union which can be attained or conceived as between things so unlike in themselves.

So then, just as a cloud which is penetrated by the force and brightness of the sun's rays, filled and (if the word be allowable here) saturated with light, is itself like a sun, however it be looked at; just so, when Christ unites, not only His virtue and light, but His very Body and Spirit, with the faithful and just, and in some sort mingles His very Soul with their souls, and His Body with their bodies, in the way I have described, Christ looks out from their eyes, speaks from their tongues, works through their senses; their faces, their countenances, their movements are Christ, Who thus occupies them wholly. So intimately does He take possession of them that, though His Nature in no way destroys or corrupts their own, there will be nothing seen in them at the Last Day, nor will any nature be found in them other than His Nature. There will be that one Nature in all; and both He and they will be one and the same in Himself.

Strong indeed, Sabino, is that tie, and so fast a bond of union that in nothing which Nature has formed or art invented are the divers parts knit together with so fine and so invisible a bond as this. Indeed, it is like the union of matrimony, but so much the stronger and more excellent as the rite is the straiter and more pure. It is purer than betrothal or marriage after the flesh ; and even so, or more, does it excel such marriage in the intimacy of its union. For whereas in the one there is defilement of the body, in the other there is deification both of soul and flesh. Here there is mutual affection between the wills of two persons ; there all is one will and one desire. Here the body of the one is master of the other ; there, without destruction of her substance, Christ the Spouse transforms His Bride into His own Body, in the manner aforesaid. Here, men often stray ; there, they walk ever securely. Here, we find continually anxiety and care, sworn foes of concord and union ; there, that rest and security which helps and favours the state of those at one. Here, the union of two is to bring into the world a third ; there, one union leads to another, one embrace to another, and its fruit is oneness for evermore.

Here, happiness is but weak, delight of base alloy and brief
duration; there, both are so great that they submerge alike body
and soul—so noble, that they are glory—so pure, that sorrow
neither precedes nor follows them, nor is joined nor mingled
with them.

The Birth of Christ in the Soul

The birth of the soul in Christ signifies properly that the
stain of sin, which made the soul in form like to the devil, is
taken away, and that we receive the grace and righteousness
which God implants in us, and which is as an image of Christ,
so that we are fashioned after His likeness.   But the birth of
Christ in us is not only that the gift of grace comes to the soul,
but that Christ's very Spirit comes and is united with it,—nay,
is infused throughout its being, as though He were soul of its
soul indeed.   And thus, infused and absorbed by the soul, this
Spirit takes possession of its faculties and powers, not fleet-
ingly nor in haste, nor merely for a short time as happens in
the glories of contemplation and in the raptures of the spirit,
but abidingly, and with a settled peace, in like manner as the
soul reposes in the body.   And Christ Himself says of it thus:
'He that loveth Me shall be loved of My Father, and We will
come unto him, and make Our abode in him.'[1]
So then, we are born in Christ when we receive His grace
and grow in its likeness; but Christ is born in us when He
comes by His Spirit to dwell in our souls and bodies.   When
He comes, I say, to dwell, and not alone to bring delights and
favours.   Although Marcelo told us yesterday, then, of how
we are born in God, there remains yet room to-day to tell of
the birth of Christ in us.   Of this, since we have mentioned and
explained its difference from the other, its essence being the
coming of Christ to dwell in the soul, let us now say first, that
it may be the better understood, in how different a manner He
dwells in the soul, when He reveals Himself in prayer; and

[1] Joh. 14²¹,²³,—a composite quotation.

afterwards we will tell how and when Christ begins to dwell in us, and the strength which His birth and life within us bring, and the degrees and stages of growth which mark it.

With respect to the first-named, between that advent and union with ourselves of the spirit of Christ which we call His birth, and His appearances to the souls of the just and the proofs of His presence which He gives in prayer, the principal difference is this. In what we call His birth, the spirit of Christ is united with the very being of the soul, and begins to work His virtue upon it, embracing it closely without its perception or knowledge. And there He rests, hidden as it were in its very depths: as Isaiah says, 'Sing and rejoice, O daughter of Zion, for the Lord of Israel is within thee.'[1] And even as He rests within its depths, He sheds over it the rays of His power, and moves it secretly. And by this movement, and the obedience of the soul thus moved, it becomes ever a more spacious dwelling, a larger room and a room more fitly prepared.

But in the inspiration and the graces which come through prayer, all the business of Christ is with the powers of the soul, —the will, the understanding, the memory. At times He touches even the bodily senses, and communicates Himself to them in diverse and wondrous ways, in such degree as these feelings are possible to the human body. So entirely is the soul overwhelmed with superfluity of sweetness that the over-plus passes to others. Whence these seasons of enlightenment and graces, or this union 'in sweetness of the soul with Christ in prayer, has something in it of the lightning flash: I mean that its brilliance is quickly over. For our powers and feelings, while this mortal life endures, are of necessity compelled to busy themselves with other thoughts and cares, without which man lives not, nor can live.

---

[1] He means, presumably, Isa. 62[11] (Vulg.: Dicite filiæ Sion: Ecce Salvator tuus venit, etc.), but the passage is much nearer to Zeph. 3[14-15]: Lauda filia Sion; jubila, Israel; rex Israel Dominus in medio tui; or to Zech. 2[10]: Lauda et laetare, filia Sion, quia ecce ego venio, et habitabo in medio tui, ait Dominus; or to Zech. 9[9] (q.v.).

And together with this difference there comes another. For, in the union of the spirit of Christ with our spirits, which we call the birth of Christ, His Spirit is as a soul with respect to our soul, and does within it the work of a soul, moving it to act as it ought in all that offers, inspiring it with a strength to be up and doing, and so working in it and moving it that by Its aid the soul works together with It. But in Christ's presence as revealed to the faithful in prayer, when He gives them inspiration and joy, the greater part of the soul and its powers are at rest, and He alone works secretly in them repose and blessings which cannot be described. And thus the first is a living union while the second brings but delight and favour; the one is life and existence itself,—the other brings those things which make life sweet; in the one the soul is inhabited and possessed by God, in the other it tastes but something of His felicity. The first, then, is given abidingly and for ever, because if it fail there can be no life, while the second is fleeting and soon passes away, because it is a thing more of favour than of need, and because in this life, which is given us for work, the delight, so long as it lasts, turns us away from work and in its stead gives fruition. This is the one; and, as to the other of which I spoke, I will say of it in this wise:

Christ is born in us whensoever we fall to considering our lives, when we see and abhor their wretchedness and confusion, when we meditate on the wrath of God which we have deserved, and when in our grief and our desire to appease Him, we turn with faith, love and contrition, to the mercy of God and the ransom wrought by Christ. It is then that Christ is born within our souls.

And we say that He is born in us because then His very spirit enters our soul; He becomes its familiar friend, works in it His grace, which is, as it were, a ray or a refulgence of His Presence, takes up His abode in the soul and makes it beautiful. And thus it is that Christ begins to live in the soul; namely, when He begins to work in and through it the works proper to Himself, for the most sure and certain signs of life are works.

CHRIST THE PRINCE OF PEACE

Even did reason not prove, and there were no other way of knowing how desirable a thing is peace, this glorious spectacle of the heavens unveiled before us now, and the harmony of the wondrous lights which shine in them afford us testimony enough. For what is that but peace, or at the least a perfect image of the same, which we now see in the heavens and which gives so much delight to our eyes? If peace, as St. Augustine briefly and truly concludes, is a tranquil order, or calm and steadfastness in that which good order requires,—it is that very thing which this image reveals to us now. For here the host of the stars, placed as it were in order and arrayed in ranks, gives forth its wondrous light; each member inviolably keeps its place; none usurps the room of its neighbour nor hinders it in its office, far less, forgetful of its own, breaks the sacred and eternal law which Providence has given it. Rather do all of them, united among themselves, and as it were considerate of each other, the greater sharing their lights with the less, show signs of love, and in a manner do reverence to each other. All of them at certain seasons moderate their light and power, which they reduce to one peaceful uniformity of power, composed of divers parts and aspects, beyond all measure powerful and universal.

If we may so express it, they are not only a bright and lovely example of peace, but also a proclamation, a hymn of praise sung by an exceeding multitude of voices, declaring to us how excellent are those virtues which peace contains in itself and which it brings to all things. The which voice and proclamation makes itself heard without noise of words in our souls, and its efficacy and persuasiveness are clearly manifest from the effect which there it makes. For our souls, perceiving how lovely and precious a thing is peace, begin to seek peace in themselves, and to set themselves throughly in order.

For, if we consider the secret things that come to pass within ourselves, we shall find that this order and harmony among the stars, as we contemplate it, brings rest to our souls; that, as our eyes are fixed intently upon the heavens, our desires and troubled affections, which surged tumultuously in our breasts by day, are gradually lulled to rest, we know not how; and that, sinking, as it were, to sleep, these desires are calmed, restored to their rightful place, and brought imperceptibly into subjection and due order. We shall find, too, that, as they are humbled and stilled, the reason, which is chief and lord of the soul, rises above the rest, recovers its right and its strength, and, as if inspired by this glorious heavenly vision, conceives high thoughts, which are worthy of itself, and in some sort mindful of its first beginning, sets all that is mean and vile in its proper place, and tramples it underfoot. Thus, with reason enthroned once more as empress of the soul, and its other parts reduced to their fit rank, the whole man is in an ordered and peaceful state.

But what of ourselves, who are reasonable beings? The rude and insensible works of creation, the elements,—the earth, the air—the animals, order themselves, and go to rest, when the sun sets and the resplendent host of heaven appears. See you not how silence is now over all things, as though they gazed in this most beauteous mirror, and forthwith were composed and at peace, returning to their places and offices, and contented with them?

Without any doubt peace is that good part which is in all things everywhere: wherever men see it they love it. And not peace alone, but the sight of its very image arouses our love, and makes us burn with longing to approach it, for we tend easily and without effort to approach our greatest good. And if we confess the truth, as confess it we needs must, not only is peace sought generally by all, but it alone and nought else is so sought and desired and pursued. For all our work, so long as we live this life, and all our desire and labour, is directed towards the attainment of this good part, this peace. It is the goal to which all direct their thoughts, the consummation to which all aspire. For if the merchant takes a ship and ploughs the seas, it is to be at peace with his ambition, which ever importunes and assails him. And the labourer tilling the soil in the sweat of his brow seeks peace by driving stern penury from him, so far as he may. So also he who follows pleasure, covets honour or cries out for

revenge : all these, beneath their several aims, seek peace. For
they pursue some good thing which they lack, or flee from some
evil which molests them.

And because both that good thing which the desire pursues,
and the evil which is borne in fear and sorrow, disturb the repose
of the soul, and are as enemies making war upon it, it is clear
that all man's deeds are nought but efforts to flee from war and
to pursue peace. And if this peace is our great and only good,
who may be its Prince—that is, its chief fountain-head and source
—save Him who is the author and begetter of all that is good,
Jesus Christ, our Lord and our God? For if to possess peace
is to be free from evils which afflict us and desires which torment,
and to enjoy quietness and rest, it is He alone Who can free our
souls from fear, and enrich them with such manner of good things,
that there remains no more which they can desire.

The Life Removed [1]

How tranquil is the life
Of him who, shunning the vain world's uproar,
May follow, free from strife,
The hidden path, of yore
Trod by the few who conned true wisdom's lore!

For he with thoughts aloof
By proud men's great estate is not oppressed,
Nor marvels at the roof
Of gold, built to attest
The Moor's skill and on jasper piles to rest.

He cares not though his name
Be raised aloft, to winds of rumour flung,
He cares not for the fame
Of cunning flatterer's tongue,
Nor that which truth sincere would leave unsung.

[1] " How have I ever loved the life removed," Shakespeare, *Measure for
Measure*, I, iv.

What boots it my content
That the vain voice of fame should favour me,
If in its service spent
I find myself to be
Vexed by dull care and gnawing misery?

O hills, O streams, O fields,
O solitary refuge of delight,
Since my ship well-nigh yields
To the storm, your solace bright
I seek, and flee this sea's tempestuous might.

Sleep broken by no fear
Be mine, and daytime clear and bright and free,
Shunning the look severe,
Lofty exceedingly,
Of him whom gold exalts or ancestry.

Me may the birds awake
With their sweet unpremeditated song ;
May I those cares forsake
That e'er to him belong
Who lives not in his independence strong.

I to myself would live,
To enjoy the blessings that to Heaven I owe,
Alone, contemplative
And freely love forgo
Nor hope, fear, hatred, jealousy e'er know.

Upon the steep hill-side
An orchard I have made with my own hand,
That in the sweet springtide
All in fair flower doth stand,
And promise sure of fruit shows through the land.

And, as though swift it strove
To see and to increase that loveliness,
From the clear ridge above
A spring pure, weariless,
Running to reach that ground doth onward press.

And straightway in repose
Its course it winds there tree and tree between,
And ever as it goes
The earth decks out with green
And with gay wealth of flowers strows the scene.

The air in gentle breeze
A thousand scents for my delight distils,
It moves among the trees
With softest sound that fills
The mind, and thought of gold or sceptre kills.

Treasures and gold be theirs
Who to a frail bark would entrust their life:
I envy not the cares
Of those whose fears are rife
When the north wind with the south wind is at strife.

In the storm's strain the mast
Groans, and clear day is turned to eyeless night,
While to the skies aghast
Rise wild cries of affright
And they enrich the sea in their despite.

But me may still suffice
With plenty and meek peace a humble fare,
And the wrought artifice
Be his of gold plate rare
Who dreads not o'er the raging sea to fare.

And while in misery
Others are pledged to fierce ambition's throng,
Afire insatiably
For power nor sure nor long,
May I in pleasant shade recite my song.

Yea, lying in the shade,
My brow with ivy and bay immortal crowned,
My ear attentive made
To the sweet, tuneful sound
Of zither touched by fingers' skill profound.

[Translation by Aubrey F. G. Bell,
adapted by E. A. P.]

The Heavenly Life

Fair realm of radiant light,
O meadow of the blest, that neither hail
Nor lightning-flash may blight,
Where pleasure without fail,
Springing from richest soil doth e'er prevail.

With purple flowers and white
His head is crowned as, onward journeying,
To pastures of delight,
With neither crook nor sling,
The Shepherd his loved flock in thee doth bring.

He goes, and after him
Follow his happy sheep : their pasturage
Are flowers that wax not dim
But their desire assuage,
And cropped, still suffer neither change nor age.

In the blest mountain's fold
He guides, and zealous for their welfare goes,
Bathes them in waters cold
And plenteous fare bestows
The Pastor-Pasture whence all blessing flows.

When in the highest sphere
The sun to the heaven's zenith doth attain,
His flock around him, here
Resting will he sustain
His sacred ear's delight with music's strain.

Immortal ecstasy
The soul drinks as he strikes the sounding lyre;
Gold is mere mockery
In this consuming fire
Of endless blessings that outrun desire.

O voice! O music! might
But some faint strain descend into my sense,
In transports of delight,
That my soul, journeying hence,
Might lose itself in thee, O love immense!

Ah, then would it indeed
Beloved, know thy noontide resting-place,
And win, from prison freed
Of suffering, to thy grace,
Nor ever from thy fold its steps retrace.

[Translation by Aubrey F. G. Bell,
adapted by E. A. P.]

A NIGHT OF STARS

When I behold the sky
With stars innumerable spangled bright,
And then the earth descry,
Encompassèd with night,
Buried in sleep, oblivion infinite,

Sorrow and love arise
And with a burning fever fill my breast,
And ever from my eyes
The tears flow without rest
Till my tongue speaks at last, with grief oppressed :

O dwelling of great might,
Temple of lovely light incomparable,
My soul, that to thy height
At birth aspired, what spell
Doth in this dark, low prison-house compel?

What mortal folly thus
From truth's possession can remove our sense,
So that, oblivious
Of heavenly gifts, it thence
Strays into shadowy lands and vain pretence?

Man lives imprisonèd
In sleep and recks not of his destiny,
While still with silent tread
At Heaven's swift decree
Hour after hour his life doth from him flee.

Ah, mortal men, awake
And turn your thoughts intent upon your loss!
Shall souls divine forsake
Such blessings for the cross
Of life unreal and dull delusion's dross?

O, skyward lift your eyes,
Upward to this eternal heavenly sphere,
And you will then despise
The vain delights that here
Beguile our life, its every hope and fear.

O, how may we compare
The fleeting span of this low earthly scene
With that great region where
In noblest forms are seen
What is and what shall be and what hath been.

Who sees the eternal fires
With fixèd laws move on their heavenly way,
How each with each conspires,—
Uneven their array,
Yet varying they one ordered scheme obey;

How in the moon's clear train
As she her silver sphere doth onward move,
Goes light of wisdom's rain,
And gleaming there above,
Follows, serenely fair, the star of love;

But blood-red angry Mars
Chooses unto himself another way,
While girt with myriad stars
Jove in his blest array
Benignly calms the heavens with steadfast ray;

And yonder in the height
Whirls Saturn, father of the Age of Gold,
And after him the bright
Stars in fair choir enroll'd
Their light and all their treasure still unfold:

Who may all this descry
And pleasure still in this vile earth retain?
Who will not groan and sigh
To rive the imprisoning chain
Wherein his soul exiled from Heaven hath lain?

Lo, here lies sweet content,
Reigns peace, and on a rich and lofty throne
Sits holy love, and blent
Together in its zone
Delight and honour evermore at one.

Here beauty infinite
Unveils itself, and light, quintessence pure,
Transparent gleams: no night
Its radiance may obscure,
Spring's flowerèd splendour here is ever sure.

O fields of truth most fair!
O meadows ever fresh indeed and bright!
O mines of riches rare!
O fountain of delight,
Deep valleys with a thousand blessings dight!

[Translation by Aubrey F. G. Bell,
adapted by E. A. P.]

II. ORIGINAL VERSIONS

HERNANDO DE ZÁRATE

WORKS. *Discursos de la paciencia cristiana* (1593). Possibly also: *Certamen de la Concepción de Nuestra Señora* (1586).

BIBLIOGRAPHY. *Discursos de la paciencia cristiana*, in *Biblioteca de Autores Españoles*, Vol. XXVII, pp. 419-684. Bibliographical article in *Diccionario Enciclopédico Hispano-Americano*, Vol. XXIII.

LA GLORIA DEL CIELO

La gloria del cielo que Dios tiene guardada para sus amigos, no hay lengua humana que pueda decir cuál es; antes dice san Pablo que ni ojos vieron ni orejas oyeron, ni jamás cayó en pensamientos de hombres, lo que Dios tiene allí aparejado para los que le temen. Pero según lo que de la fe y los libros santos sabemos, algunos rastros alcanzamos, de dónde lo demás se puede conjeturar.

Pero cuánta gloria será ver a Dios rostro a rostro, en que consiste esencialmente nuestra bienaventuranza, no puede caer debajo de nuestra imaginación, pues ni sabemos cuál es el rostro de Dios, qué es su esencia y sustancia, ni todos alcanzan el cómo y con qué lumbre se ha de ver. Y por eso contentarémonos con sacarlo por conjeturas; como hizo un pintor, según cuenta Plinio, que, mandado hacer un gran jayán en una pequeña tabla, pintó en ella una figura de un hombre, pequeña como la tabla era, pero a los pies de la figura pintó un sátiro que le estaba con una vara de medir midiendo el dedo pulgar. De donde el discreto que la mirase coligiese, multiplicando en proporción, las varas que tendría en todo el cuerpo por las del dedo, y hallaría que era grandísimo gigante.

Y así hizo el Señor cuando quiso darles a los apóstoles una vislumbre de su gloria, para que entendiesen cuál ha de ser la suya, y les mostró en el monte Tabor un rascuño della, pues fué sola la gloria del cuerpo, y desta sola la claridad, y desta una pequeña parte,

cuanta bastaba para aquel monte; porque de otra manera estando él
tan claro como el sol, no fuera tan secreta la claridad como él quiso
que fuese y como al cabo fué; mayormente que no falta quien diga
que fué este misterio de noche. Pues así será en este discurso, donde
no pretendemos dar sino una vislumbre de la gloria, pues no se trata
della de propósito, sino cuanto della se conjeture su grandeza, cuanto
cupiere entre gente que vive en este cuerpo mortal, para que de ahí
se saque el valor y excelencia de los trabajos, mediante los cuales
se merece.

Pues para este fin consideremos que cada ángel, aunque sea el
menor de todos, es mejor y más perfecta criatura en su naturaleza
que todas las corporales. Lo segundo, que toda la multitud de
ángeles que Dios crió, se exceden unos a otros en perfección, pues
no hay dos de una misma especie y naturaleza, como los hombres
son, sino que así como no hay dos números que sean iguales, sino
todos, aunque son infinitos, se exceden unos a otros, y tanto mayores
son cuanto más se apartan de la unidad, así son los ángeles, y tanto
más perfectos cuanto menos se apartan del sumo bien y perfección,
que es Dios, aunque con infinita distancia ninguno puede llegar a él;
y por eso su perfección se mide por lo que menos lejos está dél, y no
por el cuanto está más cerca.

Pues a esta cuenta, si en las cosas corporales hay tantas cosas
buenas que ver y entender, ¿ qué será ver el más perfecto ángel que
está más cerca o menos lejos de Dios? Y si deste a la naturaleza
infinita y perfección de Dios hay infinita distancia en perfección,
¿ qué será ver la misma esencia de Dios? Verdaderamente no sin
causa es menester nueva y más alta lumbre y nuevas y soberanas
fuerzas, pues para imaginarlo son menester bien grandes; y si siendo
el Bautista tan santo, que algunos le cuentan luego después de la
Madre de Dios, y después de haber gastado Cristo un buen rato en
sus alabanzas, dice al cabo que el menor de los bienaventurados es
mayor que él, ¿ qué tanto bien será uno de los que en aquel dichoso
reino son mayores? No hay que ponderar más de lo que el Evangelista dice, que seremos semejantes a Dios, porque le veremos tal
cual él es. Pues cuanto a este punto no hay más que encarecer de
la gloria del alma, pues que por ella seremos dioses por participación,
que es el ser semejante a Dios.

Discursos de la Paciencia Cristiana, IV.

ALONSO DE OROZCO

WORKS. [None of his Latin works, and only the most important of those written in Spanish, are here named.] *Vergel de Oración y Monte de Contemplación* (1544); *Desposorio Espiritual* (1551); *Regimiento del Alma* (1551); *Las siete palabras que la Virgen sacratísima nuestra Señora habló* (1556); *Historia de la reina Sabá* (1565); *Epistolario cristiano para todos los estados* (1567); *Libro de la Suavidad de Dios* (1576); *Victoria de la muerte* (1583); *Arte de amar a Dios y al próximo* (1585); *De Nueve Nombres de Cristo* (first printed in *La Ciudad de Dios*, Vols. XVI, XVII, 1888; an interesting work to compare with Luis de León's closely related *De los Nombres de Cristo*).

BIBLIOGRAPHY. *Obras del venerable padre Fray Alonso de Orozco*, Barcelona, 1882, 2 vol. [Includes only the *Epistolario cristiano* and *Victoria de la Muerte.*] *Obras del Beato Alonso de Orozco*, Salamanca, 1895. On the question of the *Nombres de Cristo* of Orozco and Luis de León see *La Ciudad de Dios*, Vols. XVI, XVII, and also XC, 422-432, XCI, 33-43, 109-115, XCV, 161-179; Fray Juan Márquez: *Vida del venerable padre Fray Alonso de Orozco*, Madrid, 1648; F. A. Gante, *Vida de Alonso de Orozco*, Madrid, 1719; Fr. Tomás Cámara, *Vida y escritos del Beato Alonso de Orozco*, Valladolid, 1882.

DE LA GRAN SUAVIDAD QUE DIOS COMUNICA EN LA ORACIÓN Y CONTEMPLACIÓN

Regina Saba videns sapientiam Salomonis non habuit ultra spiritum (3 Reg. 10). Viendo la Reina Saba la sabiduría de Salomón, quedó sin espíritu admirada. Habiendo tratado en el capítulo pasado de la devoción que es gran don de Dios, y como habilita y dispone el ánima para todas las cosas espirituales, en manera que corre con alegría por el camino del cielo obrando con suavidad y alegría lo que sin esta devoción hace a secas y pesadamente, ahora será bien ver qué riquezas y deleites grandes comunica nuestro inmenso Dios al ánima, que se ejercita en la oración y contemplación de las cosas divinales.

Esta suavidad nos representa la admiración de la Reina Saba, la cual oyendo a Salomón hablar cosas tan delicadas y de tan gran sabiduría: quedó como desmayada, robada y fuera de sí. Es aquí de considerar una cosa: si a las palabras de un sabio que no era más que hombre pecador y mortal, fueron bastantes para poner en admiración a esta Reina tan entendida, las palabras de Jesu Cristo nuestro Redentor, ¿cuanto más nos habían de mover y transportar, levantando nuestra ánima sobre todo lo criado? Bien sabía lo que dijo la esposa y bien gustaba de la palabra divina cuando decía: Mi ánima se ha derretido y regalado, como habló el Amado. El enternecerse el corazón cuando el Cristiano oye a Dios, nace de sentir un fuego divinal que no hay quien le pueda declarar por palabras, porque la lengua es tartamuda, para declarar los sentimientos del espíritu. Y por tanto son cosas altas y soberanas y que exceden todo entendimiento. Y si se pudiesen decir ya no serían tan excelentes. Regálase el ánima cuando oye a Dios hablar, y acábasele su espíritu proprio: porque así ablandando el corazón se imprima como en cera blanda el conocimiento del Señor que la habla. Dilátase el ánima, porque crece su afecto, y creciendo y dilatándose el amor, todas las virtudes se aumentan. . . .

O bendita el alma a quien Dios así habla, no por ángeles, ni por los predicadores solamente, no por los libros ni por las criaturas, sino por sí mismo. El Santo Rey David en un psalmo dice así: Oiré lo que habla en mí el Señor. Luego en nuestro corazón se asienta como en cátedra, y desde allí nos dice admirables avisos, allí nos reprehende nuestros descuidos, nos da ánimo para ir adelante con la vida y ejercicios espirituales, y a la manera que el capitán anima a los soldados para dar batalla, así nuestro Salvador nos exhorta, cuando interiormente nos habla. Aquí es menester que el oído esté desocupado de todo el ruido del mundo, y que cierre la puerta a todo y ponga silencio a sus pensamientos: porque como la voz es delicada y suave, pide gran atención y cuidado. Oiré lo que habla Dios en mí.

Y ¿ qué platica con el alma, o Santo Rey David? Dícenos que el Señor hablará paz para el pueblo. ¿ Qué puede hablar el que se llama príncipe de paz, según dice Esaias: si no paz? sus labios destilan miel como lo vió la Esposa, tratando siempre de paz con nosotros que es muy dulce y suave a todos. San Agustín, en el libro de la ciudad de Díos, dice que todas las cosas desean paz, y San Dionisio afirma lo mismo, porque la paz es cosa celestial. Esta paz es una quietud y sosiego del ánima, un gusto de aquella paz perfecta que se da en la gloria. O paz divina, en ti reposen nuestros corazones, en ti como en centro descansen nuestras ánimas, cesando todo bullicio y turbación de pensamientos mundanos. O puerto quieto adonde nuestros deseos navegan, recíbenos para que en ti hallemos holganza.

Bien parece ser fruta de aquel árbol precioso que es la caridad, pues tiene admirable sabor esta paz celestial. El fruto de la caridad, dice el Apóstol, es paz y gozo en el Espíritu Santo. O desventurados los que huyen de tal tesoro, empleándose en vicios y maldades, haciendo guerra a sus mismas conciencias y no gustando de esta paz. Escrito está : No tendrán paz los malos. Mas los amigos de Dios, los que llegan a orar y contemplar y oran a Dios dentro de sí mismos, y oyendo aquella música tan suave, gozarán de gran paz y quietud, quedando admirados como aquí leemos de la Reina Saba, que de oír la gran sabiduría de Salomón, quedó como sin fuerzas admirada. . . .

Es cosa grande que el ánima subida en la contemplación, aun estando en carne mortal puede ser robada hasta ver a Dios en su esencia, no usando de los sentidos, como de sí mismo lo afirma San Pablo. Y este es un estado medio entre los que son bienaventurados en el cielo, y los que vivimos acá en la tierra, según dice Santo Tomás. Mas aunque esto sea así, oigamos el consejo de Salomón. Hallaste, hermano, miel, come la que te basta, porque si te hartares no la tornes a lanzar. Miel es la contemplación y oración, tome cada uno con tiento y discreción lo que le basta. No exceda según su estado y fuerzas ; no desee robavientos ni novedades : que suele el demonio entender en estos negocios como lo hemos visto en nuestros tiempos. Humíllese el Cristiano, entienda en remediar pobres y consolar afligidos, ore y contemple las grandezas de Dios y no quiera más sentir de lo que Dios le quiere dar. Diga con David cuando va a orar : Señor, como un animal soy hecho delante vos. Aquí me presento delante mi Rey y Señor, nada quiero gustar sino lo que Vos queréis que sienta, para vuestra gloria y provecho mío.

Nuestro padre declarando aquello del Psalmo : cuán grande es, Señor, la multitud de vuestra dulcedumbre, la cual escondisteis a los que os temen : dice así. Esconde Dios a los que le temen su dulzura, porque se humillen : y para que con más diligencia busquen a Dios. Mucho han de mirar esta sentencia los que tratan en la oración con Dios. Esperen al Señor, no se desmayen cuando no gustan tanto como desean. Y miren que el Señor sabe mejor lo que hace, que ellos lo que piden. Aristóteles dice : La ley de los amigos es tener un querer y un no querer, ser una y no dos las voluntades. Pues dime, hermano que amas a Dios, ¿cómo no guardas la ley de amistad? ¿Porque no sujetas en todo tu querer al de tu amigo Cristo Jesús? ¿Quieres ver si has mucho aprovechado? Por aquí lo entenderás : si la sequedad te sabe a devoción, porque lo quiere así el Señor : si en la enfermedad hallas contento de salud : y si la pobreza te sabe a riqueza : y finalmente si en la afrenta y deshonra hallas sabor de honra, gustando de la voluntad suavísima de tu

12

Redentor y Señor, y teniéndote mortificada la tuya, aun en los gustos espirituales. Todo esto es señal de tu gran aprovechamiento : y haslo de estimar en mucho y dar gracias a Dios.

Historia de la Reina Saba,
Capítulo XXII.

Del último grado de contemplación que consiste en contemplar a Dios en sí mismo

Haec est generatio quærentium faciem Dei Jacob. Esta gente siempre busca al Señor y quiere ver el rostro glorioso de Cristo, verdadero Jacob. En este último grado, hermano, se da fin a nuestro intento deseado, adonde habemos de trabajar no tan solamente de hallar a nuestro Dios por su imagen que fué el grado primero, considerándole en nosotros mismos. Ni le hemos de seguir por las pisadas, contemplándole en sus criaturas, que fué el grado segundo. Ni menos considerarle humanado padeciendo por nosotros en la Cruz, que fué el grado tercero, sino por más alta manera contemplarle en su esencia y perfectísimo Ser, sin otro rodeo alguno.

Aquí el Águila ha de volar sobre sí misma, según vió el profeta Ezechiel. Dos vuelos ha de dar, el primero que suba más alto que el hombre, y el león y el becerro, que eran tres figuras acompañadas al Aguila. El segundo vuelo es que el alma vuele sobre sí misma, desechando toda razón natural. Por la figura del hombre que en aquella visión vió el profeta, podría ser entendido el grado primero de contemplación según el cual cada uno ha de contemplar a Dios en sí mismo. Por la figura del león se podrá denotar el grado segundo, adonde se contempla Dios en sus criaturas. Y por la similitud del becerro, que era sacrificio limpio en la ley, se podría denotar el grado tercero, en el cual se contempla Dios hecho hombre y ofreciéndose en sacrificio por los pecados del mundo en la cruz. Por el águila que vuela más alto hemos ahora de entender este grado último de contemplación, en el cual se emplean los que aquí dijo el santo profeta David, que no sólo buscan al Señor. Esto es contemplar según los tres grados ya dichos, mas aun haciendo fuerza a sí mismos ponen los ojos en el sol : contemplando en su rueda la perfección admirable y ser de su Criador, que se llama rostro de Jacob.

Mas quiero os avisar, hermano, que quien ha de ver el rostro del Luchador poderosísimo, nuestro inmenso Dios, ha de haber luchado consigo mismo, siendo varón acabado en la vida activa, y habiéndose ejercitado por algún tiempo en estos tres grados pasados de contemplación, porque San Gregorio dice : Vale mucho más al que se siente inhábil para la contemplación ejercitarse en la vida activa : con humildad y si menester fuere toda la vida, que no con presunción darse a la contemplación, a donde por algún error mereciéndolo su soberbia sea engañado. Esto es lo que nuestro Redentor dijo : Si tu ojo derecho te escandaliza sácale, porque más te vale ir al cielo con un ojo, que no con entrambos al infierno. Muy mejor te será que te salves en la vida activa : que es como ojo siniestro, que no si presumieres de seguir la vida contemplativa sintiéndote inhábil : pierdas el mérito de lo uno y de lo otro. . . .

Monte de Contemplación,
Capítulo XII.

FRANCISCO DE OSUNA

Works. *Abecedario espiritual que trata de las circunstancias de la sagrada pasión del hijo de Dios.* (Four parts issued during the author's lifetime, from 1525 to 1530; the completed work, of six parts, appeared after his death, Sevilla, 1554); *Gracioso convite de las gracias del santísimo sacramento del altar* (1530); *Norte de los estados* (1541); *De las cinco llagas de Nuestro Señor Jesucristo; De Mystica Theologia,* in Spanish and Latin; and a number of works in Latin only.

Bibliography. *Tercera parte del libro llamado Abecedario Espiritual,* ed. M. Mir (in Nueva Biblioteca de Autores Españoles, Vol. XVI). Fray Juan de San Antonio : *Bibliotheca universal franciscana,* Madrid, 1732. E. Boehmer : *Franzisca Hernandez und Frai Franzisco Ortiz,* Leipzig, 1865 (pp. 233-310).

VIGILANCIA QUE DEBE TRAER CONSIGO EL QUE EN PURO ESPÍRITU SE QUIERE LLEGAR A DIOS

Antes que comencemos a declarar este Abecedario, será bien poner tres razones que parecen necesarias a toda persona que se quiere llegar a Dios y a todo ejercicio espiritual comunes.

La primera es que la amistad y comunicación de Dios es posible en esta vida y destierro ; no así pequeña, sino más estrecha y segura que jamás fué entre hermanos ni entre madre e hijo. Esta amistad o comunicación de Dios al hombre, no por llamarse espiritual deja de tener mucho tomo y certidumbre, y no hablo de aquella divina aceptación, ni de aquella duda que tienen los mortales ignorando si están en gracia o no, porque de ella hablaremos en otro lugar ; mas hablo de la comunicación que buscan y hallan las personas que trabajan de llegar a la oración y devoción, la cual es tan cierta, que no hay cosa más cierta en el mundo, ni más gozosa, ni de mayor valor ni precio.

No pienses que los que andan llorosos y tristes al mundo, hambrientos y mal vestidos y alcanzados de sueño, menospreciados y perseguidos, los ojos sumidos y perdida la color, casi en los huesos, enemistados con los disolutos, no pienses que se contentan con estas asperezas, pues que a ti se te hace grave esta vida teniendo las cosas a tu voluntad; desfallecerían sin duda éstos en breve si no saliese Dios Nuestro Señor a los recibir abiertos los brazos de su amistad con mayor alegría y consuelo verdadero que la madre recibe a su hijo chiquito que se viene a ella huyendo de las cosas que le afligen. Abre la madre sus brazos al niño, y allende de lo abrazar, ábrele sus pechos y mátale su hambre, y junta su rostro con el de su hijo, y cesa el gemir y lágrimas, perdido el miedo.

.   .   .   .

La segunda razón es que, pues Dios no es aceptador de personas, esta comunicación no es a ti, oh hombre quien quiera que seas, menos posible que los otros; pues que no eres menos hecho a imagen de Dios que todos los otros, ni creo que tienes menos deseo de ser bienaventurado que los otros; empero, según te ha hecho no Dios, sino tu libertad, pienso que dirás que la edad y el oficio o la complexión o la enfermedad o el ingenio te excusan y apartan de esto. No sé qué te responda, sino aquello que dice el sabio (Prov. XVIII a.): El que se quiere apartar del amigo, achaques busca, y todo tiempo será reprehensible. Si a ti satisfacen tus excusas, no lo sé: a mí te sé decir que escandalizan; y digo con San Agustín, que totalmente no te creo, porque no hay causa que poder tan tuyo te quite. Si dijeses no poder ayunar, ni disciplinarte, ni traer áspera vestidura, ni trabajar, ni caminar, creeríamoste; mas si dices que no puedes amar, no te creemos. Si esto dice San Agustín del amor de los enemigos, con muy mucha más razón se podrá decir del amor de Dios, para el cual hay muy muchos más motivos que no para el otro.

La tercera razón es, que para buscar esta comunicación por cualesquier medios que sean, es menester un cuidado en el ánima que no la deje sosegar, el cual se endereza solamente a buscar a Dios: este intento o cuidado no se puede bien entender sino por semejanzas de fuera. Vemos que el que perdió alguna cosa anda congojoso buscándola, y mira una vez y otra cada lugar, no ve cosa que no se le antoja ella. El que va camino, si es buen caminante, lleva en el corazón un gran cuidado de acabar su jornada, todas las cosas ordena a este fin ; por el camino va en su corazón caminando más adelante ; el cuidado lo hace madrugar y soñar de noche que ha llegado donde iba ; si se cansa, el pensar que lo ha de hacer le da fuerzas. El que saca oro tiene tanta codicia, que cada terroncico se le antoja tener oro y a cada golpe espera sacar algo, y por la codicia no cesa hasta que de toda parte le falta el favor. El que pesca está muy atento al corchuelo para ver si pican, y no piensa sino los que ha tomado y ha de tomar todavía con cuidado de su negocio. Sin este intento y cuidado solícito no creo que ninguno halló a Dios por cualquiera vía que fuese ; el cual no se ordena sino a buscar a Dios sin determinar el cómo ni en qué manera.

Tercer Abecedario Espiritual,
Trat. I, Cap. I.

Del Recogimiento del Anima

Por la causa ya dicha de la mucha excelencia tiene este ejercicio muchos nombres, así en la Escritura sagrada como en los libros de los santos y doctos varones, ca unos la llaman Teología mística, que quiere decir escondida, porque en el secreto escondimiento del corazón la enseña el buen maestro Jesús, que para sí solo quiso reservar este magisterio, del que dió a sus siervos menos parte y facultad para enseñar a otros que de cualquier otra ciencia, queriendo, como principal maestro, guardar para sí la principal doctrina, porque entre las ciencias la Teología es reina y señora, que llama, según dice el Sabio (Prov. IX a.), a sus doncellas todas las otras ciencias al alcázar de la fe para que sirvan allí a su señora la Teología, la cual aún es en dos maneras : una se llama especulativa o escudriñadora, que es lo mismo, y otra escondida, que es la que se trata o a la que se intitula este tercer alfabeto ; no que en él presuma yo enseñarla, pues ninguno de los mortales la enseñó, porque Cristo guardó para sí este oficio de enseñar en secreto a los corazones en que viviese aquesta Teología escondida como ciencia divina y mucho más excelente que la otra Teología de que hablamos primero, que se llama escudriñadora ; y esto de que nuestro tratado habla no quiere escudriñar, sabiendo que está escrito que el escudriñador de la Majestad será detenido y oprimido de la gloria muy grande de Dios. Esta Teología se dice más perfecta o mejor que la primera, según dice Gerson, porque de la primera como de un principio se sirve y en ella como en estribos se esfuerza para subir más arriba por el escalera del amor.

La primera Teología enseña Dios para que lo contemplemos ser suma verdad, y esta de que hablamos, presuponiendo aquello que no duda, pasa a amarlo así como sumo bien. La otra pertenece al entendimiento, que aun los demonios tienen harto alumbrado en la fe, pues que, según está escrito (Jacob. II c.) creen y tiemblan ; mas esta pertenece a la voluntad enamorada del sumo bien, lo cual pertenece a los justos amadores de Dios. La otra Teología con la fe perecerá cuando a la fe sucediere la visión como premio ; mas esta Teología se perfeccionará añadiendo amor, y ya no será escondida, mas a todos será manifesta dende el pequeño hasta el mayor.

La primera Teología, que se llama escudriñadora, usa de razones y argumentos y discursos y probabilidades según las otras ciencias ; y de aquí es que se llama Teología escolástica y de letrados, la cual si alguno quiere alcanzar ha menester buen ingenio y continuo ejercicio y libros y tiempo, y velar, trabajar teniendo enseñado maestro, la cual también es menester para cualquiera de las otras ciencias. Empero la Teología escondida de que hablamos no se alcanza de esta manera tan bien como por afición piadosa y ejercicio en las virtudes teologales que la alumbren y los dones del Espíritu Santo y bienaventuranzas evangélicas que la perfeccionen proporcionablemente a los tres actos jerárquicos que son purgar, alumbrar y perfeccionar ; y porque muchas veces acontece aún en los animales, cuanto más en los hombres, que adonde hay menos conocimiento hay mayor afección y amor como vemos en los muchachos, que mientras menos conocen aman más a sus padres, y en los novicios, que en los primeros o el primer año son más devotos con su simplicidad que no después que son doctores.

Síguese de lo ya dicho claramente que para hallar esta más alta Teología no es menester gran ciencia inquirida o buscada por trabajo, aunque la infusa no debe faltar ni falta a los que se disponen, porque habiendo conocido mediante la fe que Dios es todo deseable y todo amable y todo amor, si nuestra afición estuviere purgada y dispuesta y ejercitada, no sé por qué será impedida de ese transformar y encender y levantar en aquél que conoce ser todo un terrón y pedazo, o, por mejor decir, fuente de amor. . . .

Llámase también esta manera de orar arte de amor, porque sólo por amor se alcanza y con ella más que con otra arte o industria alguna se multiplica el amor, y también porque el Dios de amor,

Cristo, la enseña a los de corazón amoroso. Muchas veces se vencen por arte los que no pueden ser por fuerza vencidos, como parece en David, que más por arte que por fuerza venció a Goliat; y los elefantes son por arte de los cazadores flacos vencidos; donde este ejercicio se llama arte para que los de pocas fuerzas venzan al fortísimo y traigan a sus entrañas preso y le echen los grillos y esposas del amor diciendo con la esposa (Cant. III b.): Preso lo tengo y no lo soltaré.

Esta arte se llama de amor, el cual se dice ser fuerte así como la muerte, que a todos vence, donde en esto se da a entender que este ejercicio contiene en sí arte y fuerza, que son las dos cosas mejores para vencer todas las cosas.

Llámase también unión, porque llegándose el hombre de esta manera a Dios se hace un espíritu con él por un trocamiento de voluntades, que ni el hombre quiere otra cosa de lo que Dios quiere, ni Dios se aparta de la voluntad del hombre, mas en todo son a una, como las cosas que perfectamente están unidas, que casi se niegan de sí y se conforman totalmente en un tercio; lo cual acaece en este negocio, donde si antes Dios y el hombre tenían diversas voluntades, después concuerdan en uno sin quedar ninguno descontento. Y de esto resulta quedar el hombre unido consigo mismo y con sus prójimos; lo cual si todos tuviésemos sería la muchedumbre de los creyentes un ánima y un corazón en el Espíritu Santo juntos, en el cual se hallan el Padre y el Hijo hechos un principio para lo producir, y él nos hace a todos una cosa por amor, para nos producir en gracia y reducirnos hechos uno a Dios, por no tener que llevar a cada uno por sí.

Llámase también este ejercicio profundidad, la cual contiene escuridad y hondura; porque este ejercicio se funda en la hondura y profundo corazón del hombre, el cual debe estar escuro; esto es, privado de humano conocimiento, para que de esta manera estando tinieblas, sobre él venga el Espíritu de Dios sobre las aguas de sus deseos a decir que se haga luz divina.

. . . .

Llámase también advenimiento del Señor al ánima, porque mediante él visita el Señor a los suyos que con suspiros lo llaman.

Y dícese alteza que levanta el ánima, y amistad o abramiento del corazón devoto al de Cristo.

Y llámase ascensión espiritual con Cristo, y captividad con que sujetamos a Él nuestro entendimiento.

Y cielo tercero donde son arrebatados los contemplativos.

¿Para qué diré más? Es aqueste ejercicio un refugio do nos debemos retraer viendo las tempestades cercanas; es una contina resistencia contra los príncipes de las tinieblas, que secretamente nos combaten; es restitución que hacemos a Dios dándole todo lo que en nosotros se halla suyo sin reservar cosa. Es una resurrección a vida espiritual, donde es dada al justo potestad en el cielo de su ánima y en la tierra de su cuerpo; es una reverencia que contino tenemos a Dios estando con temor delante de El; es un rosal de virtudes, y es el reino de Dios que por conquista hemos de ganar y por maña, pues que dentro lo tenemos, y también cada día lo demandamos; y es sacerdocio real, con que, siendo de nosotros señores, nos ofrezcamos a Dios; es un silencio que en el cielo de nuestra ánima se hace, aunque breve y no tan durable como el justo desea; es un servicio que a solo Dios hacemos, adorando su sola Majestad; es silla que le tenemos aparejada para que se detenga en nuestra casa interior; es tienda de campo para andar por el desierto; es torre fortísima de nuestro amparo, dende do hemos de atalayar las cosas celestiales, y vaso de oro para guardar el maná en el arca de nuestro pecho; es valle en que abunda el trigo que tiene grosura y redaño y es victoria que vence el mundo menor, sujetándolo enteramente a Dios; es viña que hemos de guardar con vigilancia y sombra del que deseamos, do gustamos de su fruto; es unción enseñadora del Espíritu Santo, y huerto por todas partes cerrado, del cual damos la llave a solo Dios, que entre cuando quisiere.

Tercer Abecedario Espiritual,
Trat. VI, Caps. 2, 3.

DE TRES MANERAS DE ORACIÓN

La primera forma o manera de oración es vocal; y según ésta decimos que oran los que rezan el oficio divino y los que dicen otras cualesquier oraciones, pronunciándolas por la boca en alabanza del Señor. Entre las cuales la beatísima oración del Pater noster tiene primado. . . . El que esta oración dice devotamente, pide al Padre en el nombre del Hijo que la compuso, y por tanto es de Él oída más prestamente; y tanto más presto que las otras, cuanto al Padre eterno era más amado el autor de ésta que de todas las otras cosas parejas.

Mandónos el Señor que cuando orásemos no hablásemos mucho, sino que multiplicásemos más la afección y amor que no las palabras; lo cual guardó el mismo Señor en esta oración haciéndola breve y comenzándola con estas palabras: Padre nuestro; despertando en la primera el amor de Dios, pues lo llamamos Padre, y en la segunda el amor del prójimo, pues que en esta palabra 'nuestro' lo hacemos nuestro hermano e hijo de Dios por gracia; y oramos también por él en ella como por nosotros en llamar al Señor Padre universal de todos.   Al fin de todas las otras oraciones añade la Iglesia: Esto sea hecho por nuestro Señor Jesucristo.   Esto no es menester añadirse en la oración del Señor, porque en el estilo, según dice San Cipriano, conoce el Padre las palabras de su Hijo, y también porque el mismo Señor la solía muchas veces decir cuando vocalmente oraba en persona suya y de todos sus fieles; los cuales supieron primero esta oración que otra ninguna, porque esta les predicaban los apóstoles; y no se lee que alguno de ellos hiciese oración común para enseñar a otros que rezasen sino esta. . . .

Son tantas las excelencias de aquesta cristianísima oración, que así como hallamos escrito cántico de cánticos, fiestas de fiestas, cosas santas de cosas santas, así debemos llamar a ésta oración de oraciones. . . .

Aunque, según hemos dicho, esta oración del Señor tenga primado entre todas las otras oraciones vocales, no por eso debe el hombre dejar las otras, ca de otra manera engendraríase fastidio; y más que hallamos haber hecho algunas santas personas otras oraciones aprobadas, y también que muchas veces es cosa muy buena orar el hombre vocalmente con palabras compuestas de propia afección. . . . La Escritura está llena de oraciones semejantes . . . y esta manera de orar vocalmente es muy impetrativa, que alcanza del Señor presto lo que demanda, y por tanto la deberían usar mucho los fieles devotos en sus necesidades, declarándolas al Señor, con breves palabras compuestas por ellos mismos; y no solamente antes del sueño, mas antes de toda obra deberían todos orar de esta manera, encomendando al Señor particularmente cada cosa, familiarmente hablando con El, formando palabras convenientes a la propia afección, mediante las cuales unas veces quejándose delante de él manifiesta sus necesidades, otras confiesa sus pecados, otras demanda misericordia y gracia y favor contra los peligros y fatigas del mundo que a sí o a los suyos empecen.

La segunda manera de orar es cuando dentro en nuestro corazón, sin pronunciar por la boca las palabras vocalmente, sólo nuestro corazón habla con el Señor, y dentro en nosotros le demandamos todo lo que hemos menester. Entonces como en escondido, sin que nadie nos oiga, hablamos con el Señor a solas cuando se suelen hacer mayores las mercedes, lo cual es como hablar al oído de Dios. De esta manera oraba David, el cual decía a Dios (II Reg. III d.) : Tu siervo ha hallado su corazón para orar a ti. . . .

A esta manera de oración que el corazón hace a Dios callando la lengua se reducen todos los santos y devotos pensamientos, así de la pasión del Señor como de la Iglesia y del Juicio y de cualquiera cosa otra devota ; porque claro está que decimos estar orando los que están meditando y pensando en la sacra pasión, y aún los que según deben piensan sus pecados, pues no los piensan sino para demandar misericordia de ellos.

Para esta manera de oración, que consiste en santos pensamientos, es menester que el hombre encomiende a la memoria las historias devotas y misterios del Señor y muchas cosas buenas de las que oyere y leyere, las cuales han de ser como leña que sustenta el fuego en el altar del Señor. Es empero de saber que los más fructuosos pensamientos que el hombre puede tener son los de la sagrada pasión. . . . Aunque esta segunda manera de orar, que es tener y usar el hombre de santos pensamientos, no parezca convenir a los principiantes ni a los idiotas, no les es del todo ajena, porque algunas veces son obligados a tener santos pensamientos, pues son obligados a desear la bienaventuranza y a otras cosas muchas soberanas ; así como amar a Dios sobre todas las cosas, lo cual no pueden hacer sin pensar en El, porque condición es del amor pensar algún tiempo en el amado ; y son también obligados a la recepción de los santos sacramentos, que presupone alguna meditación y santos pensamientos, donde el hombre se apareja para tan grandes cosas.

Y dije el deseo de la felicidad, porque nunca lo tendremos si en ella nunca pensamos ; mas empero son obligados a esta manera de oración los religiosos y personas retraídas que han dejado el mundo para vacar a la contemplación, y tienen o deben tener muy mayor oportunidad por el lugar santo de la religión, que está dedicado y constituido para más perfectamente orar ; que así como es cosa común a los buenos seglares en el mundo orar vocalmente, así debe ser común esta segunda manera de oración a los buenos religiosos en su monasterio, que debe ser casa de oración y no cueva de ladrones ;

lo cual será si comen las limosnas ajenas no para orar, sino para murmurar y vaguear, que es contra la voluntad del que las dió; lo cual se reduce a rapiña o hurto. Onde todo aquel que usa de la cosa ajena no a la voluntad e intención buena de su dueño, cierto es que usurpa lo que no es suyo y que se pueda decir ladrón; y cosa clara es que la voluntad de los que nos dan limosna es por que tengamos oportunidad de orar sin derramamiento al Señor; lo cual si no hacemos vamos contra la primera intención del bienhechor, al cual quedamos, según veo, deudores; ca puesto que nos da por amor de Dios su limosna, dánosla con tal condición que mediante ella sirvamos mejor al mismo Señor Dios; y si así no fuese, no nos la daría sino en caso de extrema necesidad, donde se tiene objeto a conservar la vida del prójimo.

.   .   .   .

La tercera manera de oración se dice mental o espiritual, con que se alza lo más alto de nuestra ánima más pura y afectuosamente a Dios con las alas del deseo y piadosa afección esforzada por el amor; el cual mientras mayor es tiene menos palabras y más comprehensoras y que hacen más al caso; porque el amor, si es verdadero, no sabe buscar rodeos de razones compuestas, mas callando obra grandes cosas, y sabe que si de las criaturas se aparta y se recoge a Dios, será de Él enteramente recibido, y tanto más enteramente cuanto más recogido fuere y con mayor fervor.

De los que así oran dice el Señor en el Evangelio: Los verdaderos adoradores han de adorar al Padre en espíritu y verdad, porque espíritu es Dios, y conviene adorarlo en espíritu y verdad, y tal es quiere El que lo adoren. Cuanto mayor conformidad hubiere entre el que ora y el Señor a quien ora, tanto será mas acepta la oración; así que, pues el Padre es puro espíritu en sí mismo y que ninguna cosa participa de cuerpo, tanto será nuestra oración a El más agradable cuanto fuere más apartada de la imaginación y aun de los pensamientos del corazón; porque no pueden ser tan elevados que no sean harto bajos en comparación del Señor; mas los deseos que abrazan a Dios desnudo y sin corporal semejanza y el amor que no cura de palabras ora con más pureza a Dios, y en manera más espiritual y más inmediata, porque no dice el ánima que así ora sino aquello de los Cánticos (Cant. II d.): Mi amado a mí y yo a mi amado. No pueden ser dichas palabras más espirituales ni más recogidas, ni más comprehensoras, ni que más declaren el fin de la oración a los que la sienten.

Lo que más puede hacer Dios con su amigo es darse a él, y lo que más puede hacer el hombre es darse a Dios; empero, porque lo segundo no podemos perfectamente hacer sin su favor, dijo la esposa primero: Mi amado a mí que no yo a mi amado. Empero han de notar que este darse el hombre a Dios y Dios al hombre es una dádiva tan perfectamente dada, que cuando se da parece que Dios está en el hombre todo y enteramente. Quiero decir que si la fé no alumbrase al hombre que tiene a Dios, casi diría que en sí incluye Dios todo y que fuera de esto no está. Vese el ánima del justo algunas veces tan llena de Dios, que le parece ponerle término la pequeñez de sus pechos, como de verdad él sea interminable. La dádiva con que algunas veces se dan las personas recogidas a Dios es asimismo tan copiosa, que ninguna cosa guardan para sí; en tal manera que pierden la elección y la voluntad, y por el mucho acordarse y darse a Dios están de sí tan olvidados como si no fuesen.

De estas tres maneras de oración dice el Sabio (Prov. XXII c.): Mira cómo en tres maneras te la he declarado. Estas tres maneras declara la glosa interlineal diciendo que son en palabra, que es la oración vocal, y en pensamiento, que es la oración del corazón, y en obra, que es la oración espiritual del recogimiento; el cual si es verdadero tanto excede a las dos maneras primeras como la obra a la palabra y al pensamiento.

Tercer Abecedario Espiritual,
Trat. XIII, Caps. 1-4 *passim.*

De lo que debes hacer para buscar este amor

Pues que el demonio se trabaja de nos quitar este amor, que es fruto del espíritu y señal que mora Dios en nosotros, y superabundancia de gracia y ración que se da a este nuestro siervo, que es el cuerpo, para que sirva con alegría, razón es que nosotros trabajemos por conservar aqueste amor. Lo primero apartándonos de todo pecado, aunque sea venial; porque el amador verdadero estudia de huir toda ofensa, no mirando a la pena que le es debida, sino al amado, que en todo mal pequeño y grande se ofende. Lo segundo trabajemos en toda virtud no dejando perder todo bien que hacer pudiéremos, siendo muy solícitos en las cosas de piedad que valen mucho. Lo tercero, guardemos nuestro amor de se enconar en cosa que sea, poseyendo las cosas como prestadas, para que no pongamos en ellas el amor, sino en Dios. Lo cuarto usemos provocarnos desadormeciendo nuestro corazón para que a menudo pueda producir obras de amor entrañal.

La primera de estas cosas nos quitará el miedo de llegarnos a Dios. La segunda nos dará osadía para ir a El hasta lo abrazar. La tercera nos dará fuerzas para arrebatar el reino de los cielos con gran ímpetu y fuerza de amor. Lo cuarto nos hará ligeros y mañosos en esto para lo obrar fácilmente; y si lo queremos hacer muy alegremente, usemos entre nosotros pensamientos que despierten el amor, y así pronunciemos palabras amorosas a Dios, que sean como quien sopla el fuego con aire fresco de palabras deleitosas que aplacen y convidan nuestra voluntad, si son dichas con fe viva, apartada toda imaginación y pensamientos de cosas que hayamos visto y oído, sino que todo el negocio se trate de fuera de nuestros términos, pensando que en espíritu hablamos con el amantísimo Dios; y no en cuerpo, ca nuestra ánima no es cuerpo, ni Dios es corporal en su deidad, al cual debemos hablar. . . .

Tercer Abecedario Espiritual,
Trat. XVI, Cap. 10.

DE TRES MANERAS DE SILENCIO

Tres maneras de callar hay en el recogimiento, o tres maneras de silencio, dejando las otras que no hacen tanto al caso. La primera es cuando cesan en el ánima todas las fantasías e imaginaciones y especies de las cosas visibles, y así calla a todas las cosas criadas; lo igual deseaba el santo Job cuando decía (Job III c.): Ahora durmiendo cállase; y en mi sueño holgaría con los reyes y cónsules de la tierra que edifican para sí soledumbres. Dormimos a las cosas temporales y callamos dentro en nosotros, según dice San Gregorio, cuando dentro en el secreto de nuestra ánima nos retraemos a la contemplación del Criador; y los santos, que son llamados aquí reyes cónsules, edifican para sí soledumbres, cuando ninguna cosa de este mundo desean ni son apremiados en el corazón por algunos tumultos de deseos desordenados; mas desechan todos los ilícitos movimientos de la cama de su corazón con la diestra mano de la santa consideración, despreciando todas las cosas transitorias y las desmedidas cogitaciones que de ellas nacen; y como desean solamente la morada eterna y no aman cosa de este mundo, gozan de gran tranquilidad en su ánima.

El segundo callar que hay en el recogimiento es cuando el ánima quietísima en sí misma tiene una manera de ocio espiritual, sentándose con María a los pies del Señor y diciendo: Oiré lo que hablará en mí el Señor Dios. Y a esta dice el Señor: Oye, hija, y mira e inclina tu oreja y olvida tu pueblo y la casa de tu padre.

Bien se compara al oír esta segunda manera de callar, porque el oyente no tan sólo calla a lo demás, empero quiere que todo le calle a él, para que así más entero se convierta al que le habla, mayormente si no sabe dónde está, como en el caso presente; ca, según se dice en el Evangelio, oímos la voz de Dios, que es su inspiración, y no sabemos dónde va ni dónde viene; por lo cual nos conviene callar mucho y estar muy atentos a El; así que tenemos dos maneras de callar: la una cesando en nosotros la imaginación y los pensamientos que voltean en nuestra memoria; la otra es un olvido aún de nosotros mismos, con una total conversación de nuestro hombre interior a sólo Dios.

El primer callar es de las cosas a nosotros; el segundo de un sosiego quietísimo en que nosotros callamos a nosotros mismos y nos ordenamos a Dios con una sujeción receptiva y muy aparejada; lo cual se figura en los santos animales de Ecequiel, de los cuales se dice: Como fuese hecha una voz sobre el firmamento, que estaba encima de la cabeza de ellos, deteníanse en pie, y sujetaban sus alas. La voz, según dije, es la divina inspiración que se recibe en el oído del ánima sin expresión de palabra, sino con sola la presencia de Dios que se da a sentir; y por esto dice Job que furtiva y calladamente oyó la palabra escondida que le fué dicha y recibió las venas o rastros de su ruído pequeño.

Esta voz inspirada es hecha sobre el firmamento, que es la más alta parte de la razón, que se junta inmediatamente a Dios por amor. Los animales santos y alados, que son los contemplativos, se dice estar entonces en pie, porque cuando esta voz se hace en el ánima ella se levanta a cosas grandes y está suspensa casi trasportada en Dios, como los apóstoles cuando lo vieron subir al cielo; y de esta manera fué mandado a Ecequiel que se levantase sobre sus pies para que Dios le hablase; así que el estar en pie es una admiración callada, según dice San Gregorio, que nos hace estar colgados de Dios como lo había Job escogido para su ánima, en la cual casi cesa toda operación de las potencias para que disminuyéndose así el ánima reciba la sabiduría.

Sujetar las alas es aplicar las fuerzas más altas para recibir el influjo divino que se infunde en el ánima; en lo cual, según dice la glosa, tienen los contemplativos por ningunas sus fuerzas; aplícanlas empero a Dios callando, para que faltando en sí mismos se hallen en El como aquel que decía: No quiso ser consolada mi ánima; acordéme de Dios y deleitéme, ejercitéme y faltó mi espíritu.

El tercer callar de nuestro entendimiento se hace en Dios, cuando se transforma en El toda el ánima y gusta abundosamente la suavidad suya, en la cual se adormece como en celda vinaria, y calla, no deseando más, pues que se halla satisfecha, antes se duerme aun a sí misma, olvidándose de la flaqueza de su condición, por se ver tan endiosada y unida a su molde, y vestida de su claridad como otro Moisén después de haber entrado en la niebla que estaba encima del monte, lo cual más de verdad aconteció a San Juan cuando después de la cena se echó sobre el pecho del Señor, y por entonces calló todo lo que sintió.

Acontece en este tercero estar tan callado el entendimiento y tan cerrado, o por mejor decir ocupado, que ninguna cosa entiende de cuantas le dicen, ni juzga cosa de las que pasan acerca de él, porque no las entiende aunque las oye; según lo cual me contó un viejo a quien yo confesaba, el cual había más de cincuenta años que se ejercitaba en estas cosas, y díjome, entre otros misterios, que le acontecía muchas veces oír algunos sermones y cosas de Dios de las cuales ninguna palabra entendía; tan acallado y ocupado estaba su entendimiento de dentro, que ninguna cosa criada podía formar en él; y decíale yo que entonces se debía ir a retraer, a lo cual respondía que las voces le eran como sonido de órganos, en las cuales había placer su ánima, aunque no las entendía, y como que contrapunteaba sobre ellas y alababa al Señor por una manera que se puede sentir, empero no se puede dar a sentir a otro.

Tercer Abecedario Espiritual,
Trat. XXI, Cap. 4.

BERNARDINO DE LAREDO

WORKS. *Subida al Monte Sión por la via contemplativa* (1535), which contains also a number of letters, and a work upon the glories of St. Joseph, entitled *Josephina.* He also published certain works on Medicine.

BIBLIOGRAPHY. Biographical articles in *Diccionario Enciclopédico Hispano-Americano*, Vol. XI, and *Enciclopedia Universal Espasa*, Vol. XXIX. Olmilla y Puig, *Discurso inaugural de la Real Academia de Medicina*, Madrid, 1904.

QUE LA QUIETUD FRECUENTADA MUESTRA LEVANTAR EL ÁNIMA CON LAS ALAS DEL AMOR

Cuantas veces en este tercer libro se dijere ciencia infusa o sabiduría escondida, o secreta o mística teología o ejercicio de aspiración, hase de entender que significa un súbito y momentáneo levantamiento mental, en el cual el ánima por divino enseñamiento es alzada súbitamente a se ayuntar por puro amor, por vía de sola afectiva a su amantísimo Dios, sin que antevenga medio de algún pensamiento ni de obra intelectual o del entendimiento, ni de natural razón. Notando como otra vez se apuntó que esta obra sobrepuja a la razón y al entendimiento humano, así como decimos con gran verdad que los misterios de nuestra fe católica y sin mancilla ni se fundan sobre razón natural ni admiten comprehensión, así como el misterio altísimo de la Encarnación del Verbo Divino y del Santísimo Sacramento del Altar, y así de muchos misterios. Así habemos de entender que excede la razón y entendimiento esta operación divina, con la cual momentáneamente el anima es levantada con las alas del amor y ayuntada con su Dios sin medio de pensamiento de cualquier cosa criada cuantas veces place a la dignación divina.

Y puesto que esta soberana operación de parte nuestra tiene en sí dificultad a los principios, pero perseverando esforzadamente en este levantamiento de la afectiva, viene a tal facilidad que digan los altos contemplativos que casi cuantas veces al ánima bien amaestrada le pluguiere, tantas se podrá alzar momentáneamente a su Dios, y ayuntarse a Él por amor. Y cerca de esto dice San Dionisio y lo afirman los altos contemplativos Herp y Henrique de Balma, que esto se hace en la ánima ejercitada cuan a menudo le place y con tal facilidad que no saben señalarla.

Y es de notar que el ánima en esta unión, en este alzarse a su Dios, no pone de parte suya más que su libre querer, porque el que obra es nuestro Dios, y obrando frecuentemente con este querer que puede poner el ánima, y con alzar la afectiva avivada con el amor, con el cual la aviva Dios, viene a la felicidad que cierto permite Nuestro Señor que aun en estos tiempos haya quien pueda decir y presentar más testigos que es muy gran verdad aquesta.

Es de ver con regaladas entrañas que la facilidad de este bienaventurado alzamiento no viene por la frecuencia y solicitud del ánima, mas por la continuación de las veces que es visitada de su amantísimo Dios, disponiéndose con limpia disposición, porque cuanto más veces es el ánima visitada de su vivificador, tanto es más agravada para más veces poder demandar y recibir el amor. Por modo que tantas veces visita Nuestro Señor y Médico amoroso la ánima que está enferma de su amor, que hace que venga el ánima a tiempo que no quiera ni sepa escaparse de los dardos del amor, por no carecer del médico que con mirarla la sana tan perfectamente que tantas cuantas veces se queja súbitamente de su viva enfermedad, tantas tenga tan presto y tan pronto el remedio y visitación de su enamorado médico que no acabe de sentirse lastimada del amor, antes que el que la lastima la tenga ya remediada.

Y acerca de esto es de ver que no ha de haber, ni nunca hubo algún Rey tan poderoso que por fuerte batería ni por mucha munición pudiese vencer otro Rey ni otro señor con tanta felicidad, cuanto el ánima enamorada puede con el solo amor vencer, tomar y tener a su amoroso Señor. La causa de esto es aquesta. Como su clemencia le tenga vencido, y sobre este vencimiento venga el combate del ánima enamorada y sean los golpes del amor, necesario es que quien combate sea presa y que en esta su prisión tome preso el combatido, y el sea siempre en nuestro amparo.

Subida del Monte Sion,
3ª Parte, Cap. IX.

QUE EL SUEÑO DE LAS POTENCIAS DEL ÁNIMA HACE DESPIERTO AL VUELO DEL VIVO AMOR

En el capítulo 2 del libro de los Cánticos dice el esposo de la Iglesia, Cristo Jesús nuestro Amor, esta palabra meliflua, conviene a saber: Mi paloma una sola es, etc. En otro lugar la llama paloma mía demandándole que le abra. Pues como esté declarado en el capítulo 17 ser la Iglesia heredad de Jesu Cristo, y cualquier ánima justa ser parte de esta heredad, y a esta su Iglesia llama nuestro Dios paloma, resta que como el ánima conoce a la Santa Iglesia (cuya parte es) desea recibir de esta admirable paloma plumas de vivos deseos, despertados por su perfecta doctrina, porque con las tales plumas pueda levantar vuelo amoroso a su amantísimo Dios, en quien está su verdadero consuelo.

Y por esto ha dicho la autoridad del psalmista en persona de la ánima enamorada: ¿Quién me dará plumas de paloma? Es a saber: Quien podrá poner en mí los deseos y la afición que tiene la Santa Iglesia para buscar a mi Dios en contemplación perfecta. Y porque perseverando en esta mortalidad no es al ánima posible el verdadero descanso sin grande interpolación, entienda un consejo que a cualesquier ánimas justas da el psalmista en el psalmo 67, teniendo figura de la Santa Madre Iglesia heredad de nuestro Dios, esposa de Jesu Cristo, paloma nuestra sin hiel, la cual queriendo criar sus plumas en sus hijos y de Dios les dice de esta manera: Si durmieseis en medio de dos términos, o lugares, o heredades, o, según dice la glosa, en la autoridad de dos testamentos, seríais como paloma que tiene plumas de plata, o si es paloma de plata, así lo serán sus plumas, y las espaldas de esta paloma serán tales como el oro que es de polido color.

Dice pues: Si durmieseis etc. El sueño sobre cosas temporales significa tener pequeño cuidado de ellas. Ahora, pues, del descuido que tiene el ánima justa de todo lo que no es Dios viene el sueño espiritual, en el cual adormidas las potencias de estas ánimas, se infunden y se transforman en el amor de su Dios, en pureza de substancia, en tal manera que el ánima en tal modo de dormir en su quietud interior no recibe operación de alguna de sus potencias, ni en su comprehensión toca alguna cosa criada, y así es todo espiritual. A este sueño descansado, a este dormir las potencias, a este reposo del ánima, a este vuelo de espíritu en la contemplación quieta, a esta vía de aspiración convida el Profeta: y para poder volar en esta aspiración desea en las ánimas plumas. Y dice que sean plumas de paloma, porque es ave amorosa, que figurando la Iglesia nos figura el mismo amor en el Santísimo Espíritu.

Pues dice la autoridad: Si durmieseis etc. Donde es de ver que aqueste sueño pacífico, este bendito dormir que junta el ánima a Dios había gustado David cuando en el Psalmo 4 decía así: En la sosegada pacificación del secreto escondimiento, en el cual se halla Dios dentro en lo interior del ánima, dormiré y tendré descanso en la paz de este mi Señor.

Síguese en la autoridad.   Entre dos términos o entre dos suertes. Donde se debe notar que el ánima que está diestra en quieta contemplación, así duerme a las cosas temporales, y así se descuida de ellas, por llegarse más a Dios, que también por amor suyo no se sabe descuidar de las cosas que le obliga la caridad y obediencia, y el cumplir tasadamente con su propria poquedad cuanto a sus no fingidas necesidades.   Ahora, pues, el descuido de estas cosas variables la aparta de todo lo transitorio, cuanto toca a su afición ; y los deseos encendidos de los bienes sempiternos la levantan al siglo que ha de durar para siempre.   De manera que el descuido de lo presente y el deseo de lo futuro hace al ánima estar como amortiguada, como dormida y suspensa en medio de dos suertes, conviene a saber, de aquesta muerte presente y la vida advenidera.   Así que el sueño es aquí la suspensión y el tácito callamiento.   Y los dos términos son este siglo transitorio, y aquel siglo sempiterno.

Subida del Monte Sion,
3ª Parte, Cap. XIX.

LA CONTEMPLACIÓN PERFECTA TRAE CONSIGO LA PIEDAD Y LA CARIDAD Y AMOR

Es de entender que cuando el contemplativo se allega a la perfección poco tiene puesto el ojo en su ganancia o devoción o provecho : porque todo su estudio es en tener conformidad desnuda, simple y entera con la voluntad de Dios : y aquesta conformidad gran merecimiento tiene : y es de muy mucho provecho en solo el deseo de padecer cualquier cosa que venga, con deliberada determinación por amor de Jesu Cristo : cuya vida inocentísima tiene puesta en su ánima por espejo de todos sus interiores y exteriores movimientos.

Es empero de notar que nunca el merecimiento de cualquier buen deseo se allega a la perfección hasta que sea deseo vivo.   Quiero decir que si proponéis paciencia o cualquier otra virtud, mucho merecimiento es, pero cuando se os ofrece grande ocasión de perderla y veis vos que la tenéis y perseveráis en ella, entonces conocéis bien que está vivo aquel deseo que el ánima concibió.   Yo no digo que vos dejéis de sentir controversia dentro en vos, porque cuando no se siente y esto es por vía natural, poco es el merecimiento, y no es menester aviso virtuoso para la tal resistencia : mas cuando vuestro próximo o sus cosas con razón o sin ella os lastima las entrañas, y os da torcimientos dentro en vuestro corazón, y miráis en el espejo que en vuestra ánima tenéis y halláis en él a vuestro dechado Cristo, que es todo manso y humilde, y os le conformáis por solo amor de su amor recibiendo de su mano cuanto el mundo os ofreciere en lo próspero y adverso : esta es ya muy próspera perfección.

Y para perficionar esta alta perfección siempre ha de estar desterrado cualquier proprio provecho como queda ya notado. Y cierto está que el ánima que desea recibir con alegría y por amor de Cristo Jesús cualquier trabajo o trabajos tiene muy grande ventaja a quien deseare el contrario en cualquier prosperidad, porque aquel hallara lo que desea adonde quiera que fuere : y este que busca lo próspero, con trabajo lo hallará y guardarlo ha con sospecha, y durarle ha poco espacio.

Queda entendida de aquí la sentencia del capítulo pasado que dice : la recatada vida del contemplativo discreto será muy gran descanso, y padecer trabajos por amor de Jesu Cristo, cuantos el mundo ofreciere le serán consolación. Y si a veces porque somos hombres algún descuido se ofrece o retoque de desconsolación, o resistencia de sensualidad, la misma conformidad que anda vestida en la ánima, la reduce y vuelve en sí. De manera que nunca se le ofrece algo al contrario que le pueda por media hora, ni aun dos Credos contristar siendo Dios su ayudador.

Y es de notar, que el ánima que así tiene el mundo y sus ofrecimientos puestos debajo de ambos los pies de la razón y afición, no hay de que pueda temer, porque nada le es contrario, todo está a su voluntad, pues no sabe escoger nada, mas recibe cuanto viene como de mano de Dios, o permitido por él, teme empero en ella la pronta humildad las faltas que hacer puede en el servicio y amor de su amantísimo bien, este tal se llama temor de hijos, y lanza siempre de sí, y de su ejercicio cualquier temor de siervos, es a saber, de los que sirven porque no sean castigados. Así es, que el amor en estos priva, desbarata, y anihila el temor de la muerte y del juicio, y del purgatorio y infierno, y de cuantas contrariedades se pueden imaginar. . . .

Subida del Monte Sion,
Cap. XXXI.

SAN PEDRO DE ALCÁNTARA

Works. *Tratado de la oración y meditación* (1533); *Breve introducción para los que comienzan a servir a Dios, Tres cosas que debe hacer el que desea salvarse, Oración devotísima, Petición especial de Amor de Dios;* together with the Constitutions of his Order, and a number of letters, written chiefly to St. Teresa.[1] The writings mentioned by name above were all published in an undated edition at Lisbon, about the year 1560.

Bibliography. *Tratado de la oración y meditación:* (1) reimpreso por un sacerdote devoto del Santo [Pablo Lafuente], Madrid, 1882, (2) publicado, con un pequeño devocionario, por Fr. A. de Ocerin Jáuregui, Madrid, 1916; *The Life of St. Peter of Alcántara*, by Armel O'Connor, Bedworth, 1915. [A brief, popular biography.] *A Golden Treatise of Mental Prayer*, translated into English by G. W. Brussels, 1632. Reprinted in a revised form, Liverpool, 1843. *A Golden Treatise of Mental Prayer*, translated by G. W. Bullock from Lafuente's edition of the *Tratado*, edited by G. S. Hollings, London, 1905.

DE ALGUNOS AVISOS QUE SE DEBEN TENER EN ESTE SANTO EJERCICIO

OCTAVO AVISO

El último, y mas principal aviso sea, que procuremos en este santo ejercicio de juntar en uno la meditación con la contemplación, haciendo de la una escalón para subir a la otra, para lo cual es de saber que el oficio de la meditación es considerar con estudio y atención las cosas divinas, discurriendo de unas en otras, para mover nuestro corazón a algún afecto, y sentimiento de ellas, que es como quien hiere un pedernal, para sacar alguna centella de él.

Mas la contemplación es haber ya sacado esta centella; quiero decir, haber ya hallado este afecto, y sentimiento que se buscaba, y estar con reposo, y silencio gozando de él, no con muchos discursos y especulaciones del entendimiento, sino con una simple vista de la verdad. Por lo cual dice un santo doctor, que la meditación discurre con trabajo, y con fruto; mas la contemplación sin trabajo, y con fruto. La una busca, la otra halla; una rumia el manjar, la otra lo gusta; la una discurre, y hace consideraciones; la otra se contenta con una simple vista de las cosas, porque tiene ya el amor y gusto de ellas: finalmente, la una es como medio, la otra como fin; la una como camino y movimiento; y la otra como término de este camino, y movimiento.

De aquí se infiere una cosa muy común, que enseñan todos los

[1] *Cf.* St. Teresa's *Libro de su vida*, Ch. XXVII, XXX. *Moradas*, Ch. IV.

maestros de la vida espiritual (aunque poco entendida de los que la leen) conviene saber, que así como alcanzado el fin cesan los medios, como tomado el puerto cesa la navegación; así cuando el hombre, mediante el trabajo de la meditación, llegare al reposo, y gusto de la contemplación, debe por entonces cesar de aquella piadosa y trabajosa inquisición. Y contento con una simple vista, y memoria de Dios (como si lo tuviese presente) gozar de aquel afecto que se le da, ora sea de amor, ora de admiración, o de alegría, o cosa semejante. La razón, porque esto se aconseja, es, porque como el fin de todo este negocio consista más en el amor, y afectos de la voluntad, que en la especulación del entendimiento cuando ya la voluntad está presa, y tomada de este afecto, debemos excusar todos los discursos, y especulaciones del entendimiento, en cuanto nos sea posible, para que nuestra ánima, con todas sus fuerzas, se emplee en esto, sin derramarse por los actos de otras potencias.

Y por eso aconseja un doctor, que así como el hombre se sintiere inflamar del amor de Dios, debe luego dejar todos estos discursos, y pensamientos, (por muy altos que parezcan) no porque sean malos, sino porque entonces son impeditivos de otro bien mayor, que no es otra cosa más que cesar el movimiento llegado el término, y dejar la meditación, por amor de la contemplación. Lo cual señaladamente se puede hacer al fin de todo el ejercicio, que es después de la petición del amor de Dios, de que arriba tratamos; lo uno, porque se presupone ya entonces, que el trabajo del ejercicio pasado, habrá parido algún afecto y sentimiento de Dios, pues (como dice el sabio) *más vale el fin de la oración, que el principio;* y lo otro, porque después del trabajo de la meditación y oración, es razón que el hombre dé un poco de huelga al entendimiento, y le deje reposar en los brazos de la contemplación, pues en este tiempo deseche el hombre todas las imaginaciones que se le ofrecieren, acalle el entendimiento, quiete la memoria, y fíjela en nuestro Señor, considerando que está en su presencia, no especulando por entonces cosas particulares de Dios.

Conténtese con el conocimiento que de él tiene por fe y aplique la voluntad y el amor, pues éste solo le abraza, y en él está el fruto de toda la meditación, y el entendimiento es casi nada lo que de Dios puede conocer y puédele la voluntad mucho amar. Encíerrese dentro de sí mismo en el centro de su ánima, donde está la Imagen de Dios, y allí esté atento a él, como quien escucha al que habla de alguna torre alta, o como que le tuviese dentro de su corazón, y como que en todo lo criado no hubiese otra cosa sino sola ella o solo él. Y aun de sí misma, y de lo que hace se había de olvidar, porque (como decía uno de aquellos padres) *aquella es perfecta oración, donde el que está orando, no se acuerda que está orando.*

Y no sólo al fin del ejercicio, sino también al medio, y en cualquier otra parte que nos tomare este sueño espiritual, cuando está como adormecido el entendimiento de la voluntad, debemos hacer esta pausa y gozar de este beneficio, y volver a nuestro trabajo, acabado de digerir y gustar aquel bocado, así como hace el hortelano cuando riega una era, que después de llena de agua detiene el hilo de la corriente y deja empapar, y difundirse por las entrañas de la tierra, seca la que ha recibido, y esto hecho, torna a soltar el hilo de la fuente, para que aun reciba más y más, y quede mejor regada. Mas lo que entonces el ánima siente, lo que goza la luz, y la hartura, y la caridad, y paz que recibe, no se puede explicar con palabras, pues aquí está la paz, que excede todo sentido, y la felicidad que en esta vida se puede alcanzar.

Algunos hay tan tomados del amor de Dios que apenas han comenzado a pensar en él, cuando luego la memoria de su dulce nombre les derrite las entrañas, los cuales tienen tan poca necesidad de discursos y consideraciones para amarle, como la madre o la esposa, para regalarse con la memoria de su hijo o esposo, cuando le hablan de él; y otros, que no sólo en el ejercicio de la oración, sino fuera de él, andan tan absortos, y tan empapados en Dios, que de todas las cosas, y de sí mismos se olvidan por él, porque si esto puede muchas veces el temor furioso de un perdido, ¿cuánto más lo podrá el amor de aquella infinita hermosura, pues no es menos poderosa la gracia, que la naturaleza, y que la culpa?

Pues cuando esto el ánima sintiere, en cualquier parte de la oración que lo sienta, en ninguna manera lo debe desechar, aunque todo el tiempo del ejercicio se gastase en esto, sin rezar o meditar las otras cosas, que tenía determinadas, si no fuesen de obligación. Porque, así como dice S. Agustín, *que se ha de dejar la oración vocal, cuando alguna vez fuese impedimento de la devoción; así también se debe dejar la meditación, cuando fuese impedimento de la contemplación.*

Donde también es mucho de notar, que así como nos conviene dejar la meditación por la afección, para subir de menos a más; así por el contrario a veces convendrá dejar la afección por la meditación, cuando la afección fuese tan vehemente, que se temiese peligro a la salud, perseverando en ella, como muchas veces acaece a los que sin este aviso se dan a estos ejercicios, y los toman sin discreción, atraídos con la fuerza de la divina suavidad. Y en tal caso como esto (dice un doctor), que es buen remedio salir algún afecto de compasión, meditando un poco en la Pasión de Cristo, o en los pecados y miserias del mundo, para aliviar y desahogar el corazón.

Tratado de la Oración y Meditación,
Primera parte, Cap. XII.

JUAN DE AVILA

PRINCIPAL WORKS. *Epistolario espiritual* (1579) (a collection of letters on spiritual and moral subjects, not prepared by the author for publication); *Tratado del 'Audi Filia'* (1588), his most famous work; *Pláticas para sacerdotes, Meditaciones, Tratados del Santísimo Sacramento del Altar* and minor writings (mainly short treatises on the festivals of the Church). The first collected edition of Juan de Avila's works appeared in 1588; in this was included the biography written by Luis de Granada.

BIBLIOGRAPHY. *Obras del Beato Juan de Avila,* ed. J. Fernández Montaña, 4 vols., Madrid, 1901; *Epistolario espiritual,* ed. V. García de Diego, Madrid, 1912; (also *B.A.E.,* Vol. XIII); *The Audi Filia; or a rich cabinet full of spirituall jewells.* Translated out of Spanish by L. T. St. Omer, 1620; *Certain selected Spirituall Epistles.* Translated from the Spanish, Rouen, 1631; *Letters of Blessed John of Avila,* translated and selected from the Spanish by the Benedictines of Stanbrook, London, 1904 [a small selection only]; P. Rousselot: *Les Mystiques Espagnols,* Paris, 1867, pp. 145-171; A. Catalán Latorre: *El Beato Juan de Ávila, su tiempo, su vida y sus escritos, y la literatura mística en España,* Zaragoza, 1894; P. Gerardo de San Juan de la Cruz: *Vida del maestro Juan de Ávila,* Toledo, 1915; A. Arenas: *La patria del beato Juan de Ávila,* 99 pp., Valencia, 1918, [In *Anales del Instituto General y Técnico de Valencia*]; The biographies of Juan de Avila by Luis de Granada (*q.v.*) and Luis Muñoz (1634: *B.A.E.,* Vol. XIII), are also fairly accessible.

CARTA A UNA DONCELLA ENFERMA, CONSOLÁNDOLA EN SUS TRABAJOS

Señora, sabido he que vuestra merced está mala; y no me pesa de ello, porque si es de alguna demasía de penitencia que ha hecho, bien se le emplea el castigo; y si no es sino que Nuestro Señor lo envía, sea muy en buena hora la parte que de la cruz le da: y aunque por una parte me dé pena su pena, cuanto sabe Nuestro Señor, por otra me alegro, porque veo clara la ganancia de quien yo deseo ver muy ganada. No quiero yo para mis hijos consuelo, sino azotes, que después será tiempo de los consuelos. Ahora, Señora, no se quiten sus ojos de la cruz, ni su corazón de quien en ella se puso : no descanse hasta que le sepa bien el padecer, que en ello se parece el amor : no haya piedad de sí misma, que en el cielo y en la tierra tiene quien de ella la tenga muy de corazón, y lo que le viene muy mirado viene, y pasado por mano de quien la ama muy de verdad : no se entibie la fe en los peligros y necesidades, ni el amor entre los trabajos.

Cuando el fuego es grande no se apaga con el viento, antes crece : y así, cuando uno ama a Dios de burla, con un soplillo que le soplan se apaga su fuego como candelilla. Mas el verdadero amor crece en los trabajos ; porque más fuerza pone a sufrir, mientras más viene que sufrir ; y como sea de Dios, vence a los trabajos, y ninguna agua basta para apagar este fuego que del cielo descendió. Para amar la llamó Dios, y no es cosa el amor para regalaros : convíenele aborrecerse para amar a Cristo, y negarse para confesarle, y ser cruel para sí misma, para ser suave y blanda al Señor. Si le quiere y desea gozar, pierda a sí misma. Si le quiere ver, por lanzas se ha de meter : si le desea aposentar en su corazón, eche de él a sí misma y a toda cosa criada : sola la quiere Dios, y atribulada, no por malquerencia, sino después que su Hijo bendito fué atribulado, no quiere ver a sus hijos vestidos de otra librea. Esto es lo que delante sus ojos parece hermoso, ver en nosotros la imagen de su unigénito Hijo ; y así como no hay cosa que de tan buena gana mire una ánima como a Jesucristo atormentado en la cruz, y mientras más atribulado y afeado está, más hermoso le parece, así mientras más padeciéremos, mejor pareceremos a Dios. Y no es mucho que el ánima que a Dios desea bien parecer se ponga este afeite con que a Dios enamore, pues que las mujeres del mundo hacen muchas cosas y muy a su costa para contentar a hijos de hombres. Señora, mudarse tienen los cueros para parecer bien a Dios.

Con agua fuerte se apura el oro, y quitada la tierra sale resplandeciente del crisol. Hayamos vergüenza de ser tan flojos en empresa tan grande como es agradar a Dios ; que si lo sintiésemos cobraríamos ánimo para derramar la sangre por Él, porque más hermoso le pareciésemos. . . . La empresa del amor no es palabra, sino dolor, crudos tormentos, deshonra del mundo, desamparo de criaturas y ausencia del amparo del Criador ; y con todo esto ha de haber buen rostro, no quejas, no caimiento de corazón ; mas a semejanza del mártir que le sacaban las entrañas y peinaban con peines de hierro, y no sonaba en su boca sino Jesús, y en su corazón: "Bendito sea Dios," y propósito de pasar más si Dios era servido. Don y merced es padecer por Cristo, y no la da sino a quien Él mucho ama.

Epistolario Espiritual.

Carta a un Religioso,
Animándole al perfecto amor de Dios

Muy Rdo. Padre: *Pax Christi.* Pues que Nuestro Señor Jesucristo no es servido que yo esté por ahora donde gozase de la comunicación de vuestra merced y de esos señores colegiales como deseo, sea su nombre bendito, y súfrolo en paciencia; en lo cual creo que no hago poca penitencia, porque difícil cosa es de sufrir estar apartado de quien el hombre ama; y de verdad nunca tanto deseé la corrección de Vuestra Reverencia como ahora, porque creo que fuera para mucho servicio de Nuestro Señor; mas pues al que le aman todas sus cosas le parecen bien, hablaré un poquito por ausencia, hasta que Dios dé la presencia. Deseo mucho, señor mío, que buscásemos a Dios nuestro bien; y esto no como quiera, mas como quien busca un deseado tesoro, por amor del cual vende todo lo que tiene, creyendo quedar rico con tener una sola cosa, en lugar de muchas que poseía.

¡Oh Dios y Señor, y descanso de lo de dentro de nuestro corazón! ¿Y cuando comenzaremos, no digo a amarte, mas siquiera a desearte amar? ¿Cuándo tendremos un deseo de Ti, digno de Ti? ¿Cuándo nos ha de mover ya la verdad, más que la vanidad; la hermosura, que lo feo; el descanso, que el desasosiego; el Criador tan lleno y suficientísimo, que la criatura pobre y vacía? ¡Oh Señor, y quién abrirá nuestros ojos para conocer que fuera de Ti no hay cosa que harte ni que permanezca! ¿Quién nos descubrirá algo de Ti, para que enamorados de Ti vayamos, corramos, volemos y nos estemos siempre contigo? ¡Ay de nosotros, que estamos lejos de Dios, y tan poca pena tenemos de ello, qui ni aun lo sentimos! ¿Adónde están los entrañables suspiros de ánimas, que una vez han gustado a Dios, y después se les aparta algún tanto? ¿Adónde lo que decía David (Psalm CXXXI): *Si diere sueño a mis ojos, y descanso a mis párpados, hasta que halle casa para el Señor?*

Y esta casa somos nosotros cuando no nos perdemos repartiéndonos en cosas diversas ; mas nos recogemos en unidad de deseo y amor, y entonces nos hallamos y somos cosas de Dios. Creo que es la causa de nuestra tibieza lo que uno decía, que quien a Dios no ha gustado, ni sabe qué cosa es haber hambre, ni tampoco hartura. Y así nosotros ni tenemos hambre de Él, ni hartura en las criaturas ; mas estamos helados, ni acá ni allá, llenos de pereza y desmayados, y sin sabor en las cosas de Dios, y propios para causar vómito al que quiere sirvientes no tibios ; mas encendidos en fuego, el cual Él vino a traer a la tierra, y no quiere sino que arda, y porque ardiese ardió Él mismo, y fué quemado en la cruz, como la vaca rufa lo era fuera de los reales, para que tomando nosotros de aquella leña de la cruz, encendiésemos fuego y nos calentásemos, y respondiésemos a tan grande amador con algún amor, mirando cuan justa cosa es que seamos heridos con dulce llaga del amor, pues vemos a Él, no sólo herido, mas muerto de amor.

Justo es que nos prenda el amor de quien preso por nosotros fué entregado en manos tan crudas. Entremos en la cárcel de su amor, pues Él entró en la del nuestro, y por eso fué hecho como manso cordero delante de los que le maltrataban. Y esta cárcel le hizo estar quedo en la cruz ; porque muy mayores y más recias fueron las cuerdas y prisiones de nuestro amor, que los clavos y sogas que le apretaron aquéllos al cuerpo, y el amor al corazón. Y, por tanto, átese nuestro corazón con su amor, atadura de salud, y no queramos tal libertad que estemos fuera de su cárcel ; porque así como está mal sano el que de su amor no está herido, así es mal libre quien de su cárcel no está preso.

No le resistamos ya más ; dejémonos vencer de sus armas, que son sus beneficios, con los cuales quiere matarnos, para que vivamos con Él ; quiere quemarnos, para que consumido este hombre viejo, conforme a Adán, nazca el hombre nuevo por el amor, conforme a Cristo. Quiere derretir nuestra dureza, para que así como un metal líquido con el calor se imprime bien la forma que quisiere el artífice, así nosotros, tiernos por el amor, que hace derretirse en oyendo hablar al amado, estemos muy aparejados y sin resistencia, para que Cristo imprima en nosotros la imagen que Él quiere, y la que quiere es la del mismo Cristo, que es la del amor ; porque Cristo es el mismo amor, y Él nos mandó que nos amásemos como Él nos amó. Y San Pablo nos dice (Galat. II) que andemos en el amor como Cristo nos amó y se entregó por nosotros ; de manera que si no amamos, desemejables estamos a Él, tenemos ajeno rostro, no le parecemos, somos pobres, desnudos, ciegos, sordos y mudos y muertos, porque sólo el amor es el que aviva todas las cosas, y Él es el que es cura espiritual de nuestra ánima, sin el cual está ella tal, cual está el cuerpo sin ella.

Amemos, pues, señor mío, y viviremos ; amemos, y seremos semejables a Dios, y heriremos a Dios, que con sólo amor es herido ; amemos, y será nuestro Dios, porque sólo el amor le posee ; amemos, y serán nuestras todas las cosas, pues que todas nos servirán, según está escrito : los que aman a Dios en todas las cosas tienen buen fin (Rom. VIII). Si este amor nos place, pongamos la segur de la diligencia a la raíz de nuestro amor propio, y hagamos caer a este nuestro enemigo en la tierra.

Epistolario Espiritual.

LUIS DE GRANADA

WORKS. *Contemptus Mundi,* a translation of the *Imitatio Cristi* (1536) ; *Libro de la Oración y meditación* (1554); *Libro llamado Guía de Pecadores* (1556) ; *Manual de Oraciones* (1557); *Compendio de Doctrina Cristiana* (1559) ; *Escala Espiritual* (1562); *Memorial de la vida cristiana* (1566) ; with *Adiciones* (1574) ; *Guía de Pecadores* [1] (1567) ; *Introducción del Símbolo de la Fe* (1582-88) ; *Doctrina Espiritual* (1587) ; *Vida del Beato Juan de Ávila* (1588) ; together with short lives of several other persons, sermons, minor writings and some fifty letters.

BIBLIOGRAPHY. *Obras,* edición crítica y completa por Fr. Justo Cuervo, Madrid, 1906 ff. (In progress) ; *Considerations on Mysteries of the Faith,* translated and abridged by O. Shipley, London, 1862 ; P. Rousselot : *Les Mystiques Espagnols,* Paris, 1867, pp. 172-213 ; Fr. Justo Cuervo : *Biografía de Fray Luis de Granada,* Madrid, 1896 ; Fr. Justo Cuervo : *Fray Luis de Granada y la Inquisición,* Salamanca, 1915 ; Fr. Justo Cuervo : *Fray Luis de Granada, verdadero y único autor del Libro de la Oración,* Madrid, 1918.

In the sixteenth and early seventeenth centuries many translations of the *Guía de Pecadores* and others of Fray Luis' works were published, often in abridged form, in English and French. A number of these may be seen in the British Museum.

DE LA MAR

Tiene también otra cosa la mar, la cual como criatura tan principal, nos representa por una parte la mansedumbre, y por otra la indignación y ira del Criador. Porque¿ qué cosa más mansa que el

[1] This is an amplification of the earlier and similarly named work, and the version which is celebrated in many languages.

mar cuando está quieto y libre de los vientos, que solemos llamar mar de donas, o cuando con un aire templado blandamente se encrespa, y envía sus mansas ondas hacia la ribera, sucediendo unas a otras con un dulce ruido, y siguiendo el alcance las unas de las otras, hasta quebrarse en la playa? En esto pues nos representa la blandura y mansedumbre del Criador para con los buenos. Mas cuando es combatido de recios vientos, y levanta sus temerosas ondas hasta las nubes, y cuanto más la levanta a lo alto, tanto más profundamente descubre los abismos, con lo cual levanta y abaja los pobres navegantes, azotando poderosamente los costados de las grandes naos (cuando los hombres están puestos en mortal tristeza, las fuerzas y las vidas ya rendidas) entonces nos declara el furor de la ira divina, y la grandeza del poder que tales tempestades puede levantar y sosegar, cuando a Él le place. Lo cual cuenta el Real Profeta entre las grandezas de Dios, diciendo: Vos, Señor, tenéis señorío sobre la mar, y vos podéis amansar el furor de sus ondas. Vuestros son los cielos, y vuestra la tierra, y vos criastes la redondez de ella, con todo lo que dentro de sí abraza, y la mar y el viento cierzo que la levanta, vos lo fabricastes.

Quédanos otra excelencia de la mar tan grande, que el ingenio y la pluma temen acometerla. Porque¿ qué palabras bastan, no digo yo para explicar, sino para contar por sus nombres (si los hubiera) las diferencias de pescados que hay en este elemento? ¿Qué entendimiento, qué sabiduría fué aquélla, que pudo inventar, no digo ya tantas especies, sino tantas diferencias de figuras de peces de tan diferentes cuerpos, unos muy pequeños, otros de increíble grandeza, y entre estos dos extremos, otras mil diferencias de mayores y menores? Porque él es el que crió la ballena, y crió la rana, y no trabajó más en la fábrica de aquel pece tan grande, que en la de éste tan pequeño. Hay algunos oficiales que cortan de tijera en seda o en papel mil diferencias de figuras y quimeras de la manera que quieren, porque el papel y la seda obedecen a la voluntad y ingenio del cortador. Pues¿ qué cortador fué aquél tan primo, que supo cortar y trazar tantas diferencias de figuras como vemos en los peces de la mar, dando a todas sus propiedades y naturalezas tan diversas? Porque el que corta con tijera, no hace más que formar una figura, sin darle más de lo que representa. Mas este soberano Cortador junto con la figura dió ánima, y vida, y sentidos, y movimiento, y habilidades para buscar su mantenimiento, y armas ofensivas y defensivas para su conservación, y sobre todo esto una fecundidad tan grande para conservar su especie, que si no la hubiéramos visto, fuera totalmente increíble.

Porque ¿ quién contará los huevos que tiene un sábalo, o una pescada en rollo, o cualquier otro pece? Pues de cada huevecico de éstos se cría un pece tan grande como aquél de do salió, por grande que sea. Sola el agua como blanda madre, por virtud del Criador, lo recibe en su gremio, y lo cría hasta llegarlo a su perfección. Pues ¿ qué cosa más admirable? Porque como la divina Providencia crió esta pescadería para sustentación de los hombres, y los que han de pescar no ven los peces en el agua de la manera que los cazadores ven la caza en la tierra o en el aire, ordenó él que la fecundidad y multiplicación de los peces fuese tan grande, que la mar estuviese cuajada de ellos, para doquiera que cayese la red, hallase qué prender. Muchas y cuasi innumerables son las especies de aves y de animales que hay en la tierra, mas sin comparación son más las que hay en la mar, con parecer que este elemento no era dispuesto para recibir moradores que lo poblasen, ni para darles los pastos que vemos en la tierra, para que los sustentasen.

Pues ¿ qué diré de las diferencias de mariscos que nos da la mar? ¿ Qué de la variedad de las figuras con que muchos imitan los animales de la tierra? Porque peces hay que tienen figura de caballo, otros de perro, otros de lobo, y otros de becerro, y otros de cordero. Y porque nada faltase por imitar, otros tienen nuestra figura, que llaman hombres marinos. Y allende de esto, ¿ qué diré de las conchas, de que se hace la grana fina, que es el ornamento de los reyes? ¿ Qué de las otras conchas, y veneras, y figuras de caracoles grandes y pequeños, fabricados de mil maneras, más blancos que la nieve, y con eso con pintas de diversos colores, sembradas por todos ellos? ¡ Oh admirable sabiduría del Criador! ¡ Cuán engrandecidas son, Señor, vuestras obras! Todas son hechas con suma sabiduría, y no solamente la tierra, mas también la mar está llena de vuestras maravillas.

Introducción al Símbolo de la Fe,
Parte I, Cap. 8.

DE LA HERMOSURA DEL CIELO

Pues la hermosura del cielo ¿ quién la explicará? ¡ Cuán agradable es en medio del verano en una noche serena ver la luna llena y tan clara, que encubre con su claridad la de todas las estrellas!

¡ Cuánto más huelgan los que caminan de noche por el estío con esta lumbrera, que con la del sol, aunque sea mayor! Mas estando ella ausente, ¿ qué cosa más hermosa y que más descubra la omnipotencia y hermosura del Criador, que el cielo estrellado con tanta variedad y muchedumbre de hermosísimas estrellas, unas muy grandes y resplandecientes, y otras pequeñas, y otras de mediana grandeza, las cuales nadie puede contar sino solo aquél que las crió? Mas la costumbre de ver esto tantas veces nos quita la admiración de tan grande hermosura y el motivo que ella nos da para alabar aquel soberano pintor que así supo hermosear aquella tan grande bóveda del cielo.

Si un niño naciese en una cárcel, y creciese en ella hasta edad de veinte y cinco años sin ver más de lo que estaba dentro de aquellas paredes, y fuese hombre de entendimiento, la primera vez que salido de aquella escuridad viese el cielo estrellado en una noche serena, ciertamente no podría éste dejar de espantarse de tan grande ornamento y hermosura y de tan gran número de estrellas que vería a cualquier parte que volviese los ojos, o hacia oriente o occidente, o a la banda del norte o del mediodía, ni podría dejar de decir: ¿ quién pudo esmaltar tan grandes cielos con tantas piedras preciosas y con tantos diamantes tan resplandecientes? ¿ Quién pudo criar tan gran número de lumbreras y lámparas para dar luz al mundo? ¿ Quién pudo pintar una tan hermosa pradería con tantas diferencias de flores, sino algún hermosísimo y potentísimo hacedor? Maravillado de esta obra un filósofo gentil, dijo: *Intuere cœlum et philosophare.* Quiere decir: mira al cielo, y comienza a filosofar. Que es decir: por la grande variedad y hermosura que ahí verás, conoce y contempla la sabiduría y omnipotencia del autor de esta obra. Y no menos sabía filosofar en esta materia el Profeta, cuando decía: Veré, Señor, tus cielos, que son obra de tus manos, la luna y las estrellas que tú formaste.

Y si es admirable la hermosura de las estrellas, no menos lo es la eficacia que tienen en influir y producir todas las cosas en este mundo inferior, y especialmente el sol, el cual así como se va desviando de nosotros (que es por la otoñada) todas las frescuras y arboledas pierden juntamente con la hoja su hermosura, hasta quedar desnudas, estériles y como muertas. Y en dando la vuelta y llegándose a nosotros, luego los campos se visten de otra librea, y los árboles se cubren de flores y hojas, y las aves, que hasta entonces estaban mudas, comienzan a cantar y chirriar, y las vides y los rosales descubren luego sus yemas y capullos, aparejándose para mostrar la hermosura que dentro de sí tienen encerrada. Finalmente es tanta la dependencia que este mundo tiene de las influencias del cielo, que por muy poco espacio que se impida algo dellas (como acaece en los eclipses del sol y de la luna y en los entrelunios) luego sentimos alteraciones y mudanzas en los cuerpos humanos, mayormente en los más flacos y enfermos.

Introducción al Símbolo de la Fe,
Parte I, Cap. 4.

DE LA VIDA UNITIVA

Pues según esto, cuando el hombre en esta vida mortal llegare a un tal grado de amor que despreciadas todas las cosas perecederas, en ninguna tome gusto ni contentamiento desordenado, sino que todo su gusto, todo su amor, todos sus cuidados y deseos y pensamientos sean en Dios, y esto con tan grande continuación que siempre o cuasi siempre traiga su corazón puesto en él, por no hallar descanso fuera de él, y hallarlo en solo él, cuando de esta manera muriendo a todas las cosas, viviere a solo Dios, y con la grandeza de su amor triunfare de todos los otros amores, entonces habrá entrado en la bodega de los vinos preciosos del verdadero Salomón, donde embriagado con el vino de este amor, se olvidará de todas las cosas y de sí mismo por él.

Bien veo que pocos pueden llegar a este grado, y que las necesidades de la vida y las obligaciones de justicia, y la misma caridad nos pide muchas veces (si decirse puede) que dejemos a Dios por Dios: pero todavía se dice esto así para que veamos el término a donde habemos de caminar, en cuanto nos fuere posible, porque aunque nadie puede llegar a él, pero más cerca llegarán los que extendieren sus ánimos y propósitos a cosas mayores, que los que pusieren raya a sus deseos en más bajo lugar.

Conforme a lo cual dice un sabio: En todas las cosas buenas habemos de desear lo sumo, porque a lo menos alcancemos siquiera lo mediano. Y con este afecto y deseo decía S. Bernardo: Muera, Señor, mi ánima no sólo muerte de justos, sino también de ángeles: conviene saber, que esté tan muerta a todas las cosas del mundo, y tan fuera de ellas, como lo están no solamente los justos, sino también los ángeles, si esto fuese posible. Porque el deseo muy abrasado y encendido no tiene cuenta con las propias fuerzas, no reconoce términos, no se mide con la razón, no desea solamente lo posible, porque no mira lo que puede, sino lo que quiere.

Este amor llaman los teólogos místicos unitivo, porque su naturaleza es uñir de tal manera al que ama con la cosa amada, que no halla reposo fuera de ella, por lo cual siempre tiene el corazón puesto en ella.

Memorial de la Vida Cristiana,
Trat. VII, Cap. 2.

ORACIÓN

Pues ¿ quién es, Señor, toda esta bienaventuranza mía y mi último fin, sino vos ? Vos sois, Señor, el término de mis caminos, el puerto de mi navegación, el fin de todos mis deseos. Pues ¿ por qué no os amaré yo con este amor ? El fuego y el aire rompen los montes, y hacen estremecer la tierra cuando están debajo de ella, por subirse a su lugar natural. Pues ¿ por qué no romperé yo por todas las criaturas, por qué no haré camino por hierro y por fuego, hasta llegar a vos, que sois el lugar de mi reposo ? Con ninguna cosa viene bien la vasera sino con el vaso para que fué hecha. Pues ¿ cómo siendo mi ánima una como vasera que vos criasteis para vos, puede venir bien con otra cosa que con vos ? Acordaos pues, Dios mío, que como yo soy para vos, así vos sois para mí. No huyáis pues, Señor, de mí, porque vos pueda yo alcanzar. Muy despacio camino, muchas veces me paro en él, y vuelvo atrás : no os canséis, Señor, de aguardar a quien no os sigue con pasos iguales.

Oh Dios mío y salud mía, ¿ cómo me detengo tanto, cómo no corro con suma ligereza al sumo bien, en quien están todos los bienes ? ¿ Qué se puede desear, que no se halle en ese piélago de bondad, mejor que en los charquillos turbios de las criaturas ? Aman los hombres las riquezas, y aman las honras, y la vida larga, y el descanso, y la sabiduría, y la virtud, y los deleites, y otras cosas semejantes, y ámanlas con tan grande amor, que muchas veces se pierden por ellas. ¡ Oh locos y rústicos amadores, que amáis la sombra y despreciáis la verdad, andáis a pescar por las lagunas sucias y dejáis la mar ! Si cada una de estas cosas por sí sola merece ser amada, ¿ cuánto más lo debe ser aquél que vale más que todas las cosas ? Si su padre del profeta Samuel pudo con verdad decir a su mujer, que lloraba por no tener hijos, que él solo le valía más que diez hijos, ¿ con cuánto mayor razón diréis vos, Señor, al ánima

14

del justo que le valéis más que todas las criaturas? Porque ¿qué descanso, qué riquezas, que deleites se pueden hallar en las criaturas, que no estén con infinita ventaja en el Criador? Los deleites del mundo son carnales, sucios, engañosos, breves y transitorios. Alcánzanse con trabajo, poséense con cuidado, piérdense con dolor, duran poco y dañan mucho: hinchen el ánima y no la hartan, engáñanla y no la mantienen, y no la hacen por eso más bienaventurada sino más miserable, y más sedienta, y más alejada de Dios y de sí misma, y más allegada a la condición de las bestias. Por esto dijo S. Agustín: Miserable es el ánimo enlazado con la afición de las cosas inferiores, y así es despedazado cuando las pierde. Y entonces viene a conocer su miseria con la experiencia del mal que por causa de esta afición padece, aunque también era miserable antes que lo padeciese. Mas a vos, Señor, ninguno os pierde, sino el que por su voluntad os deja: mas el que os ama, entra en el gozo de su Señor, y no tendrá por qué temer, sino antes estará muy bien en el que es infinito bien. . . .

Ámeos pues yo, Señor, con estrechísimo y ferventísimo amor. Tienda yo los brazos de todos mis afectos y deseos para abrazaros, esposo dulcísimo de mi ánima, de quien espero todo el bien. La yedra se abraza con el árbol por tantas partes, que toda ella parece hacerse brazos para afijarse más en él, porque mediante este arrimo sube a lo alto, y consigue lo que es propio de su perfección. Pues ¿ a qué otro árbol me tengo yo de arrimar para crecer y alcanzar lo que me falta, sino a vos? No crece tanto esta planta, ni extiende tanto la hermosura de sus ramas, abrazada con su árbol, cuanto crece el ánima en virtudes y gracias, abrazada con vos. Pues ¿ por qué no os amaré yo con toda mi ánima y con todas mis fuerzas y sentidos? Ayudadme vos, Dios mío y Salvador mío, y subíme a lo alto en pos de vos, pues la carga desta mortalidad pesada me lleva tras sí. Vos, Señor, que subistes en el árbol de la cruz para atraer todas las cosas a vos, vos que con tan inmensa caridad juntasteis dos naturalezas tan distintas en una persona, para haceros una cosa con nosotros, tened por bien de uñir nuestros corazones con vos con tan fuerte vínculo de amor, que vengan a hacerse una cosa con vos, pues para esto os juntasteis con nosotros, para juntarnos con vos.

Consideraciones de las perfecciones divinas, V, i.

SANTA TERESA DE JESÚS

WORKS. *Vida de la Santa Madre Teresa de Jesús [Libro de su vida]* (1562) ;
Las Constituciones (1564) ; *Libro de las Fundaciones* (1573) ; *Camino de
Perfección* (1565) ; *Conceptos del Amor de Dios* (1566) ; *Exclamaciones o
Meditaciones del Alma a su Dios* (1569) ; *Las Moradas* (1577) ; *Los Avisos*
(1580) ; together with verse compositions of various dates, a few minor
works of little importance, and some five hundred letters, covering the period
1561-1582.

BIBLIOGRAPHY. [The literature on St. Teresa is so voluminous, almost every
month, even now, adding some large or small contribution, that only a few
works of outstanding interest and a few English translations can be mentioned
here.]

MODERN EDITIONS OF THE WORKS. *Obras de Santa Teresa*, novísima edición,
corregida y aumentada, por D. Vicente de la Fuente, Madrid, 1881, 6 vols. ;
Obras de Santa Teresa de Jesús, Madrid, 1916, 4 vols. ; *Las Moradas*, ed.
T. Navarro Tomás, Madrid, 1916 ; *Castillo Interior*, ed. Viada y Lluch,
Barcelona, 1917 ; *Vida de Sta. Teresa*, in Colección Española Nelson. [The
first is the standard edition ; the remaining titles are of easily accessible popular
editions of single works.] See also *Biblioteca de Autores Españoles*, Vols.
LIII, LIV.

ENGLISH TRANSLATIONS. (All, unless otherwise stated, translated by the Bene-
dictines of Stanbrook and published by Thomas Baker, London.) *Life of
St. Teresa*, translated by David Lewis, 4th edition, 1911 ; *The Way of
Perfection*, 1911 ; *Minor Works of St. Teresa* (Conceptions, Exclamations,
Maxims and Poems), 1913 ; *The Book of the Foundations*, translated by
David Lewis, 1913 ; *Letters of St. Teresa*, 1919 ff. ; *The Interior Castle or
the Mansions*, 3rd edition, 1921. [Earlier translations by John Dalton may
also be read ; they date from the middle of the nineteenth century.]

COMMENTARIES. *Vida de Sta. Teresa de Jesús*, por el P. Francisco de Ribera,
nueva edición aumentada por el P. Jaime Pons. Barcelona : Gustavo Gili,
1908 ; G. Cunninghame Graham, *Santa Teresa*, new edition, London, 1907 ;
J. Domínguez Berrueta, *Santa Teresa de Jesús y San Juan de la Cruz*,
Bocetos psicológicos, Madrid, 1915 ; M. Mir, *Santa Teresa de Jesús*, Madrid,
1912, 2 vols. ; P. Rousselot, *Les Mystiques Espagnols*, Paris, 1867, pp.
308-378 ; A. Whyte, *Santa Teresa, an appreciation*, London, 1897. A. Morel-
Fatio : " Les Lectures de Ste.-Thérèse," in *Bulletin Hispanique*, 1908, pp.
17-67 ; J. A. Zugasti, *Santa Teresa y la Compañía de Jesús*, Madrid, 1914 ;
Edmond Cazal, *Sainte Thérèse*, Paris, 1921.

DEL LIBRO DE SU VIDA

Eramos tres hermanas, y nueve hermanos : todos parecieron a
sus padres (por la bondad de Dios) en ser virtuosos, sino fuí yo,
aunque era la más querida de mi padre ; y antes que comenzase a
ofender a Dios, parece tenía alguna razón : porque yo he lástima,

cuando me acuerdo las buenas inclinaciones que el Señor me había dado, y cuán mal me supe aprovechar de ellas. Pues mis hermanos ninguna cosa me desayudaban a servir a Dios.

Tenía uno casi de mi edad, que era el que yo más quería, aunque a todos tenía gran amor y ellos a mí; juntábamonos entrambos a leer vidas de santos: como veía los martirios que por Dios los santos pasaban, parecíame compraban muy barato el ir a gozar de Dios, y deseaba yo mucho morir así; no por amor que yo entendiese tenerle, sino por gozar tan en breve de los grandes bienes que leía haber en el cielo. Juntábame con este mi hermano a tratar qué medio habría para esto. Concertábamos irnos a tierra de moros, pidiendo por amor de Dios, para que allá nos descabezasen: y paréceme que nos daba el Señor ánimo en tan tierna edad, si viéramos algún medio, sino que el tener padres nos parecía el mayor embarazo. Espantábanos mucho el decir en lo que leíamos que pena y gloria era para siempre. Acaecíanos estar muchos ratos tratando de esto, y gustábamos de decir muchas veces para siempre, siempre, siempre. En pronunciar esto mucho rato era el Señor servido me quedase en esta niñez imprimido el camino de la verdad.

De que ví que era imposible ir a donde me matasen por Dios, ordenábamos ser ermitaños, y en una huerta que había en casa procurábamos, como podíamos, hacer ermitas poniendo unas pedrecillas, que luego se nos caían, y así no hallábamos remedio en nada para nuestro deseo; que ahora me pone devoción ver, cómo me daba Dios tan presto lo que yo perdí por mi culpa. Hacía limosna como podía, y podía poco. Procuraba soledad para rezar mis devociones, que eran hartas, en especial el rosario, de que mi madre era muy devota, y así nos hacía serlo. Gustaba mucho cuando jugaba con otras niñas hacer monasterios, como que éramos monjas; y yo me parece deseaba serlo, aunque no tanto como las cosas que he dicho.

Acuérdome que cuando murió mi madre quedé yo de edad de doce años, poco menos: como yo comencé a entender lo que había perdido, afligida fuíme a una imagen de Nuestra Señora y supliquéla fuese mi madre con muchas lágrimas. Paréceme que aunque se hizo con simpleza, que me ha valido; porque conocidamente he hallado a esta Virgen Soberana en cuanto me he encomendado a ella, y en fin, me ha tornado a sí. Fatígame ahora ver y pensar en qué estuvo el no haber yo estado entera en los buenos deseos que comencé.

¡Oh Señor mío! pues parece tenéis determinado que me salve,

plega a vuestra Majestad sea así, y de hacerme tantas mercedes como me habéis hecho, ¿ no tuvierais por bien, no por mi ganancia, sino por vuestro acatamiento, que no se ensuciara tanto posada a donde tan contino habíais de morar? Fatígame, Señor, aun decir esto porque sé que fué mía toda la culpa; porque no me parece os quedó a vos nada por hacer para que desde esta edad no fuera toda vuestra. Cuando voy a quejarme de mis padres tampoco puedo, porque no veía en ellos sino todo bien y cuidado de mi bien. Pues pasando de esta edad, que comencé a entender las gracias de naturaleza que el Señor me había dado (que según decían eran muchas) cuando por ellas le había de dar gracias, de todas me comencé a ayudar para ofenderle.

Libro de su vida,
Cap. I.

EL HUERTO DEL ALMA

Ha de hacer cuenta el que comienza, que comienza a hacer un huerto en tierra muy infructuosa, y que lleva muy malas yerbas, para que se deleite el Señor. Su Majestad arranca las malas yerbas, y ha de plantar las buenas. Pues hagamos cuenta que está ya hecho esto, cuando se determina a tener oración una alma, y lo ha comenzado a usar; y con ayuda de Dios hemos de procurar como buenos hortelanos que crezcan estas plantas, y tener cuidado de regarlas para que no se pierdan, sino que vengan a echar flores que den de sí gran olor para dar recreación a este Señor nuestro, y así se venga a deleitar muchas veces a esta huerta y a holgarse entre estas virtudes.

Pues veamos ahora de la manera que se puede regar para que entendamos lo que hemos de hacer y el trabajo que nos ha de costar, si es mayor la ganancia, o hasta qué tiempo se ha de tener. Paréceme a mí que se puede regar de cuatro maneras: o con sacar el agua de un pozo, que es a nuestro gran trabajo; o con noria y arcaduces, que se saca con un torno; yo la he sacado algunas veces, es a menos trabajo que este otro, y sácase más agua; o de un río o arroyo, esto se riega muy mejor, que queda más harta la tierra de agua, y no se ha menester regar tan a menudo, y es menos trabajo mucho del hortelano; o con llover mucho que lo riega el Señor sin trabajo ninguno nuestro, y es muy sin comparación mejor que todo lo que queda dicho.

Ahora, pues, aplicadas estas cuatro maneras de agua de que se ha de sustentar este huerto, porque sin ella perderse ha, es lo que a mí me hace al caso, y ha parecido que se podrá declarar algo de cuatro grados de oración, en que el Señor por su bondad ha puesto algunas veces mi alma. Plega a su bondad atine a decirlo, de manera que aproveche a una de las personas que esto me mandaron escribir, que la ha traído el Señor en cuatro meses, harto más adelante que yo estaba en diez y siete años: hase dispuesto mejor, y así sin trabajo suyo riega este verjel con todas estas cuatro aguas; aunque la postrera aún no se le da sino a gotas; mas va de suerte, que presto se engolfará en ella con ayuda del Señor: y gustaré se ría, si le pareciere desatino la manera del declarar.

De los que comienzan a tener oración, podemos decir son los que sacan agua del pozo; que es muy a su trabajo, como tengo dicho, que han de cansarse en recoger los sentidos, que como están acostumbrados a andar derramados, es harto trabajo. Han menester irse acostumbrando a no se les dar nada de ver ni oir, y a ponerlo por obra las horas de oración, sino estar en soledad, y apartados pensar su vida pasada; aunque esto, primeros y postreros, todos lo han de hacer muchas veces: hay más, y menos de pensar en esto, como después diré. Al principio andan con pena, que no acaban de entender, que se arrepienten de los pecados; y sí hacen, pues se determinan a servir a Dios tan de veras. Han de procurar tratar de la vida de Cristo, y cánsase el entendimiento en esto. Hasta aquí podemos adquirir nosotros, entiéndese con el favor de Dios, que sin éste ya se sabe no podemos tener un buen pensamiento.

Esto es comenzar a sacar agua del pozo; y aún plega a Dios la quiera tener, mas al menos no queda por nosotros, que ya vamos a sacarla y hacemos lo que podemos para regar estas flores; y es Dios tan bueno, que cuando por lo que su Majestad sabe (por ventura para gran provecho nuestro) quiere que esté seco el pozo, haciendo lo que es en nosotros, como buenos hortelanos, sin agua sustenta las flores y hace creer las virtudes: llamo agua aquí las lágrimas, y aunque no las haya, la ternura y sentimiento interior de devoción.

¿Pues qué hará aquí el que ve que en muchos días no hay sino sequedad, y disgusto, y desabor, y tan mala gana para venir a sacar el agua, que si no se le acordase que hace placer y servicio al Señor de la huerta, y mirase a no perder todo lo servido, y aún lo que espera ganar del gran trabajo que es echar muchas veces el caldero en el pozo y sacarle sin agua, lo dejaría todo? Y muchas veces le acaecerá aun para esto no se le alzar los brazos, ni podrá tener un buen pensamiento; que este obrar con el entendimiento, entendido va que es el sacar agua del pozo.

Pues, como digo, ¿qué hará aquí el hortelano? Alegrarse y consolarse, y tener por grandísima merced de trabajar en huerto de tan gran Emperador: y pues sabe le contenta en aquello, y su intento no ha de ser contentarse a sí, sino a él, alábele mucho que hace de él confianza, pues ve que sin pagarle nada tiene tan gran cuidado de lo que le encomendó; y ayúdele a llevar la cruz, y piense, que toda la vida vivió en ella, y no quiera acá su reino, ni deje jamás la oración; y así se determine, aunque por toda la vida le dure esta sequedad, no dejar a Cristo caer con la cruz.

Libro de su vida,
Cap. 11.

MORADAS QUINTAS

Pareceros ha que ya está todo dicho lo que hay que ver en esta Morada, y falta mucho, porque como dije, hay más y menos. Cuanto a lo que es unión, no creo sabré decir más. Mas cuando el alma a quien Dios hace estas mercedes se dispone, hay muchas cosas que decir de lo que el Señor obra en ella; algunas diré, y de la manera que pueda.

Para darlo mejor a entender, me quiero aprovechar de una comparación, que es buena para este fin: y tambien para que veamos como, aunque en esta obra que hace el Señor no podemos hacer nada; mas para que su Majestad nos haga esta merced, podemos hacer mucho disponiéndonos. Ya habréis oído sus maravillas en cómo se cría la seda (que sólo Él puede hacer semejante invención), y cómo de una simiente, que es a manera de granos de pimienta pequeños (que yo nunca la he visto, sino oído, y así si algo fuere torcido, no es mía la culpa). Con el calor en comenzando a haber hoja en los morales, comienza esta simiente a vivir (que hasta que haya este mantenimiento de que se sustenta, se está muerta), y con hojas de moral se crían, hasta que después de grandes les ponen unas ramillas, y allí con las boquillas van de sí mismos hilando la seda, y hacen unos capuchillos muy apretados, a donde se encierran, y acaba este gusano, que es grande, y feo, y sale del mismo capucho una mariposita blanca muy graciosa.

¿Mas si esto no se viese, sino que nos lo contaran de otros tiempos, quién lo pudiera creer? ¿Ni con qué razones pudiéramos sacar, que una cosa tan sin razón como es un gusano, y una abeja, sean tan diligentes en trabajar para nuestro provecho, y con tanta industria, y el pobre gusanillo pierda la vida en la demanda? Para un rato de meditación basta esto, hermanas, aunque no os diga más, que en ello podéis considerar las maravillas, y sabiduría de nuestro Dios. ¿Pues qué será si supiésemos la propiedad de todas las cosas? De gran provecho es ocuparnos en pensar estas grandezas, y regalarnos en ser esposas de Rey tan sabio y poderoso.

Tornemos a lo que decía. Entonces comienza a tener vida este gusano, cuando con la calor del Espíritu Santo se comienza a aprovechar del auxilio general que a todos nos da Dios, y cuando comienza a aprovecharse de los remedios que dejó en su Iglesia así a continuar las confesiones, como con buenas lecciones, y sermones, que es el remedio que un alma que está muerta en su descuido, y pecados, y metida en ocasiones puede tener. Entonces comienza a vivir, y vase sustentando en esto, y en buenas meditaciones, hasta que está crecida, que a mí me hace al caso, que esto otro poco importa. Pues crecido este gusano (que es lo que en los principios queda dicho de esto que he escrito) comienza a labrar la seda, y edificar la casa a donde ha de morir. Esta casa querría dar a entender aquí, que es Cristo. En una parte me parece he leído, u oído, que nuestra vida está escondida en Cristo, o en Dios, que todo es uno: o que nuestra vida es Cristo. En que esto sea, o no, poco va para mi propósito.

Pues veis aquí, hijas, lo que podemos con el favor de Dios hacer, que su Majestad mismo sea nuestra morada, como lo es en esta oración de unión, labrándola nosotras. Parece que quiero decir, que podemos quitar, y poner en Dios, pues digo que él es la Morada, y la podemos nosotros fabricar para meternos en ella. Y como si podemos; no quitar de Dios, ni poner, sino quitar de nosotros, y poner como hacen estos gusanitos, que no habremos acabado de hacer en esto todo lo que podemos, cuando este trabajillo, que no es nada, junte Dios con su grandeza, y le dé tan gran valor, que el mismo Señor sea el premio de esta obra. Y así como ha sido él que ha puesto la mayor costa, así quiere juntar nuestros trabajillos con los grandes que padeció su Majestad, y que todo sea una cosa.

Pues ea, hijas mías, priesa a hacer esta labor, y tener este capuchillo, quitando nuestro amor propio, y nuestra voluntad, el estar asidas a ninguna cosa de la tierra, poniendo obras de penitencia, oración, y mortificación, obediencia, todo lo demás que sabéis. Que así obrásemos como sabemos, y somos enseñadas de lo que hemos de hacer. Muera, muera este gusano (como lo hace en acabando de hacer para lo que fué criado) y veréis cómo vemos a Dios, y nos vemos tan metidas en su grandeza, como lo está este gusanillo en este capucho. Mirad que digo, ver a Dios, como dejo dicho, que se da a sentir en esta manera de unión.

Pues veamos qué se hace este gusano; ¿qué es para lo que he dicho todo lo demás? ¿Qué? Cuando está en esta oración, bien muerto está al mundo, sale una mariposita blanca. ¡Oh grandeza de Dios, y cuál sale un alma de aquí, de haber estado un poquito metida en la grandeza de Dios, y tan junta con él, que a mi parecer nunca llega a media hora! Yo os digo de verdad, que la misma alma no se conoce a sí; porque, mirad la diferencia que hay de un gusano feo a una mariposita blanca, que la misma hay acá. No sabe de dónde pudo merecer tanto bien (de dónde le pudo venir, quiso decir, que bien sabe que no le merece): vese con un deseo de alabar al Señor, que se querría deshacer, y de morir por él mil muertes. Luego le comienza a tener de padecer grandes trabajos, sin poder hacer otra cosa. Los deseos de penitencia grandísimos, el de soledad, el de que todos conociesen a Dios; y de aquí le viene una pena grande de ver que es ofendido. Y aunque en la Morada que viene se tratará más de estas cosas en particular, porque aunque casi lo que hay en esta Morada, y en la que viene después, es todo uno, es muy diferente la fuerza de los efectos; porque como he dicho, si después que Dios llega a un alma aquí, se esfuerza a ir adelante, verá grandes cosas. ¡Oh, pues ver el desasosiego de esta mariposita, con no haber estado más quieta, y sosegada en su vida! Es cosa para alabar a Dios, y es, que no sabe a dónde posar, y hacer su asiento, que como le ha tenido tal, todo lo que ve en la tierra, le descontenta, en especial, cuando son muchas las veces que le da Dios de este vino, casi de cada una queda con nuevas ganancias!

Ya no tiene en nada las obras que hacía siendo gusano, que era poco a poco tejer el capucho: hanle nacido alas, ¿cómo se ha de contentar, pudiendo volar, de andar paso a paso? Todo se le hace poco cuanto puede hacer por Dios, según son sus deseos. No tiene en mucho lo que pasaron los santos, entendiendo ya por experiencia cómo ayuda el Señor, y transforma un alma, que no parece ella, ni su figura; porque la flaqueza que antes le parecía tener para hacer penitencia, ya la halla fuerte: el atamiento con deudos, y amigos, o hacienda, que ni le bastaban actos, ni determinaciones, ni quererse

apartar, que entonces le parecía se hallaba más junta; ya se ve de
manera, que le pesa estar obligada, a lo que para no ir contra Dios,
es menester hacer. Todo le cansa, porque ha probado, que el
verdadero descanso no le pueden dar las criaturas.

Moradas, V,
Cap. 2.

POESÍAS

Pues nos dais vestido nuevo,
Rey celestial
Librad de la mala gente
Este sayal.

SANTA TERESA

Hijas, pues tomáis la cruz,
Tener valor,
Y a Jesús, que es vuestra luz
Pedid favor :
Él os será defensor
En trance tal.

CORO

Librad de la mala gente
Este sayal.

SANTA TERESA

Inquieta este mal ganado
En la oración,
El ánimo mal fundado,
En devoción :
Mas en Dios el corazón
Tened igual.

CORO

Librad de la mala gente
Este sayal.

SANTA TERESA

Pues vinisteis a morir
  No desmayéis;
Y de gente tan civil
  No temeréis,
Remedio en Dios hallaréis
  En tanto mal.

CORO

Librad de la mala gente
  Este sayal.
Pues nos dais vestido nuevo,
  Rey celestial,
Librad de la mala gente
  Este sayal.

VILLANCICO

¡ Oh hermosura que excedéis
A todas las hermosuras!
Sin herir dolor hacéis,
Y sin dolor deshacéis
El amor de las criaturas.

Oh ñudo que así juntáis
Dos cosas tan desiguales,
No sé por qué os desatáis,
Pues atado fuerza dais
A tener por bien los males.

Quien no tiene sér juntáis
Con el Sér que no se acaba:
Sin acabar acabáis,
Sin tener que amar amáis,
Engrandecéis vuestra nada.

SAN JUAN DE LA CRUZ

WORKS. *Subida del Monte Carmelo y Noche Oscura* (1583); *Llama de Amor Viva* (1584); *Cántico Espiritual* (1584); *Tratado de las Espinas de Espíritu, Tratado breve del conocimiento obscuro de Dios afirmativo y negativo, y modo de unirse el alma con Dios por amor, Avisos y sentencias espirituales,* together with some Poems, Letters and Minor Works, the dates of which are not known.

BIBLIOGRAPHY :—

EDITIONS. *Obras del místico doctor San Juan de la Cruz,* ed. P. Gerardo de San Juan de la Cruz, Toledo, 1912-14, 3 vols. [See also Biblioteca de Autores Españoles, Vols. XXVII, XXXV.]

ENGLISH TRANSLATIONS. *The complete works of St. John of the Cross,* translated by D. Lewis, London, 1864, 2 vols. (2nd edition, 1889); *The Ascent of Mount Carmel,* translated by David Lewis, London, 1906; *A Spiritual Canticle of the Soul,* translated by David Lewis, London, 1909; *The Living Flame of Love, with Letters, Poems and Minor Writings,* translated by David Lewis, London, 1912; *The Dark Night of the Soul,* translated by David Lewis, 4th edition, London, 1916.

COMMENTARIES. M. Domínguez Berrueta, *El misticismo en la poesía,—San Juan de la Cruz,* Madrid, 1894; R. Encinas y López de Espinosa, *La poesía de San Juan de la Cruz,* Valencia, 1905; M. Muñoz Garnica, *San Juan de la Cruz,* Jaén, 1875; P. Rousselot, *Les Mystiques Espagnols,* Paris, 1867, pp. 379-408; David Lewis, Life of St. John of the Cross, 1897.

EN UNA NOCHE ESCURA

(i) *Se trata de la Noche del Sentido*

Esta noche, que decimos ser la contemplación, dos maneras de tinieblas o purgaciones causa en los espirituales, según las dos partes del hombre; conviene a saber, sensitiva y espiritual. Y así, la una noche o purgación sensitiva con que se purga o desnuda un alma será según el sentido, acomodándole al espíritu; y la otra es noche o purgación espiritual, con que se purga y desnuda el alma según el espíritu, acomodándole y disponiéndole para la unión de amor con Dios. La sensitiva es común y que acaece a muchos, y estos son los principiantes, de los cuales trataremos primero. La espiritual es de muy pocos, y estos ya de los ejercitados y aprovechados, de que trataremos después.

La primera noche o purgación es amarga y terrible para el sentido. La segunda no tiene comparación, porque es muy espantable para el espíritu, como luego diremos; y porque en orden es primero y acaece

la pupila de la lechuza, y cuanto el sol se mira más de lleno, más tinieblas causa en la potencia visiva, y la priva, excediéndola, por su flaqueza. De donde, cuando esta divina luz de contemplación embiste en el alma que aun no está ilustrada totalmente, le hace tinieblas espirituales; porque, no solamente la excede, sino también la escurece y priva el modo de su inteligencia natural.

Que por esta causa san Dionisio y otros místicos teólogos llaman a esta contemplación infusa rayo de tiniebla; conviene a saber, para el alma no ilustrada y purgada, porque de su grande luz sobrenatural es vencida la fuerza natural intelectiva y privada de su modo de entender natural. Por lo cual David también dijo: *Nubes, et caligo in circuitu eius ;* que cerca de Dios y en derredor de él está escuridad y nube, no porque ello así sea en sí, sino para nuestros entendimientos flacos, que en tan inmensa luz se ciegan y quedan ofuscados, no alcanzando tan gran alteza. Que por eso el mismo David lo declaró, diciendo: *Prae fulgore in conspectu eius nubes transierunt ;* Por el gran resplandor de su presencia se atravesaron nubes; es a saber, entre Dios y nuestro entendimiento. Y esta es la causa por que en derivando Dios de sí al alma, que aun no está transformada, este esclarecido rayo de su sabiduría secreta le causa tinieblas escuras en el entendimiento.

Y que esta escura contemplación también le sea al alma penosa a estos principios está claro; porque, como esta divina contemplación infusa tiene muchas excelencias en extremo buenas, y el alma que las recibe, por no estar purgada, tiene muchas miserias, de aquí es que, no pudiendo caber dos contrarios en un sujeto, el alma de necesidad haya de penar y padecer, siendo ella el sujeto en que se hallan estos dos contrarios, haciendo los unos contra los otros, por razón de la purgación que de las imperfecciones del alma por esta contemplación se hace.

Lo cual probaremos por inducción en esta manera. Cuanto a lo primero, porque la luz y sabiduría de esta contemplación es muy clara y pura, y el alma en que ella embiste está escura y impura; de aquí es que la pena mucho el recibirla, así como cuando los ojos están de mal humor, enfermos y impuros, del embestimiento de la clara luz reciben pena, y esta pena en el alma, a causa de su impureza, es inmensa cuando de veras es embestida de esta divina luz, que, embistiendo en el alma esta luz pura, a fin de expeler la impureza de ella, siéntese el alma tan impura y miserable, que le parece estar Dios contra ella, y que ella está hecha contraria a Dios. . . .

La segunda manera en que pena el alma es a causa de su flaqueza natural y espiritual ; porque, como esta divina contemplación embiste en el alma con alguna fuerza, a fin de la ir fortaleciendo y domando, de tal manera pena en su flaqueza, que casi desfallece ; particularmente algunas veces, cuando con alguna más fuerza la embiste, porque el sentido y espíritu, así como si estuviese debajo de alguna inmensa y escura carga, está penando y agonizando tanto, que tomaría por partido y alivio el morir. . . .

Cosa de grande maravilla y lástima que sea aquí tanta la flaqueza y impureza del ánima, que, siendo la mano de Dios de suyo tan blanda y suave, la siente el alma aquí tan grave y contraria, con no cargar ni asentarla, sino solamente tocar, y eso misericordiosamente, pues lo hace a fin de hacer mercedes al alma, y no de castigarla.

Noche Escura del Alma,
Lib. II, Cap. 5.

¡OH LÁMPARAS DE FUEGO!

Suponiendo primero que las lámparas tienen dos propiedades, que son lucir y arder, para entender este verso es de saber que Dios, en su único y simple ser, es todas las virtudes y grandezas de sus atributos ; porque es omnipotente, es sabio, es bueno, es misericordioso, es justo, es fuerte, es amoroso, y otros atributos y virtudes que de él no conocemos acá. Y siendo él todas estas cosas, estando unido con el alma, cuando él tiene por bien de descubrírsele en muy particular noticia, echa ella de ver en él estas virtudes y grandezas todas en único y simple sér perfecta y profundamente conocidas, según se compadece con la fe. Y como cada una de estas sea el mismo ser de Dios, que es Padre, Hijo y Espíritu Santo, siendo cada atributo de estos el mismo Dios, y siendo Dios infinita luz y infinito fuego divino, como arriba queda dicho, de aquí es que según cada uno de estos atributos luzca y arda como verdadero Dios.

Y así, según estas notas que el alma allí tiene de Dios conocidas en unidad, le es al alma el mismo Dios muchas lámparas, pues de cada una tiene noticia, y le dan calor de amor cada una en su manera, y todas ellas en un simple sér, y todas ellas una lámpara ; la cual lámpara es todas estas lámparas, porque luce y arde de todas maneras.

Lo cual echando de ver el alma, esta sola le es muchas lámparas ;

porque, aunque ella es una, todas las cosas puede y todas las virtudes tiene y todos espíritus coge ; y así, podemos decir que luce y arde de muchas maneras en una manera, porque luce y arde como omnipotente, y luce y arde como sabio, y luce y arde como bueno, etc. ; dando al alma inteligencia y amor, y descubriéndosele de la manera que es capaz según todas ellas. Porque el resplandor que le da esta lámpara en cuanto es omnipotencia, le hace al alma luz y calor de amor de Dios en cuanto es omnipotente ; y según esto, ya Dios le es lámpara de omnipotencia, que le luce y arde según este atributo. Y el resplandor que le da esta lámpara en cuanto es sabiduría, le hace calor de amor de Dios en cuanto es sabio. Y así de los demás atributos ; porque la luz que le da de cada uno de estos atributos y de todos los demás, hace al alma juntamente calor de amor de Dios en cuanto es tal ; y así, Dios le es al alma en esta alta comunicación y muestras (que a mi ver es de las mayores que le puede hacer en esta vida) innumerables lámparas, que le dan luz y amor.

Estas lámparas le hicieron ver a Moisen en el monte Sinaí ; donde, pasando Dios delante de él, apresuradamente se postró en la tierra y dijo algunas grandezas de las que en él vió, y amándole según aquellas cosas que había visto, las dijo distintamente por estas palabras : *Dominator Domine Deus, misericors, et clemens, patiens, et multae miserationis, ac verax, qui custodis misericordiam in millia : qui aufers iniquitatem, et scelera, atque peccata, nullusque apud te per se innocens est ;* Emperador, Señor Dios mío, misericordioso, clemente, paciente, de mucha miseración, verdadero ; que guardas misericordia en millares, que quitas los pecados y maldades y delitos ; que eres tan justo, que ninguno hay inocente delante de ti. En lo cual se ve que Moisen los más atributos y virtudes que allí conoció y amó fueron los de la omnipotencia, señorío y misericordia, justicia y verdad de Dios, que fué altísimo conocimiento y subidísimo deleite de amor.

De donde es de notar que el deleite y arrobamiento de amor que el alma recibe en el fuego de la luz de estas lámparas es admirable, es inmenso, es tan copioso como de muchas lámparas, que cada una quema de amor, ayudando el ardor de la una al ardor de la otra, y la llama de la una a la llama de la otra ; así como la luz de la una a la otra, y todas hechas una luz y fuego, y cada una un fuego, y el alma inmensamente absorta en delicadas llamas, llagada sutilmente en cada una de ellas, y en todas ellas más llagada y más sutilmente llagada en amor de vida ; echando ella muy bien de ver que aquel amor es vida eterna, la cual es junta de todos los bienes ; conociendo

15

bien allí el alma la verdad del dicho del Esposo en los *Cantares*, que dijo: *Lampades eius, lampades ignis, atque flammarum;* que las lámparas de amor eran lámparas de fuego y de llamas.

Porque, si una sola lámpara de estas que pasó delante de Abrahan le causó grande horror, pasando Dios por una noticia de justicia rigurosa que había de hacer de los cananeos, todas estas lámparas de noticias de Dios que amigable y amorosamente lucen aquí, ¿cuánta más luz y deleite de amor causarán que causó aquella sola de tiniebla y horror en Abrahan? Y ¡ cuánta y cuán aventajada y de cuántas maneras será, alma, tu luz y deleite; pues en todas y de todas estas sientes que te da su gozo y amor, amándote según sus virtudes y atributos y condiciones! Porque el que ama y hace bien a otro según su condición y sus propiedades, le honra y hace bien. Y así, tu Esposo, estando en ti, siendo omnipotente, te da y ama con omnipotencia; y siendo sabio, sientes que te ama con sabiduria; siendo él bueno, sientes que te ama con santidad; y así en los demás. Y como él sea liberal, sientes también que te ama con liberalidad, sin algún interés, no mas de por hacerte bien, mostrándote alegremente este su rostro lleno de gracias, y diciéndote: yo soy tuyo y para ti, y gusto de ser tal cual yo soy para darme a ti y ser tuyo.

Llama de amor viva,
Canción III.

Noche Escura del Alma

En una noche escura,
Con ansias en amores inflamada,
  ¡ Oh dichosa ventura !
  Salí sin ser notada,
Estando ya mi casa sosegada.

A escuras y segura,
Por la secreta escala disfrazada,
  ¡ Oh dichosa ventura !
  A escuras, encelada,
Estando ya mi casa sosegada.

En la noche dichosa,
En secreto que nadie me veía,
Ni yo miraba cosa,
Sin otra luz ni guía
Sino la que en el corazón ardía.

Aquesta me guiaba
Más cierto que la luz de medio día
Adonde me esperaba
Quien yo bien me sabía,
En parte donde nadie parecía.

¡Oh noche, que guiaste,
Oh noche amable más que el alborada,
Oh noche, que juntaste
Amado con amada,
Amada en el Amado transformada!

En mi pecho florido,
Que entero para él solo se guardaba,
Allí quedó dormido,
Y yo le regalaba,
Y el ventalle de cedros aire daba.

El aire del almena,
Cuando ya sus cabellos esparcía
Con su mano serena,
En mi cuello hería
Y todos mis sentidos suspendía.

Quedéme y olvidéme,
El rostro recliné sobre el Amado;
Cesó todo y dejéme,
Dejando mi cuidado
Entre las azucenas olvidado.

LLAMA DE AMOR VIVA

¡Oh llama de amor viva,
Que tiernamente hieres
Mi alma en el más profundo centro!
Pues ya no eres esquiva,
Acaba ya, si quieres,
Rompe la tela deste dulce encuentro.

¡O cautiverio suave!
¡Oh regalada llaga!
¡O mano blanda! ¡Oh toque delicado,
Que a vida eterna sabe,
Y toda deuda paga,
Matando, muerte en vida lo has trocado!

¡Oh lámparas de fuego,
En cuyos resplandores
Las profundas cavernas del sentido
Que estaba escuro y ciego,
Con extraños primores
Calor y luz dan junto a su querido!

¡Cuán manso y amoroso
Recuerdas en mi seno,
Donde secretamente solo moras,
Y en tu aspirar sabroso,
De bien y gloria lleno,
Cuán delicadamente me enamoras!

PEDRO MALÓN DE CHAIDE

WORKS. *La Conversión de la Magdalena* (1592), sermons, etc.

BIBLIOGRAPHY. *La Conversión de la Magdalena*, together with a sermon on the Resurrection. (In Vol. XXVII of *Biblioteca de Autores Españoles*, pp. 275-417, *cf.* also Vol. XXXV. *El Alma en Gracia* (Tratado del Amor), Madrid, 1899. P. J. Pidal, *Estudios literarios*, Vol. II, Madrid, 1890. Bibliographical articles in *Diccionario Enciclopédico Hispano-Americano*, Vol. XII and *Enciclopedia Universal Espasa*, Vol. XXXII; P. Rousselot, *Les Mystiques Espagnols*, Paris, 1867, pp. 81-113.

LA CONVERSIÓN DE LA MAGDALENA

(i)

Ecce Mulier

Estas cuatro cosas hacían muy graves los pecados de la Madalena; y así, no es mucho que diga el Evangelista: *Ecce mulier, quæ erat in civitate peccatrix;* Veis una mujer pecadora en la ciudad. Hora no me parece que habemos aun desentrañado del todo lo que hay en estas palabras. Dos *Ecce* hallo en la sagrada Escritura, que parecen contrapuestos el uno del otro; el uno es este *Ecce mulier*, y el otro el *Ecce homo*, que se dijo del Hijo de Dios.

Cuenta el evangelista san Juan que, queriendo Pilato librar al Redentor de las manos de los judíos, sabiendo que por envidia le buscaban la muerte, por moverlos a lástima mandó azotar al Redentor; sácale desnudo con una corona de espinas en su sagrada cabeza y cubierto con una ropa vieja de púrpura; y al tiempo que salió, vuelto a los judíos, que pedían con grande instancia su muerte, les dijo: *Ecce homo;* Veis aquí al hombre; como si les dijera: Acusáis a este hombre por alborotador y revolvedor del pueblo, decís que tiene humos de rey; pues veisle aquí, que lo menos que tiene es talle de hombre, cuanto más de príncipe.

Poned pues a una parte a Cristo, llagado, atado, espinado, el rostro lleno de cardenales y salivas, el cuerpo cubierto de sangre de los azotes, y aquellos divinos ojos llenos de lágrimas; poned a otra parte a la Madalena, suelta, profana, llena de pecados, infame, sin nombre, hecha una añagaza del demonio, un despeñadero de almas. Oíd a Pilato, que dice *Ecce homo;* y volved a san Lúcas que le contrapone *Ecce mulier;* y mirad agora el misterio tan galán que ahí está : *Ecce homo*, pues *Ecce mulier* ; para que haya un *Ecce mulier* es menester que haya un *Ecce homo* ; que si este no hay, no habrá aquel. *Ecce homo*, que se hizo hombre por gracia ; *Ecce mulier*, que es mujer por flaca naturaleza. *Ecce homo*, que es justo ; *Ecce mulier*, que es pecadora. *Ecce mulier*, que peca ; pues *Ecce homo*, que lo paga. *Ecce mulier* culpada ; pues *Ecce homo* penado. *Ecce mulier*, que merece el castigo ; pues *Ecce homo*, que es el azotado. *Ecce mulier* suelta ; pues *Ecce homo* atado. *Ecce homo*, que siendo Dios se hizo hombre ; pues *Ecce mulier*, que siendo pecadora queda santa. *Ecce homo*, que muere porque esta viva ; pues *Ecce mulier*, que vive porque este muere. *Ecce homo*, que le presentan por esta mujer a Pilato ; pues *Ecce mulier*, que la presentan por este hombre al Padre. Pilato da este *Ecce homo* a los hombres para su rescate ; Cristo da esta *Ecce mulier* al Padre para su regalo.

¡ Oh trueque soberano ! ¡ Dulce bien nuestro, que te pones en competencia de una pecadora porque tu amor te fuerza, y tu Padre te lo manda ! Mirad, hombres, el gran amor de vuestro Dios, que dice : « Tomad un Dios y dadme un hombre ; tomad mi Hijo y dadme una pecadora.» Pues dime, gran Señor, ¿ y éste es trueque que se puede sufrir? ¿ No ves que te engañan más que en la mitad? Dar un Dios por un hombre ¿ quién tal vió? El justo por un homicida, el inocente por el culpado, el señor por el siervo, el hijo por el esclavo, el Hacedor universal por su misma hechura? ¿ Quién vió trocar la gloria por el polvo? ¿ La riqueza suma por la suma pobreza? ¿ La alteza de Dios por la bajeza del hombre? *Ecce homo*, remedio de mis males, hombre que paga mis deudas, sangre con que se lavan mis culpas, precio con que se redime mi ofensa.

Pilato te me muestra, Redentor de mi alma ; tu Padre te me da ; tú mueres por mí, tú dices : « Esta es mi sangre, que derramo por vosotros » ; tu Padre dice : « Así amé al mundo, que le dí un solo Hijo que tenía.» Pilato me dice : Pues veis al hombre que todo eso hace ; *Ecce homo* ; él me dice : *Ecce homo* ; mas yo digo : *Ecce Deus*. Hombre te me muestran, mas Dios te conozco ; Ecce homo, que muere por mí ; Ecce Deus, que resucita por sí. Ecce homo, que muestra mi flaqueza padeciendo ; Ecce Deus, que me da su fortaleza venciendo. ¡ Dulce retrato de mi remedio, que así te había yo menester para mí, que te perdieses a ti para hallarme a mí !

Conversión de la Magdalena, § XII.

(ii)

Reflexiones de la Magdalena

Pero decidme, Madalena, ¿ no será bueno que aguardéis que el Señor salga del convite? Que no es buena sazón de derramar lágrimas entre los manjares, ni es bien aguarles el contento con vuestro llanto. ¡ Ay de mí, dice María, que cada momento de tardanza me es a mí mil años de infierno! Sé que las he con Dios, y no con algún hombre. No se me importunará con mi penitencia el que no se ha cansado con mi malicia. Tiene aquel mi amado, a quien yo voy, otra más sabrosa comida que la que le da el fariseo, que es hacer la voluntad de su Padre. *El lo dice así: Meus cibus est, facere voluntatem Patris mei;* Mi manjar es hacer la voluntad de mi Padre. La voluntad de su Padre, dice él mismo que es, no perder nada de lo que su Padre le envía; luego no me querrá perder.

Pues si soy manjar suyo ¿a qué tiempo puedo yo ir mejor que cuando está comiendo? Quiero llegar antes que se levante de la mesa; que tarde llega el plato cuando son levantados los manteles. Pues ¿no veis, Madalena, que está en casa del fariseo mofador, que se pica de santo, y murmurador de vuestra penitencia? ¡Ah, que me veo a mí, y no he vergüenza de nadie! Veme mi Dios y los ángeles, ¿qué se me da a mí que me vean los hombres? Y ya que me conocen por enemiga y pecadora, conózcanme por penitente y arrepentida. Pues a lo menos, ya que vais, ¿no iríades como moza rica y noble? Enrizad ese cabello, apretadlo con un rico prendedero de oro, enlazadlo con perlas orientales, ponéos unos zarcillos con dos finas esmeraldas, un collar de oro de galanos esmaltes, y más, seis vueltas de cadenilla sobre los hombros, de quien cuelgue un águila de soberano artificio, con un resplandeciente diamante en las uñas, que caya sobre el pecho; una saya de raso estampado, con muchos follajes de oro; un jubón de raso con cordoncillo, que relumbre de cien pasos. Ponéos muchas puntas y ojales de perlas y piedras, una cinta que no tenga precio, y una poma de ámbar gris que se huela a cuatro calles. Ponéos más anillos que dedos; hacéos de dijes una tablilla de platero, que así se componen las damas de nuestro tiempo para salir a oír misa, con más colores en el rostro que el arco del cielo, a adorar el escupido, azotado, desnudo, coronado de espinas y enclavado en una cruz, Jesucristo, único Hijo de Dios.

Y ¿por cristianas se tienen? ¡Ay, que esa gala, donaire y hermosura es engañadora! *Fallax gratia, et vana est pulchritudo: mulier timens Deum, ipsa laudabitur;* Engañosa es la gracia y vana la hermosura, y sola la mujer que teme a Dios será la alabada. ¡Oh desdicha de nuestro siglo, perdición y castigo del nombre de cristianos! ¿Quién vió tan gran desventura como la que pasa en nuestras repúblicas? Entrad por esas iglesias y templos sagrados, veréis los retablos llenos de las historias de los santos; veréis a una parte pintado un san Lorenzo, atado, tendido sobre unas parrillas, y que debajo salen unas llamas que le ciñen el cuerpo; las ascuas parecen vivas, las llamas cárdenas, que parece que aun de verlas pintadas ponen miedo; los verdugos con unas horcas de hierro que las atizan, otro soplando con unos fuelles para avivarlas; parécese aquella generosa carne quemada y tostada con el fuego, y que se entreabren las entrañas y anda la llama devastando y buscando los senos de aquel pecho, jamás rendido. . . . Veréis en otro tablero pintado un san Bartolomé, desnudo, atado, tendido sobre una mesa y que le están desollando vivo. A otro lado un san Estévan, que le apedrean; tópanse las piedras en el camino, el rostro sangriento, la cabeza abierta, que mueve a compasión a quien lo mira, y él arrodillado, orando por los verdugos que le matan. Veréis en otra parte un san Pedro colgado de una cruz, un Bautista descabezado, y al fin muchas muertes de santos, y por remate en lo alto un Cristo en una cruz, desnudo, hecho un piélago de sangre, abierto el cuerpo a azotes, el rostro hinchado, los ojos quebrados, la boca denegrida, las entrañas alanceadas, hecho un retrato de muerte.

Pues decidme, cristianos, ¿para qué nos pintan estas figuras en los retablos? ¿Por qué no nos ponen a Cristo lleno de gloria, sentado sobre las coronillas de los ángeles, y a los santos vestidos de resplandor y llenos de alegría? ¿Para qué nos los representan muriendo y padeciendo trabajos? Yo creo que es porque entendamos que por los tormentos que sufrieron en la tierra llegaron a la gloria que tienen en el cielo; y así, los sigamos en los trabajos si queremos ser sus compañeros en el descanso.

Siendo pues esto así, ¿qué desatino es que os arrodilléis vos a orar delante de un crucificado, de otro desollado, delante del apedreado, del despedazado entre los dientes de los leones, y que delante de los que están tales lleguéis vos más enjoyada y pintada que si fuérades a algunas bodas? ¿Cómo no os avergonzáis de poneros delante en tal traje? Y ¿con qué ojos miraréis a los que allí veis tan lastimados? Y ¿con qué lengua les pediréis que sean vuestros abogados con Dios, que tendrán asco de volver los ojos a vos? No cura la Madalena de otro adorno ni de otras galas para ir delante los ojos de Dios, sino de solo el del alma; con ese va abrasada y hecha un horno de amor.

¡ Oh, quien viera ir a esta santa mujer por la calle, tan olvidada de sí, que aun un paño no llevó para alimpiar los pies del Rey de la gloria ! No va ya con la pompa pasada, no lleva el acompañamiento que solía, no se detiene por las calles por ser vista; antes, los ojos derrocados en el suelo y puesto el corazón en su bien y Señor, derramando tantas lágrimas, que apenas veía la calle por do pasaba, iba apriesa con ansia, diciendo entre sí :

¡ Oh nuevo y celestial Esposo de mi alma, Médico divino de mis enfermedades, detente un poco y espera a esta desventurada pecadora, que se va a derrocar a tus sagrados pies ! ¡ Oh hermosura antigua y nueva, qué tarde te conocí y que tarde te amé ! ¡ Oh pies perezosos para llegar adonde desea mi alma ! ¿ Por qué sois más pesados en llevarme a mi remedio que lo fuistes para mi perdición? Dáos priesa, pies míos, y llevadme a la fuente de mi gloria, para que allí temple el ardor que me abrasa las entrañas. Mirad, pies míos, que si tardáis se os irá vuestro remedio, y sólo os quedará el fuego del infierno que os espera. ¡ Oh resplandor de la gloria, y cómo te desea mi alma !

Conversión de la Magdalena, § XXX.

(iii)

Unum est necessarium

Pues María, aunque perdonada, habiéndose subido el Señor a los cielos . . . determina de apartarse a un desierto, adonde a sus solas pudiese gozar de la contemplación de su Amado. ¡ Oh, que dulces ratos tenía entre aquellos riscos y por aquellas breñas ! Arrebatábase en espíritu, y como si ya fuera vecina del cielo, y como si se desnudara del cuerpo mortal de que estaba vestida, así tan libremente, dejando la tierra, se subía donde vive su Amado.

Allí miraba aquellas moradas celestiales de la soberana ciudad de Jerusalén ; veíala llena de luz inmensa, sus calles y plazas que hervían de ciudadanos bienaventurados. Resonaba por aquellos ricos palacios una música que su dulzura desmaya, causada de la suavidad de las voces angélicas que alaban al gran Príncipe del mundo, sin cesar un punto. Cuando consideraba los edificios, no hechos por humanas manos, sino por sólo el querer de aquel hermosísimo Dios, no tenía ojos para tanta belleza; veía la ciudad puesta en cuadros de grandeza inmensa, cuyos cimientos eran de todas las piedras preciosas que acá conocemos, como lo dice san Juan en el *Apocalipsi*; porque estaban hechos de jaspe y zafiros, calcedonias y esmeraldas, jacintos y topacios, y de otras muchas que allí se nombran; los muros resplandecían como el sol, que no se dejaban mirar a los ojos humanos. Había en cada cuadro tres puertas, de suerte que venían a hacer doce, y cada una era de una piedra preciosa. Las torres y almenas eran cubiertas de cristal, que con los lazos que se hacían en ellas de las esmeraldas y rubíes engazados en oro purísimo y retocados de la luz y resplandor del verdadero Sol que allí resplandece, no hay pensamiento humano que descubra su no pensada hermosura. El suelo, calles y plazas desta bienaventurada ciudad son de oro limpísimo.

Aquí dura siempre una alegre primavera, porque está desterrado el erizado invierno; no la furia de los vientos combaten los empinados árboles ni la blanca nieve desgaja con su peso las tiernas ramas; aquí el enfermizo otoño jamás desnuda las verdes arboledas de sus hojas, porque allí se cumple el *folium ejus non defluet* que dijo David; antes dura una apacible templanza que conserva la frescura de cuanto tiene el cielo en un perfecto ser. Aquí las flores de los prados celestiales, azules, blancas, amarillas, coloradas, y de mil maneras, vencen en resplandor a las esmeraldas y rubíes y claras perlas y piedras del Oriente. Aquí las rosas son más hermosas y de olor más suave que las de los jardines de Jericó, las fuentes más que cristal deshecho; el agua es más dulce, el gusto de las frutas más suave.

¡Oh vida verdaderamente vida! ¡Oh gloria que sola eres gloria! ¡Oh soberana ciudad, en quien tus ciudadanos se gozan! No se sabe qué cosa es dolor, no hay enfermedad; no llega a ti muerte, porque toda es vida; no hay dolor, porque todo es contento; no hay enfermedad, porque Dios es la verdadera salud. Ciudad bienaventurada, donde tus leyes son de amor, tus vecinos son enamorados; en ti todos aman, su oficio es amar, y no saben más que amar; tienen un querer, una voluntad, un parecer; aman una cosa, desean una cosa, contemplan una cosa, y únense con una cosa: *Unum est necessarium, unum est necessarium*.

Conversión de la Magdalena, § LXII.

SONETO

¡Oh paciencia, infinita en esperarme!
¡Oh duro corazón en no quereros!
¿Que esté yo ya cansado de ofenderos,
Y que no lo estéis vos de perdonarme?

¿Cuántas veces volvistes a mirarme
Esos divinos ojos, y a doleros,
Al tiempo que os rompía vuestros fueros;
Y vos, mi Dios, callar, sufrir, y amarme?

¡Oh guarda de los hombres! vuestra saña
No mostréis contra mí, que soy de tierra;
Mirad a lo que es vuestro, y levantalde;

Que no es deleite ya lo que me engaña,
Sino costumbre que me vence en guerra;
Pues por solo pecar, peco de balde.

JUAN DE LOS ÁNGELES

PRINCIPAL WORKS. *Triunfos del Amor de Dios* (1590); *Diálogos de la Conquista del espiritual y secreto Reino de Dios* (1595); *Manual de Vida Perfecta*[1] (1608); *Lucha espiritual y amorosa entre Dios y el Alma*[2] (1600); *Tratado de los soberanos misterios de la Misa* (1604); *Vergel del ánima religiosa* (1610); *Consideraciones sobre el Cantar de los Cantares* (1607).

BIBLIOGRAPHY. *Obras místicas del P. Fray Juan de los Angeles*, ed. P. Fr. Jaime Sala (in *Nueva Biblioteca de Autores Españoles*), 2 vols. Madrid, 1912. *Diálogos de la conquista del reino de Dios*, ed. M. Mir., Madrid, 1915. *Segunda parte de la "Conquista" o Manual de vida perfecta*, ed. P. Fr. Jaime Sala, Barcelona, 1905. *Triunfos del Amor de Dios*, Reimpresión tomada y corregida de la edición hecha en Medina del Campo en el año de 1590, Madrid, 1901. J. Domínguez Berrueta, *Fray Juan de los Angeles*. In *Revista Quincenal*, Vol. IX, 1919. Biography in the first-named of the above volumes. P. Rousselot, *Les Mystiques Espagnols*, Paris, 1867, pp. 114-22. M. Menéndez Pelayo, *Historia de las Ideas Estéticas en España*, III, 132-36.

PRELUDIO A LAS CONSIDERACIONES SOBRE EL CANTAR DE LOS CANTARES

Y si algún libro requería espíritu profético era éste; y no solo eso, sino conocimiento de infinitas cosas naturales y de sus propie-

---

[1] A continuation of the *Conquista*.
[2] An enlarged and revised version of the *Triunfos*.

dades, porque a cada paso se traen aquí para significación de cosas espirituales. En solo el primer capítulo, en que me he ocupado más de dos años, he hallado tantas dificultades, que muchas veces he querido volver atrás de lo comenzado y he tenido mil tedios y desconsuelos por haberme metido en tan grande laberinto. Cuando me ponía a considerar boca en Dios, y pechos, como en las mujeres; nombre, como aceite derramado, vestidos olorosos más que los preciosos ungüentos; lecho florido, casas de madera de cedro y de ciprés, celdas y retretes, beso de esposa, negregura y hermosura, cabaña y pastores, cabritos y ovejas, etc., quedaba fuera de mí, y perdía el ánimo y deseo de escribir.

Y es lo bueno que diciendo esto me reprehendo a mí mismo, y me obligo a dar razón de mi porfía, y aun atrevimiento, en haber querido tomar empresa tan ardua y dificultosa y tan superior a mis fuerzas. Y sé que no basta para excusarme de culpa representar veinte y cuatro años de púlpito, con grande ejercicio de la Escriptura; ni el celo que siempre he tenido (por la misericordia de Dios) del aprovechamiento de las almas; ni bastara ser muy erudito y versado en lenguas, cuando lo fuera; ni la santidad y letras de Santo Tomás, cuando de uno y otro fuera dotado, pues teme el santo subir a este monte, siendo el que era, y temieron los santos todos, llenos de la ciencia del Señor y de celestiales riquezas. Pues ¿quién me ha puesto en estos cuidados?

Lo primero, los ruegos de un amigo mío, hombre gravísimo, y en letras humanas y divinas muy aventajado, el cual, conociendo mi espíritu, inclinado a cosas tiernas y de amor, ansí por lo que había leído en los *Triunfos* y *Diálogos*, como de lo que de mi trato y sermones coligió, juzgó que se le haría a Dios grande servicio, y a la república cristiana no pequeño beneficio, si me ocupase en escribir sobre este libro, en el cual todo cuanto se trata espira y huele amor. Porque, como dijimos en otra parte y diremos más de propósito, aquí se describen los castísimos y purísimos amores de Cristo y la Iglesia, o alma que mereció nombre de esposa, y que pudo decir lo que está en el primero dellos: «Béseme de besos de su boca.»

Lo segundo, una afición y inclinación a este libro, desde que tuve licencia de leer en él por razón de oficio, tan grande, que, aunque no entendía lo que leía, sentía particular gusto y consolación en el alma el rato que en él me ocupaba. Creció esta afición con los años, y confirmóse con la leción de los santos que escriben sobre él. . . .

Es un jardín espiritual para regalo de las almas, adonde podrán hacer ramilletes olorosísimos de diferentes flores para su consuelo y entretenimiento. Aquí verán qué cosa es amor de Dios, y lo que puede, y a lo que obliga, y lo que alcanza, y de lo que nos aparta. Aquí conocerán sus accidentes, tan varios, y sus estudios, tan otros de los que en nuestros tiempos vemos en personas que se dicen espirituales; con que muchos serán desengañados y reducidos a la verdad.

Lo que a mí me asegura y me da confianza que saldré con esta empresa, para gloria de Dios y edificación de su Iglesia comenzada, es no regirme por lo que yo medito o puedo por mí alcanzar (que ni soy profeta ni conozco en mí la gracia de interpretar las Escrituras), sino por lo que los santos y los varones aprobados, y hombres doctos y versados en lenguas dejaron en sus escritos: que, aunque no los habré visto todos, he visto los más y de mayor satisfación, de manera que de mío escribo pocas cosas, y esas, como enano que se pone en hombros de un gigante, no por sí, sino porque el gigante le puso sobre sí y le sirvió de atalaya. Sí: que yo enano soy y pigmeo respeto de los demás que me han precedido en esta escritura, y si algo más que ellos descubriere y atalayare, no será por ser de mayor estatura, sino por beneficio de Dios y suyo dellos, que me han dado luz, y abierto camino para todo.

En lo que más me he desvelado ha sido en buscar claridad y en quitar ofensas y estropiezos a los simples, y así se verá en la obra toda, que, demás de ser clara, el lenguaje es casto, honesto, religioso, grave y que a nadie podrá ser motivo para mal. En lo que toca a la exposición de lugares dificultosos, pongo los pareceres de todos, cuando son en parte o en todo diferentes, y elijo el que juzgo por mejor, y siempre aquel que más se llega al alma y más sirve a las costumbres. Especialmente en materia de oración y de contemplación me alargo más cuando se me ofrece ocasión para ello, porque deseo que este libro ande en poder de personas espirituales, a las cuales desengaño frecuentemente y doy admirables documentos para su pretensión, si la tienen, de aprovechar en la mística teología y comunicación con su Dios mediante los ejercicios del amor gratuito y fruitivo y seráfico, que es el fundamento destos *Cantares*.

Consideraciones sobre el Cantar de los Cantares.

Puertas para el Reino del Alma

Puerta Oriental

Maestro. Por principio y para fundamento de todo, has de saber que hay cuatro entradas o puertas para el hondón y centro del alma, que propiamente es el Reino de Dios : una al Oriente, otra al Poniente, otra al Mediodía, otra al Septentrión o Norte. La puerta del Oriente es la humildad, porque es el principio y fundamento de todo el edificio espiritual. Al Poniente está la pasión y muerte de Cristo, como lo advirtió San Gregorio (Greg. *super psal.* 63) sobre aquel verso del salmo : *Iter facite ei, qui ascendit in Occasum.* El cual dice que el ponerse el sol fué morir Cristo. La puerta del Mediodía es la abnegación de la propia voluntad, porque nunca queda tan clara y resplandeciente el alma como cuando se niega y desampara a sí misma y nada le queda de propia voluntad. Al Norte está la cuarta puerta, que es tribulación, que a veces parece cerrarnos la del cielo y la del consuelo todo. Al fin, del Cierzo o Norte vienen y se descubren todos los males y penas (Ezech. ; Hier., 1). Y aunque de cada cosa destas pudiera yo formar un largo tratado para hacer volumen y cuerpo, como lo hacen muchos de los que escriben, algunas veces de cosas de poco provecho y satisfación para el alma, porque mi primero propósito fué con brevedad enseñarte lo más necesario para la vida espiritual, diré solamente lo que no pudiere excusar de cada una destas puertas.

. . . .

Lleguemos ya a contemplar esta puerta oriental de la humildad, por la cual entró aquel soberano Pontífice y sumo sacerdote Cristo en su Reino, con tan aventajado premio y gloria como habrás oído ; reconociéndole todas las criaturas del cielo, de la tierra y del infierno por Señor, e hincando sus rodillas al sonido de aquel divino nombre Jesús, que le dió su Padre por haberse humillado hasta la muerte de cruz (Phili. 2). El camino real para Dios en ninguna parte se puede hallar sino en la verdadera mortificación de los vicios y en el verdadero ejercicio de las virtudes, en el cual has de tener constancia y perseverancia y en ningún tiempo declinar dél cuanto un cabello ni a la mano derecha ni a la mano izquierda, sino los ojos puestos en Bethsames, que quiere decir ciudad del sol, que es el cielo, caminar como aquellas vacas que llevaban el arca camino derecho, andando y bramando, sin que los becerrillos que quedaban encerrados y bramaban fuesen parte para impedir su jornada ni hacerles torcer a una u otra mano, y haciendo contra esto errarás sin duda, y cuanto más alto volares y pusieres tu nido, aunque sea entre las estrellas, por altísimas y profundísimas especulaciones, mayor será y más peligrosa tu caída. Pues si deseas aprovechar mucho en poco tiempo, asienta sobre tu corazón el nobilísimo y firmísimo fundamento de la humildad y trabaja conservarla tenazmente hasta la muerte; porque de otra manera imposible cosa es que permanezca la labor del espiritual edificio. Esta tan extremada virtud escogió Cristo particularmente para sí (Math. 11) y en vida y en muerte con palabras y ejemplos vivos quiso ser el maestro y preceptor della.

Conquista del espiritual y secreto reino de Dios,
Diálogo III.

Oración jaculatoria

Discípulo. Gran cosa debe ser la libertad de ánimo para esta manera de orar.

Maestro. Puedo afirmarte con toda verdad que sin ella, ni el Reino de Dios, ni Dios, pueden estar dentro de nosotros. Más pierde quien esta libertad pierde que vale el cielo y la tierra ni alguna otra criatura, ni todas juntas; porque ¿ de qué me sirven todas si mi corazón está asido a ellas o a la más mínima dellas, de manera que no le pueda convertir y levantar libremente al Criador ?

Discípulo. Pues ¿ qué condiciones pide esta oración ?

Maestro. Lo primero y principal es la pureza del corazón, que sin ella no somos hábiles ni estamos dispuestos para recibir las influencias de la divina gracia, mediante la cual se establece nuestra ánima en Dios y se obra en nosotros la perfecta abnegación y mortificación de las pasiones y afectos de humanidad. Y añado aquí que la perfecta abnegación y resignación total de nosotros en Dios, por la cual salimos de nosotros y de toda propiedad nos desnudamos, conformándonos en todas las cosas con el querer de Dios, es la llave para la altísima perfección, para la gracia y para la gloria. ¡ Ay amor propio, cuántos daños acarreas a las almas ! En tanto que éste vive en nosotros, continuamente está brotando vicios y engendrando malos pensamientos, y fomentando inclinaciones pésimas y deseos vanos; los cuales nos apartan de Dios, ensucian nuestras ánimas y perturban la paz interior; y al fin él es el mayor impedimento que tiene el aprovechamiento espiritual. Y porque desto queda dicho mucho en el tercero diálogo, aquí no más de amor propio ni de propia voluntad.

Dos o tres avisos te quiero dar para la libertad de aspirar. El primero, que trabajes cuanto te fuere posible por tener el corazón desnudo de fantasías o imágenes de criaturas, representaciones y formas; y principalmente de todo desordenado afecto; para lo cual ayuda mucho el huir las parlerías y chocarrerías y las ocasiones todas de ociosidades y curiosidades, y novedades y hermosuras, y de negocios y ocupaciones inútiles, y de todo aquello tras que se suele ir y a que se suele pegar el corazón. Cercena lo superfluo en el comer y en el beber, y en el vestir y en todo el ornato y aplauso exterior; y luego y muchas veces y continuamente despierta la fuerza concupiscible de tu ánima, multiplicando los deseos de amar ferventísima y castísimamente al Señor.

Pero advierte que puede haber aquí gula espiritual y daño notable para la cabeza, si con demasiado ímpetu y sin moderación se hacen estas oraciones; en las cuales muchos adulteraron deleitándose en ellas, siendo dones de Dios, más que en el mismo Dios. Por lo cual debes andar siempre con cuidado de que tu intención sea casta, pura y deiforme; esto es, conforme al beneplácito y gusto de Dios, cuya gloria sola y a solas se ha de buscar siempre sin respeto a la nuestra, así en lo próspero como en lo adverso.

Advierte lo tercero que, siendo como es nuestra ánima de tanta nobleza y capacidad, ya que no puede obrar infinitamente, porque su virtud es finita, puede a lo menos extender en infinito sus deseos. No te pedirá Dios que le ames con infinito amor, porque no puedes; empero como el deseo se extienda a las cosas imposibles, quiérele Dios extendido a lo infinito, esto es, no limitado en el honrarle y amarle y codiciarle. De manera que en las oraciones afectuosas no se ha de reparar en que sea imposible lo que se desea, o que exceda en infinito la virtud de nuestra alma y las fuerzas en el obrar, sino en que sea justo lo que se desea y enderezado a la gloria y honra de Dios.

Que cuando sola la impotencia, que está de nuestra parte, impide el efectuar lo que deseamos, el deseo será coronado de Dios como se coronara la obra si fuéramos suficientes para ello; lo cual pertenece a uno de los grados del amor violento, que Ricardo llamó insaciable, que puso a San Agustín en decir que si él fuera Dios, como lo era el

aquella limpísima y perdurable fuente de todos los bienes, adonde solamente puedo apagar mi sed y satisfacer el hambre que mi alma padece de su verdadero y sempiterno bien!

Triunfos del Amor de Dios.

Intimo del Alma

Discípulo. Parece que andas por declararme lo que tanto deseo.

Maestro. De razón ya lo habías de haber entendido por lo dicho; y pues habemos llegado a tal punto (advirtiéndote primero que es el más alto que hay en la vida espiritual y de que has de tener memoria para adelante) has de saber que el íntimo del alma es la simplicísima esencia della, sellada con la imagen de Dios, que algunos santos llamaron centro, otros íntimo, otros ápice del espíritu, otros mente. San Agustín summo y los más modernos la llaman hondón; porque es lo más interior y secreto, donde no hay imágenes de cosas criadas, sino (como queda dicho) la de solo el Criador. Aquí hay suma tranquilidad y sumo silencio, porque nunca llega a este centro ninguna representación de cosa criada, y según él somos deiformes o divinos, o tan semejantes a Dios, que nos llama la sabiduría dioses. Este íntimo desnudo raso, y sin figuras, está elevado sobre todas las cosas criadas, y sobre todos los sentidos y fuerzas del ánima, y excede al tiempo y al lugar, y aquí permanece el alma en una perpetua unión y allegamiento a Dios, principio suyo.

Cuando este íntimo (al cual la luz eterna y no criada continuamente ilustra y esclarece) se manifiesta y descubre al hombre, en gran manera la aficiona y enternece, como se dice del que halló el tesoro, que por el gozo demasiado que recibió vendió todas sus cosas y compró el campo. ¡Oh noble y divino templo, del cual nunca Dios se aparta, adonde la santísima Trinidad mora y se gusta la eternidad! . . . Aquí mana una fuente de agua viva que da saltos para la vida eterna (Ioan, 4) y es de tanta virtud y eficacia y tiene tanta suavidad, que destierra fácilmente toda la amargura de los vicios y vence y sobrepuja toda la rebeldía, contradicción y resabios de la naturaleza viciosa y mal inclinada. Porque luego que se bebe esta agua de vida, corre por toda la región del cuerpo y del ánima, y da y comunica al cuerpo y al ánima una maravillosa pureza y fecundidad.

Discípulo. Gran cosa es esa verdaderamente, y no debría el hombre aflojar ni cesar de la oración hasta que Dios le concediese beber siquiera un solo trago de tal agua.

Maestro. Una sola gota que bebieses no tendrías más sed de las cosas vanas, ni de las transitorias criaturas, sino tu sed sería de solo Dios y de su amor, en el cual cuanto más crecieres tanto más aprovecharás en la unión divina ; y cuanto más unido y más profundamente metido en Dios, tanto más claramente le conocerás, y así conocido, forzosamente ha de ser con mayor ardor amado ; y ese es el blanco de nuestras obras y ejercicios, ahí se ordenan y van a parar todos, porque si te falta este amor, todos tus trabajos (aunque sobrepujen a los que han padecido y padecen todos los hombres del mundo y los demonios) son vanos y de ningún fruto, como largamente lo hallarás escrito en nuestros *Triunfos.* Al fin, tanto tendrás de santidad cuanto de caridad, y no más. Y si te parece que me alargo en esto, oye al gran padre Augustino, que dice : Si quieres cumplir con perfección todo lo que explícita o implícitamente se contiene en las divinas Escrituras, guarda en tu alma la verdadera caridad, que ella es el fin de la ley y de los profetas.

Conquista del espiritual y secreto reino de Dios,
Diálogo I.

DIEGO DE ESTELLA

Works. *De la Vida, Loores y Excelencias del bienaventurado evangelista San Juan* (1554) ; *Tratado de la Vanidad del Mundo* (1574) ; *Meditaciones devotísimas del Amor de Dios* (1578), and a number of treatises in Latin.

Bibliography. *Meditaciones devotísimas del amor de Dios.* Ahora nuevamente impresas según la edición de Barcelona de 1578, con un prólogo de Ricardo León, Madrid, 1920 ; *De la Vanidad del Mundo,* in Colección de los mejores autores españoles, Vol. XLIV ; *The contempte of the world and the vanitie thereof,* written by the Reverend F. D. de Stella. And of late translated out of Italian into Englishe by G. C. Douay, 1584 ; *A methode unto mortification :* called heretofore, The Contempt of the World and the Vanitie thereof. Written at the first in the Spanish now reformed and published by T. Rogers, 1608 ; *Meditations on the love of God,* translated by Henry W. Pereira, London, 1898 [a scanty selection, and the translation is often poor] ; P. Rousselot, *Les Mystiques Espagnols,* Paris, 1867, pp. 123-144 ; Bibliographical article in *Diccionario Enciclopédico Hispano-Americano,* Vol. VII.

Como el amor nos lleva a Dios como a nuestro centro

Muy claro está, Señor, y muy averiguado, que así como el bien de los hombres eres tú, así toda la fuerza del amor naturalmente inclina a ese mismo hombre y le lleva a ti, como a su principio y centro, aunque muchas veces desordenadamente sea llevado a otras cosas, contra su valor y honra. Porque así como la naturaleza siempre endereza a una cosa, así también toda nuestra voluntad nos lleva a una cosa, aunque por el libre albedrío sea capaz de muchas, y por su poder se pueda volver a do quisiere. Porque en la voluntad no hay necesidad como la hay en la naturaleza, y pluguiese a tí, mi Dios, que la hubiere y un atamiento necesario, de manera que aunque no quisiésemos no pudiésemos hacer otra cosa, y nos ayuntásemos contigo, como después de esta vida por tu grande misericordia seremos a tí ayuntados.

¡ Ay de mí, que veo en los hombres un grande milagro, y muy mal milagro, y digno de ser lamentado! ¿ No tendrías, por ventura, a muy grande milagro, si vieses a un grande peñasco colgado en el aire y que lo tenía una pluma, y ver un río caudaloso que corriendo con gran ímpetu fuese bastante un papel para detenerle? ¿ Quién viendo tal cosa no se santiguaría? ¿ Quién no se maravillaría y espantaría? Pues ¿ cómo no me maravillo yo en ver hombres a quienes bastan cosas muy pequeñas para que los detengan, para que no lleguen a ti, mi Señor? Extraño caso es que un hombre que naturalmente tiene un peso gravísimo que lo lleva a ti, mi Dios, que lo detengan cosas tan livianas como las de la tierra.

Peregrinos somos en este mundo, y así nos llaman las divinas letras, y caminamos a ti, Señor, como a propia tierra nuestra y naturaleza de nuestras almas, en quien nos movemos, como dice el Apóstol, y vivimos y somos : y siempre que pecamos nos detenemos en el camino y paramos en él, y lo que es grande maravilla, y tanta que pone admiración, es que cosas tan livianas nos detienen. Mi amor es mi peso, y del amor soy llevado, donde quiera que voy. A donde acuesta mi amor, allí va mi ánima, y así como diste, Señor, a la piedra el peso para que bajase al centro, que es su lugar natural, así diste a nuestra alma un peso, que es un deseo del sumo bien, para que con ese peso llegase más ligeramente a ti. Pues si esto es así, ¡ oh mi buen Dios ! ¿ y cómo puede ser que toda ánima por ti criada, no se vaya a gran prisa hacia ti ? Pero vemos la que suspensa y colgada de un poco de viento es privada de todo bien, y se ríe y huelga y descansa.

¿ Cómo es posible que alguna criatura capaz de Vos no se vaya hacia Vos cuanto pudiere, centro infinito e infinitamente bueno y, por consiguiente, infinitamente atractivo ?　¿ Qué cosa puede detener a una criatura capaz de tanto bien ?　¡ Oh gran peso el del pecado, el cual puesto sobre las cervices de los hombres animales, las apesga y hace sentar en lo bajo, porque no suban a su esfera, para la cual son criados !

Verdaderamente, más milagro es a las ánimas no subirse a su Dios por amor, que a las peñas estarse suspensas y colgadas con un poco de viento para que no bajen a su centro, y más que detener un pliego de papel muy delgado a un impetuoso y caudaloso río para que no corra y vaya al mar.　¿ Quién nunca recibiría con paciencia su vida, si distinta y claramente conociese de cuanto bien es privado y cuanto bien pierde ?　¡ Oh, ingratísimo velo de mi carne, y de cuánta alegría me privas !　¿ Quién me detiene que no te rompa y rasgue con mis propias manos, para que vaya a ver a mi Dios y goce de El y en El descanse ?　¡ Oh de cuántos placeres y de cuán grande bienaventuranza carezco por ti y, aun lo que peor es, que conociendo todo esto y viéndolo y sabiendo que es así, te sufro, me río y no lloro ni gimo, como sería razón, días y noches sobre tan grande destierro y tanta ceguedad y miserable desventura mía !

¿ De dónde me viene a mí tan mala y tan ingrata paciencia, sino porque está el velo puesto en medio, y porque esta nube de la carne me impide que la claridad del sol no resplandezca en los ojos de mi ánima ?　Quita este velamento que impide y verás con cuán grande ímpetu se irá el alma hacia su centro.　Mira las ánimas de los santos, que, suelto ya el velo y libres, con qué prisa y con cuánta ligereza se van para su Dios.　¿ Quién las podrá impedir ?　¿ Quién las podrá detener ?　¿ Quién las podrá apartar de su lugar ?　Allí está el lleno y perfecto descanso, allí la eterna hartura de todos los movimientos y deseos del ánima.

Verdaderamente, grande es el Señor y loable, y no menos amable, sino tan amable como loable.　Aunque esté mi ánima en la ciudad del Señor, y en el monte santo suyo, allí está encendida la fuerza del amor, donde ninguna interposición de velo impide, y aún ahora, cuanto este velo es delgado y transparente, tanto más se mueve el ánima hacia su Dios, y más se esfuerza en ella el ímpetu del amor ; como al contrario acaece a muchos, los cuales tienen tan grueso el velo de la carne, con la grande abundancia de riquezas y otros bienes temporales, que muy poco y muy despacio y perezosamente se van hacia su centro. Estos tales, muy poquito o nada aman a Dios. Mas los que con vigilias y ayunos y otras abstinencias adelgazan este velo de la carne y le quebrantan, por su transparencia, en alguna manera, aun en esta vida mortal, se les trasluce en los ojos de sus almas aquella luz bienaventurada, según aquello que el Apóstol dice: Vemos ahora por espejo en enigma y oscuridad.

Y así corren los tales tras el olor de sus ungüentos, y aun algunas veces les acontece que por algunos resquicios y agujeros resplandecen aquellos rayos de la divina lumbre, siquiera por un poco de tiempo, en los ojos de sus ánimas, y se derriten luego en amor y con grande ímpetu son llevados, no ya atraídos por el olor sino por la gran hermosura. Mas ¡ay! que muy poco dura esta radiación y muy presto se pasan tan deleitables rayos. Hieren el ánima y pasan luego, y como dice Job, esconde su luz en las manos y mándala que venga otra vez, y dice de ella a su amigo que es su posesión y que a ella puede subir. Mas luego como entre las manos la enciende, sólo por entre los dedos un poco resplandecía.

Porque si con toda su lumbre quisiera resplandecer en lleno, aun a los quicios de los cielos, conviene a saber, a los espíritus celestiales, con su resplandor más cegara que alumbrara, porque serían vencidos de tan grande claridad. Porque ¿quién podrá sufrir la majestad divina, si ella no se templare?

De esta manera son entretenidos los varones espirituales en esta vida, en tanto que no ven a ti, mi Dios, claramente en la otra, donde están perfectamente en el centro de la bienaventuranza gozando de tu Divina Esencia.

Meditaciones Devotísimas del Amor de Dios, IX.

COMO EL ALMA NO SE AQUIETA SINO EN DIOS, COMO EN SU CENTRO

Como, naturalmente, mi ánima se incline a ti, mi Dios, por su amor, de aquí es que si por el pecado no estuviere afeada y estragada nuestra naturaleza, nunca tuviera necesidad que le mandaras que te amase, como ni ahora nos mandas que nos amemos a nosotros mismos, porque naturalmente harto y aun demasiado nos inclinamos a ello, ni hay necesidad que nos mandes ni amonestes a hacer aquello que de naturaleza nos viene y conviene.

Y pues naturalmente se inclina el hombre a amarte, y más a ti que a sí mismo, ¿por qué se nos manda tu santo amor, como sea más natural, y no se nos manda el de nosotros mismos? Ciertamente el pecado es causa de esto, cuando apartando los ojos el ánima de su Dios los hincó y puso en sí misma, y estancó y detuvo aquel arroyo de amor que impetuosamente corría a ti, mi Dios.

Pues luego digamos que no hubiera necesidad de tal mandamiento si la naturaleza se conservara con aquella pureza que fué criada, y de aquí es que en su primera creación ni a los ángeles ni a los hombres no leemos que tal mandamiento les dieses cuando los criastes, porque naturalmente se inclinaban a esto y no tenían necesidad de espuelas para cumplir tal mandamiento los que con ley de amor íntima y grandemente habían sido formados por su Hacedor. Mas ya olvidado nos hemos de esta ley natural, y enajenados estamos de nuestro propio natural, de tal manera que ni por mandamientos ni promesas ni amenazas ni cotidianos y grandes beneficios nunca te amamos como es razón. Mas así como el plomo que violentamente es detenido en lo alto, si lo dejan luego desciende a lo bajo, así nuestra ánima, si un poco y con violencia es arrebatada y subida a las cosas altas, luego, con su peso, se baja a las cosas terrenales y transitorias y se derrama toda por estas cosas sensibles.

Dime, pues, ánima mía; respóndeme, miserable, y declárame qué sea la causa por qué de tan buena gana te andas por las criaturas tan hambrienta y sedienta, y con tanta deshonra tuya, mendigando de ellas una gotica de aguas turbias y desabridas o salobres, que más te encienden la sed que te la matan, dejando la limpia, sabrosa y perpetua fuente de todos los bienes, en la cual sola podrías matar toda tu sed y hartarte a tu placer y voluntad.

Dime, mezquina: ¿qué cosa puedes desear que no la halles muy más enteramente en tu Dios? Si te deleita la sabiduría, sapientísimo es; si el poderío y la fortaleza, poderosísimo y fortísimo es; si quieres gloria y riquezas, mucha gloria y riquezas hay en su casa; si deleites y placeres, delectaciones hay en su mano derecha hasta el fin; si hartura y abundancia de deseos, embriagados son de la abundancia de su casa los que le poseen.

¿Pues cómo, mísera, sabiendo esto, y mucho más de lo que yo te puedo decir, dejas adrede al abismo de todos los bienes y te andas acongojada, triste y fatigada, buscando tus consolaciones y placeres por los arroyuelos de las criaturas? Menosprecias la fuente que te dan de balde, y con grandes trabajos cavas para ti pozos turbios. ¡Oh intolerable locura, desatino muy grande y ceguedad estupenda! De aquí es que indignado el Señor por esto, exclama por el Profeta, diciendo: «Espantáos cielos y sus puertas sean destruídas—dice el Señor,—porque dos males ha hecho mi pueblo. Dejaron a mí, fuente de agua viva y cavaron para sí cisternas destruidas que no pueden tener las aguas.» . . .

Deja pues, ánima mía; deja, yo te ruego, estas cisternas disipadas, deshechas y agujereadas que con tanto trabajo has cavado, y a gran prisa corre y vete a la fuente de agua viva, que es tu Dios y esposo Jesucristo, donde podrás a tu placer matar toda tu sed. Aquí serás harta de deleites, verdaderos deleites y placeres, según todo tu corazón y toda tu voluntad y como quisieres.

Sólo en el Señor hallarás quietud y descanso y no en otra cosa alguna de cuantas hay en el mundo. El solo es tu centro y propia y natural esfera; fuera de El no hallarás contento, y en El mucho bien y descanso y gloria.

Meditaciones Devotísimas del Amor de Dios, X.

COMO EL AMOR DE DIOS ENCIENDE A NUESTRA ALMA EN DESEOS CELESTIALES

Sufre, Señor, bienaventuranza mía, que te manifieste yo el deseo que de tu vista enciende tu divino amor en mi alma, no para que de nuevo conozcas algo de lo que no sabías, pues miras claramente lo secreto del corazón, sino porque no hallo en el cielo ni en la tierra a quien ir con mis quejas si no a ti, que, como Dios, todo lo ves, y como Padre te apiadas y como Todopoderoso me puedes remediar. Y también porque las penas que nacen de tu santo y casto amor contigo traen consuelo cuando se refieren a ti y cuando piensa el que las sufre cuán dichoso fin suele alcanzar de tus manos.

Mas ¿qué haré, Señor, que decir lo que de ti siento? No sé cómo el entendimiento, guiado de tu lumbre, me guió a ti y dejó la voluntad así prendada, que cuando quiere manifestar lo que en ti halla o, por mejor decir, lo que en ti hallar espera, falta consideración, cuanto más la lengua y la mano.

Poco te ama y desea quien todo lo que siente puede explicar, porque como la medida de tu amor ha de ser no tener medida, así el deseo de tu presencia se ha de manifestar con lágrimas y no con palabras. De donde viene que si quiero por alguna semejanza declararme, hallo a todas tan diferentes de lo que para llegar a su medida es menester, que mejor podré decir que no es mi deseo sino sacarle al vivo como él es. No te deseo solamente como la Esposa la vista de su querido Esposo, por más que cuente los días y las horas, porque nunca pudo llegar amor de hermosura o deleite corporal a lo que se desea la hermosura de aquel que pintó las estrellas y en cuya comparación, como dice Job, los cielos no son limpios y los ángeles en su presencia no tienen parecer. No es mi deseo como el del hijo que no puede sufrir la ausencia de su amoroso padre, con cuya venida espera mucha honra y acrecentamiento de estado, porque tú eres más que padre y contigo están todos los bienes, según aquello que dijiste a tu siervo Moisés : « Yo te mostraré todo el bien.» Y quererlos en particular referir es más dificultoso que contar las gotas de la lluvia.

Poco es lo que desea el preso y cautivo, que está en continuo peligro de vida, que llegue el verdadero amigo por cuya diligencia salga de tanto mal y vuelva a su tierra y naturaleza, porque el que te amare y llegare a ti tendrá cierta la redención del cuerpo y estará seguro de la tiranía de este mundo, y su alma alcanzará presto libertad para sujetarse del todo a ti y cesará la libre servidumbre de poderte perder, porque no estará ya más en sus manos, sino en las tuyas, y tú darás libertad para que siempre goce de ti, mas no para que se pueda apartar luego. Pone, pues, Señor, tu divino amor tan gran deseo en mí, que te desea mi alma, no como lo que acá se desea, sino como quien desea a Dios, que tal deseo a ti sólo se puede comparar, y si algo dijere que es semejante, quiero decir que le parece en algo y no que sea retrato uno de otro, por no hacer agravio en cosa que en ti toca, si la midiere con cosa baja.

Con esta salva me atreveré a decir con el Salmista : « Como el ciervo desea las aguas de las fuentes, así mi alma desea a ti, mi Dios.» Como este animal, aquejado de la sed interior y perseguido de los monteros y perros, y llegando, con apresurado camino va a las fuentes donde piensa aliviar su trabajo, sanar de las heridas y asegurar su peligro y refrescarse del excesivo calor que tiene, así mi alma, a quien enciende el interior fuego de tu santo amor y es de fuera combatida de muchos enemigos, viéndose por algunas partes derramar sangre, desea a ti, para que tu piadosa mano la cure y tu fuerte brazo la defienda y la guíes a la fuente de las aguas, adonde con las aguas frescas y que salen de golpe, se acaba la sed.

No tendrá sed quien viniere a ti, fuente de aguas vivas; no tendrá más que desear que llegase a tu presencia, según aquello de Isaías: «No tendrán hambre ni sed ni serán heridos del estío ni del sol, porque el Señor misericordioso los regirá y llevarlos ha a las fuentes de las aguas.» No tendrá entonces mi alma más que desear ni mi voluntad más que querer, porque me hartaré cuando tu gloria apareciere.

Este deseo hizo a aquel hijo pródigo que, desamparando y dejando el vil oficio en que servía a los torpes deleites, buscase con diligencia, volviendo al amor primero que te tenía, y así, llegando a tu presencia, se acabó en él la hambre que padecía y todos los otros trabajos que pasaba en el servicio del mundo. Falta el agua de tu divina consolación, como faltó a Agar fuera de la casa de Abraham; conviene, pues, a mi alma que vuelva a ti, mi Dios, ardiendo en llamas de vivo fuego de amor, porque con estos deseos encendidos en amor te busque con cuidado y vaya con diligencia a ti, Señor, donde viva y descanse. Aborrece todo lo presente quien de veras te ama y desea y todo lo que el mundo me representa es estrechura que aprieta y congoja mi corazón, acordándome de tus celestiales palacios y de las riquezas inestimables de tu gloria. ¡Oh, Señor, quien con el favor de tu espíritu se ha levantado hasta ver las grandes anchuras de tu omnipotencia y aquellas espaciosas moradas de tu santa ciudad, cuán estrecha le parecerá toda criatura! ¡Oh cómo halla luego la vista con que topar, mirando otra cualquier cosa!

No me espanto de lo que dijo tu profeta Isaías, cuando después de la contemplación de tus grandezas se volvió a mirar lo de acá abajo. «Mirad que todas las gentes son como una gotilla de agua que se rezuma de una redoma.» Estimólas como un grano, el menor que se pesa, y todas las islas como un polvo menudo. Y aún parecióle que comparándolo a algo había dicho poco y así da otra sentencia más al propio diciendo que todo es nada, y como cosa vacía y por tal se ha de estimar. La cual sentencia es de más valor que el juicio de los vanos hijos de este siglo, vecinos de acá, que se deshacen por extender los términos, como si por ser un poco más ancha la cárcel, creciese más la libertad del espíritu, para el cual es tan poco todo lo temporal. Viendo, pues, mi ánima, y habiendo por experiencia conocido cómo no hinchen sus deseos todo esto de acá, movida con el estímulo de tu santo amor, desea a ti, Señor, y arde en deseos celestiales y atormentada con la dilación, susténtase en esta vida confiando en aquello que está escrito : « Darse ha a los justos su deseo.»

Oiste, Señor, el deseo de los pobres, y la preparación de su corazón oyó tu oído. Delante de ti está todo mi deseo, el cual no es otro sino de amarte y verte, donde hay cumplimiento de deseos, donde el deseo no tenga más que desear, y el corazón, estando lleno de tu santo amor, esté seguro y cierto que nunca te dejará de amar, confirmando en tu gracia y amor. No dilates, Señor, misericordia mía y mi bienaventuranza, el cumplimiento de mi deseo, pues el amor me da empellones y me incita para que vaya a ti y te ame para siempre.

Meditaciones Devotísimas del Amor de Dios, LXXVII.

DE LOS GRADOS DEL DIVINO AMOR

No tenemos, Señor, tan en las manos este tu divino amor, que luego podamos subir a él, sino poco a poco, aunque en la verdad, si nuestra naturaleza no estuviera estragada, tomara nuestro amor principio de arriba. Mas porque está por el pecado corrupta y dañada, perdió la lumbre espiritual y tomó otro principio de amor ; así como una fuente de su principio mana abundantísima y claramente, y si la cierran con piedras y leños y lodo busca otra parte por donde salga, y la que al principio salía clara sale después turbia y sucia, corrompido su primer origen. Así es en la fuente del amor, porque se hizo otro origen turbio, hediondo, corrupto y lodoso, porque comenzamos a amar de nosotros, como hubiésemos de comenzar de Dios, porque esto, según verdad, era lo más natural. Mas depravada la naturaleza del amor, mudó el amor su origen, de manera que como hubiésemos de amar a ti, Señor y Dios nuestro, primeramente por amor de ti y todas las cosas por ti y en ti, ahora comenzando de nosotros, amamos a nosotros más que a nadie y todo lo que amamos es por nosotros. De aquí comenzamos a aprovechar en tu santo amor, poniendo el fundamento y principio en nosotros, amándote no tanto por ti como por nosotros, porque sabemos que sin ti no podemos ser, pues la continua necesidad que sabemos que tenemos de tu Divina Majestad, nos fuerza y compele que te busquemos por ayudador y que te llamemos para que nos favorezcas y nos des las cosas necesarias para esta vida. Y de aquí es que porque esto que amamos no lo podemos poseer sin ti, consiguientemente amamos a ti por nosotros como necesitados y que no nos cumple hacer otra cosa.

Y porque continuándote, Señor, a amar por la necesidad que de ti tenemos, experimentamos y conocemos tu benignidad en nosotros y tu largueza, benevolencia, suavidad y bondad, con otras muchas divinas perfecciones, de aquí viene que comenzando a olvidarnos de nosotros, en ti mismo nos comience a agradar tu bondad, siendo antes buscado al principio de nosotros como bien útil y provechoso. Este es el tercer grado del amor, porque el primero es con el que nos amamos a nosotros mismos; el segundo, con el que te amamos a ti por nosotros. Mas el tercer grado del amor es con el cual a ti y a nosotros y a todas las cosas amamos por ti solo.

Cuando Jacob iba de casa de sus padres a Mesopotamia y se durmió sobre una piedra vió en visión una escalera que tenía una punta en la tierra y otra en el cielo, y tú, Señor y Dios nuestro, estabas recostado en ella. No somos aves, ni hemos de volar de la tierra al cielo, y por eso es menester subir poco a poco por escalera, por los escalones y gradas del amor, el cual comienza en la tierra por originarse y tener su fundamento terrenal comenzando del amor propio y subiendo por sus grados y escalones hasta lo fino y más perfecto de tu santo amor, que es lo celestial, acendrado y más esmerado y puro.

Entonces, subiendo por estos grados del amor, llegamos al cielo cuando la imperfección de nuestro amor se va limando, purificando y adelgazando hasta venir a la cumbre y alteza del verdadero amor, cuando ya sin respecto alguno de nosotros mismos te amamos solamente por quien tú eres como dignísimo de ser amado, pues eres sumo bien y bondad infinita. Y porque la naturaleza flaca, imperfecta y corrupta es menester que sea ayudada y favorecida, estabas, Señor, arrimado en aquella escalera, porque con tu divino favor y auxilio de tu mano, hemos de subir al excelente y soberano amor tuyo. Toda buena dádiva y todo don perfecto viene de lo alto y desciende del Padre de las lumbres. ¿Pues cuánto más el amor, que es el más perfecto don de todos? Fuego es el amor, y como el fuego en su principio, cuando introduce su forma en la materia del leño, está impuro y lleno de humo, y después que comienza a subir a su esfera se va apurando y haciéndose más puro, sutil y claro, así el amor, aunque en su comienzo empiece al principio imperfecto, impuro y terreno, va subiendo a su propia esfera, que es Dios, y perfeccionándose hasta llegar a él y mejorándose hasta llegar al punto de su perfección.

Entonces ha subido lo que ha de subir y está como conviene y donde ha de estar cuando, olvidado el hombre totalmente de sí mismo y de todas las cosas, es transportado y transformado en su Dios, no queriendo en el cielo ni en la tierra otro bien sino el Criador y Señor de todas las cosas. Aquel es verdadero amante, que ninguna cosa quiere para sí ni pretende intereses propios ni bien alguno particular que toque a él ni en el cielo ni en la tierra y no busca en todo cuanto piensa y dice y hace sino solamente la honra y gloria de Dios y hacer su voluntad en todas las cosas. ¿ Quién alcanzará este grado de amor? Bienaventurado es aquel que a tan alto grado de amor ha venido, que olvidado de sí y de todas sus cosas y enajenado totalmente de sí, se da del todo a ti, mi Dios, y se traspasa en ti.

Tanta felicidad y bienaventuranza como ésta, no es de la presente vida, porque más es de la que está por venir que de ésta, llena de cuidados y necesidades que tiran por nuestro corazón y lo encorvan e inclinan al amor de este siglo, en el cual vive el alma cautiva aunque no quiera. Si algunas veces llegamos a este grado de excelente y puro amor, perseveramos en él. Porque en el cuerpo corruptible apesga y agrava el alma y la hace bajar con su peso cuando ya comenzaba a volar en altanería, y entremétese la importuna carne, aun a la que no se quería acordar de ella, desasosegándola y enojándola con mil clamores y desasosiegos y otras tantas vanidades, a la que había concedido, que siquiera un poco de tiempo, sosegase y deleitase con su Esposo Jesucristo.

Nunca faltan moscas importunas de vanos pensamientos y cuidados del mundo que desasosieguen al santo patriarca Abraham cuando ofrece sacrificio y ama y ora a Dios, así como el mismo Señor se lo había mandado. A este grado perfecto de amor había venido el que decía al Amado: «Encendióse mi corazón en vuestro amor, Señor mío, y esta llama tan grande mata en mí todo el fuego de la concupiscencia mala.» Porque ningún fuego consiente arder con este santo fuego, de aquí es que de concupiscencia grande se han mudado mis rehenes en blancura y pureza de castidad, tragando y deshaciendo en mí el fuego del cielo, el ardor ajeno, y mudóme del todo, y me ha deshecho y tornado en nada la potentísima fuerza del amor. Cumplido has en mí, Señor mío, lo que en otro tiempo por un Profeta en forma de saludable amenaza nos habías dicho : «Convertiré mi mano a ti y coceré tu escoria y fundiré tu estaño.»

Esto veo en mí verificado, porque todo lo que en mí era mío, se ha consumido y gastado. Todo soy tornado en nada, porque vivo yo ; y ya no yo, pero vive en mí Cristo y no lo supe. No supe tan gran sacramento ; no sabía verdaderamente el misterio de tan gran mudanza ; que convino aniquilarme y tornarme en nada para que tuviese verdadero ser y que todo yo desfalleciese en mi Dios como estaba escrito : «Desfalleció mi corazón y mi carne en Dios vivo.» Y otra vez dice : «Desfallecido ha mi alma en vuestro Salvador.» ¡ Oh, cuán bueno es este desfallecimiento cuando el alma desfallece en su Dios y de sí misma pasa en Dios, y llegándose a su Dios es hecha un espíritu con él ! Harto era, conforme a nuestra naturaleza, y harto a ella se inclinaba, que todas las cosas se amasen por aquel por quien fueron hechas.

Y este amor se ha de tener por bueno y derecho, que así es conforme a la naturaleza, y si nuestras almas no fuesen tan livianas y de tan poco peso, este grado último de amor había de ser el primero. Así había de ser y así fuera, si el pecado no se pusiera de por medio. Puedo también, Señor, amarte en tres maneras ; conviene a saber : con otras cosas y más que a otras cosas y sin otras cosas. El que con otras cosas te ama, igualándote en el amor con ellas, divide este tal el corazón y no cumple el mandamiento del amor. El que te ama más que las otras cosas, aunque ama las otras cosas lícitamente contigo, no divide su corazón, aunque de alguna manera le aparte y divierta a otras cosas. Este tal, el mandamiento cumple del amor, aunque no ha alcanzado la perfección. Mas el que ama solamente a ti, Señor, y sin otra cosa, este tal ya ha alcanzado la cumbre de la perfección y puede decir con la Esposa : «Mi amado a mí y yo a él, el cual se apacienta entre los lirios.» El primer amor edifica para el infierno. El segundo edifica sobre el fundamento de la fe, estopos, maderos y pajas. El tercero oro y plata y piedras preciosas, según la palabra del Apóstol.

Meditaciones devotísimas del Amor de Dios, LXXIV.

Como el amor transforma al amante en el amado

Tan grande y tan extraña es la fuerza del amor, que tal me conviene que sea cual es lo que amo y según aquello a que por amor me llego. No hay engrudo ni cola que así pegue como el amor, el cual así nos une y junta con el amado que transforma al amante en el que ama. El amor no es otra cosa sino una virtud mutua y unitiva. Como el hierro después de muy encendido en la fragua es hecho fuego, así mi corazón, ardiendo, Dios mío, en tu divino y santo amor, es todo en ti transformado por amor, deificado y endiosado. El hierro duro, frío, negro y oscuro, es convertido en fuego, y hecho blando, caliente, resplandeciente y claro, y tiene todas las operaciones de fuego, haciendo todos sus efectos y todo lo que hace el fuego, porque quema, alumbra y enciende.

La Escritura, Dios y Señor nuestro, te llama fuego, y tales somos nosotros llegándonos a ti por amor, porque de pecadores que éramos antes, duros como hierro, obstinados, fríos, oscuros y torpes, llegados a ti por amor y metiéndonos el amor en esa fragua de vivas llamas como te vió Moises en la zarza, somos convertidos en ti y hechos fuego, y así obramos obras divinas y somos varones espirituales, de carnales y terrenos que antes éramos. Así estaba transformado y convertido en ti el apóstol San Pablo, que vino a decir a los Gálatas: « Vivo yo, y ya no yo, porque vive en mí Cristo.»

De tal manera vivía en ti el santo Apóstol y así estaba en ti transformado, que su vida ya no era suya, y él no estaba en sí sino en el amado. Pluguiese a mi Dios y Señor, que así fuese mi alma absorta en ese piélago de infinito amor y bondad, que yo no fuese yo, sino por divina participación fuese un traslado y retrato de tu soberano bondad y clemencia.

¡Oh, quién me diese que todos mis pensamientos se volviesen en uno, y toda la fuerza de todos se emplease en arder ante tu divino acatamiento y de suerte que pudiese decir como el Profeta: « El pensamiento de mi corazón siempre está en tu presencia.» ¡Oh! pluguiese a ti, mi Dios, que no hubiese sino una lámpara que ardiese en el altar de mi alma, encendida con fuego de verdadero amor y se cebase de todo cuanto siento y oigo de tus admirables perfecciones, para que éste fuese el aceite purísimo que antiguamente mandabas quemar en el santuario. ¡Oh! pluguiese a ti, Señor, hicieses con mi alma aquel amoroso castigo con que amenazas por el profeta

Oseas, diciendo : «Cercaré tu camino con espinas y con paredes que no las puedas romper» : Pondré en todo dificultades, para que si buscares otros amores, nunca los halles y así te vuelvas para mí. Dichosa necesidad que obliga a no querer sino al que sólo merece ser amado.

Pues hagamos ya fin, ánima mía, a los vanos discursos, y recogiendo tus pensamientos, pon toda tu caída y amor en sólo tu Esposo Jesucristo. Si verdaderamente amases a Dios, olvidarte habías de todas las cosas del mundo. El Apóstol tiene todas estas cosas por estiércol, por amor de Jesucristo. Así cuando nuestro padre estaba en el estado de inocencia, mandóle Dios que comiese de los árboles del Paraíso. Fué menester que le recordase Dios que comiese porque el amor grande que le tenía pudiera ser que le hiciera olvidar de tomar el mantenimiento necesario para conservar la vida. Si con grande y verdadero amor amases a tu Dios y Señor, no tendrías tan solícito cuidado de estas cosas exteriores que tanto te distraen y derraman.

Cuanto más se llega nuestra voluntad a Dios, tanto más se aparta de nosotros mismos, y así deberíamos tenerle pegada y asida con Dios, que anduviésemos olvidados de todo lo de acá, andando todos transformados, convertidos y elevados en Dios. Si de veras, Señor, te amase, la fuerza del amor me haría que fuese como lo que amo, porque transformándome en ti, sería semejante a lo que amo. Y si la semejanza es causa de amor, subiría y así se aumentaría este amor, que se alzase con el homenaje y con todo cuanto hay en mí, no quedando cosa que no estuviese presa de tu amor. Mira, pues, alma a tu hermosura y entenderás qué hermosura debes amar. Tienes esposo y no le conoces, y siendo el más hermoso de todos, no le amas porque no viste su rostro. Si le vieses no dudarías de su hermosura ni te podría nadie detener para que no le amases.

Tan grande es la fuerza del amor, que allí verdaderamente moras donde por la contemplación amas. Este es el reino de Dios que está dentro de ti, el cual desechas cuando amas las cosas de fuera. Amando este reino de Dios, eres reina en él, y teniéndole dentro de ti gozas de infinitas riquezas que tiene consigo el amor de Dios. Y si tanto eres mejor cuanto son mejores cosas las que amas, síguese claramente que si amas al cielo eres celestial y si pones tu amor en las cosas de tierra eres tierra. Pues hace el amor tan maravillosos efectos en mi alma, que transformada por amor, soy lo que amo, amarte ha, Señor, mi corazón hasta lo último de su potencia y fuerzas

17

y virtud, y cuanto le es posible, pues por esta vía soy llevado a tan alto y noble estado y subido a dignidad tan suprema y aventajada, que todo lo criado es menos cuando no te ama, que el corazón que arde en tu divino amor.

Y este traspasamiento del amante en la cosa amada, no es violento ni forzoso ni penoso ni trabajoso, mas voluntario, libre, dulce y muy deleitable. Y de aquí es que la voluntad que así por amor se junta con la cosa amada, no puede ser por alguna violencia apartada de ella sino por su libre querer. Y pluguiese a ti, mi Dios, que fuese mi voluntad privada de tal libertad y tal querer, para que después que una vez te amare, no pueda volver atrás ni mudar el amor ni el querer, amando para siempre jamás esa suma bondad y bien infinito donde arda mi corazón perpetuamente en vivas llamas de amor. Pero queda el mismo amor libre, aunque traspase la voluntad en la cosa amada; y así mismo la voluntad siempre queda voluntad y en su libre poder y querer, aunque por el amor sea transformada en el que ama. Cosa es maravillosa que en esta transformación que hace el amor del amante en el amado, que cual es la cosa amada, tal es el amor, y cual es el amor, tal es la voluntad de donde nace.

De donde se sigue que la cosa primero y principalmente amada, da nombre, naturaleza y forma a la voluntad que ama, y de aquí se concluye, que porque es propiedad del amor trabar, convertir y transformar al amante en el amado o en la cosa amada, si la voluntad primero ama tierra, tierra se hace, y terreno se hace y terreno se llama su amor, y si cosas mortales ama, llámase mortal y humana voluntad, y si ángeles ama, angélica es, y si ama a ti, Dios y Señor nuestro, es divina.

En esto se descubre y manifiesta una gran dignidad del hombre, y es que por el amor se puede transformar y mudar en cualquier cosa que él quisiera, más alta o más baja que él. De Nabucodonosor, que como bestia seguía sus apetitos bestiales, rigiéndose por los sentidos, por los cuales solamente obran y se gobiernan los irracionales, la Escritura dice que como bestia anduvo paciendo las yerbas del campo. Y de los hombres espirituales que aman a Dios, habla David en el Salmo diciendo: «Yo dije: vosotros sois dioses e hijos del Muy Alto.» Pues puedo yo alcanzar tan alta dignidad amando, justo es, Dios mío y mi Señor, que te ame mi corazón de noche y día en todos los días que viviere. Y si dijeres, ánima mía, que entre tantas angustias y dolores de esta vida, no puedes con tristeza levantarte al amor de tu Dios, como dijo Aarón, que con ánimo triste no podía hacer fiesta a Dios, mira que estos trabajos son golpes de eslabón que te da Dios para sacar del pedernal duro de tu corazón centellas de fuego de amor, y que te aflige para que le ames. Porque ve el clementísimo Señor que no se ablanda tu corazón con beneficios, te fatiga con trabajos, porque de esta manera vayas a él por amor, y amando cobres nuevo sér y honra transformada por amor en Dios.

Meditaciones Devotísimas del Amor de Dios, LXXVI.

LUIS DE LEÓN

WORKS. *Exposición del Cantar de Cantares de Salomón* (1560); *Respuesta de Fr. Luis de León estando preso en la cárcel*; *La Perfecta Casada* (1583); *De los nombres de Cristo* (1583-5); *Exposición de Job* (published only in 1779); *Poesías*. Also some few minor works, commentaries on certain Psalms, sermons, and letters.

BIBLIOGRAPHY. *Obras*, ed. A. Merino, 1804-16 (repr. Madrid, 1885,) 6 vols. [See also *Biblioteca de Autores Españoles*, Vols. XXXV, XXXVII, LIII, LXI, LXII.] *La Perfecta Casada*, ed. E. Wallace, Chicago, 1903; ed. Bonilla y San Martín, Madrid, 1917; *De los nombres de Cristo*, ed. F. de Onís, Madrid, 1914-17; *Poesías*, ed. F. de Onís, Puerto Rico, 1920; *Proceso original que la Inquisición de Valladolid hizo al maestro Fr. Luis de León, religioso del orden de S. Agustín*, ed. M. Salvá and P. Sainz de Baranda, Madrid, 1847; J. Gonzalez de Tejada, *Vida de Fray Luis de León*, Madrid, 1863; C. A. Wilkens, *Fray Luis de León*, Halle, 1866; A Arango y Escandón, *Frai Luis de León, ensayo histórico*, 2nd ed., Mexico, 1866; F. H. Reusch, *Luis de León und die Spanische Inquisition*, Bonn, 1873; P. Rousselot, *Les Mystiques Espagnols*, Paris, 1867, pp. 214-307; M. Gutiérrez, *Fray Luis de León y la filosofía española del siglo XVI*, 2nd ed., Madrid, 1891 (with posthumous additions in *La Ciudad de Dios*, 1907-8); M. Menéndez Pelayo, *Horacio en España, passim*; F. Blanco García, *Luis de León, estudio biográfico del insigne poeta agustino*, Madrid, 1904; Conrado Muiños Sáenz, *Fr. Luis de León y Fr. Diego de Zúñiga*, Estudio histórico-crítico, Madrid, 1914; J. Fitzmaurice-Kelly, *Luis de León*, London, 1920; Adolphe Coster, *Luis de León, 1528-91* (*Revue Hispanique*, Vol. LIII). V. also *sub* Orozco.

AMOR Y UNIDAD

Porque el amor, como platicabais ahora, Juliano y Sabino, es unidad, o todo su oficio es hacer unidad; y cuanto es mayor y mejor la unidad, tanto es mayor y más excelente el amor; por donde cuanto por más particulares maneras fueren uno mismo dos entre sí, tanto sin duda ninguna se tendrán más amor.

Pues si en nosotros hay carne y espíritu, y si con el espíritu ayunta el suyo Cristo por tantas maneras, poniendo en él su seme- janza y comunicándole su vigor, y derramando por él su espíritu mismo, ¿ no os parecerá, Juliano, forzoso el decir, o que hay falta en su amor para con nosotros, o que ayunta también su cuerpo con el nuestro, cuanto es posible ayuntarse dos cuerpos? Mas ¿quién se atreverá a poner mengua en su amor en esta parte, el cual por todas las demás partes es sobre todo encarecimiento extremado? Porque, pregunto: ¿ o no le es posible a Dios hacer esta unión, o hecha no declara ni engrandece su amor, o no se precia Dios de engrandecerle? Claro es que es posible y manifiesto que añade quilates, y notorio y sin duda que se precia Dios de ser, en todo lo que hace, perfecto.

Pues si es esto cierto, ¿cómo puede ser dudoso, si hace Dios lo que puede ser hecho, y lo que importa que se haga para el fin que pretende? El mismo Cristo dice, rogando a su Padre: *Señor, quiero que yo y los míos seamos una misma cosa, así como yo soy una misma cosa contigo.* No son una misma cosa el Padre y el Hijo solamente porque se quieren bien entre si, ni sólo porque son, así en voluntades como en juicios, conformes; sino también porque son una misma substancia, de manera que el Padre vive en el Hijo, y el Hijo vive por el Padre, y es un mismo ser y vivir el de entrambos. Pues así, para que la semejanza sea perfecta cuanto ser puede, conviene sin duda que a nosotros los fieles, entre nosotros y a cada uno de nosotros con Cristo, no solamente nos añude y haga uno la caridad que el espíritu en nuestros corazones derrama; sino que también en la manera del sér, así en la del cuerpo como en la manera del alma, seamos todos uno, cuanto es hacedero y posible. Y conviene que, siendo muchos en personas, como de hecho lo somos, empero por razón de que mora en nuestras almas un espíritu mismo, y por razón que nos mantiene un individuo y solo manjar, seamos todos uno en espíritu y cuerpo divino, ayuntándose estrechamente con nuestros propios cuerpos y espíritus, los califiquen y los acondicionen a todos de una misma manera, y a todos de aquella condición y manera que le es propia a aquel divino cuerpo y espíritu, que es la mayor unidad que se puede hacer o pensar en cosas tan apartadas de suyo.

De manera que, como una nube en quien ha lanzado la fuerza de su claridad y de sus rayos el sol, llena de luz y, si aquesta palabra aquí se permite, en luz empapada, por donde quiera que se mire es un sol ; así, ayuntando Cristo, no solamente su virtud y su luz, sino su mismo espíritu y su mismo cuerpo con los fieles y justos, y como mezclando en cierta manera su alma con la suya de ellos, y con el cuerpo de ellos su cuerpo, en la forma que he dicho, les brota Cristo y les sale afuera por los ojos y por la boca y por los sentidos, y sus figuras todas y sus semblantes y sus movimientos son Cristo, que los ocupa así a todos, y se enseñorea de ellos tan íntimamente, que, sin destruirles o corromperles su sér, no se verá en ellos en el último día, ni se descubrirá otro sér más del suyo y un mismo sér en todos ; por lo cual, así él como ellos, serán un él y uno mismo.

Grande ñudo es aqueste, Sabino ; y lazo de unidad tan estrecho, que en ninguna cosa de las que, o la naturaleza ha compuesto o el arte inventado, las partes diversas que tiene, se juntaron jamás con juntura tan delicada o que así huyese la vista, como es esta juntura. Y cierto, es ayuntamiento de matrimonio tanto mayor y mejor, cuanto se celebra por modo más uno y más limpio. Y la ventaja que hace al matrimonio o desposorio de la carne en limpieza, esa o mucho mayor ventaja le hace en unidad y estrecheza : que allí se inficionan los cuerpos, y aquí se deifica el alma y la carne : allí se aficionan las voluntades, aquí toda es una voluntad y un querer ; allí adquieren derecho el uno sobre el cuerpo del otro ; aquí, sin destruir su substancia, convierte en su cuerpo, en la manera que he dicho, el Esposo Cristo a su esposa ; allí se yerra de ordinario, aquí se acierta siempre ; allí de contino hay solicitud y cuidado, enemigo de la conformidad y unidad ; aquí seguridad y reposo ayudador y favorecedor de aquello que es uno ; allí se ayuntan para sacar a luz a otro tercero ; aquí por un ayuntamiento se camina a otro, y el fruto de aquesta unidad es afinarse en ser uno, y el abrazarse es para más abrazarse ; allí el contento es aguado y el deleite breve y de bajo metal ; aquí lo uno y lo otro tan grande, que baña el cuerpo y el alma ; tan noble, que es gloria ; tan puro, que ni antes le precede ni después se le sigue, ni con él jamás se mezcla o se ayunta el dolor.

Nombres de Cristo : Libro 2°,
'Esposo.'

El Nacimiento de Cristo en el Alma

El nacer nosotros en Cristo es propiamente, quitada la mancha de culpa con que nuestra alma se figuraba como demonio, recibir la gracia y la justicia que cría Dios en nosotros, que es como una imagen de Cristo, y con que nos figuramos de su manera. Mas nacer Cristo en nosotros es, no solamente venir el don de la gracia a nuestra alma, sino el mismo espíritu de Cristo venir a ella y juntarse con ella, y, como si fuese alma del alma, derramarse por ella ; y derramado y como embebido en ella, apoderarse de sus potencias y fuerzas, no de paso, ni de corrida, ni por un tiempo breve como acontece en los resplandores de la contemplación y en los arroba-mientos del espíritu, sino de asiento y con sosiego estable, y como se reposa el alma en el cuerpo ; que él mismo lo dice así : *El que me amare será amado de mi Padre, y vendremos a él y haremos asiento en él.*

Así que, nacer nosotros en Cristo es recibir su gracia y figurarnos de ella ; mas nacer en nosotros él, es venir él por su espíritu a vivir en nuestras almas y cuerpos. Venir, digo, a vivir, y no sólo a hacer deleite y regalo. Por lo cual, aunque ayer Marcelo dijo de cómo nacemos nosotros en Dios, queda lugar para decir hoy del nacimiento de Cristo en nosotros. Del cual, pues habemos ya dicho que se diferencia y cómo se diferencia del nuestro, y que propiamente consiste en que comience a vivir el espíritu de Cristo en el alma, para que se entienda esto mismo mejor, digamos lo primero cuán diferentemente vive en ella cuando se le muestra en la oración ; y después diremos cuándo y cómo comienza Cristo a nacer en nosotros, y la fuerza de este su nacer y vivir en nosotros, y los grados y crecimiento que tiene.

Porque, cuanto a lo primero, entre esta venida y ayuntamiento del espíritu de Cristo a nosotros, que llamamos nacimiento suyo, y entre las venidas que hace al alma del justo, y las demostraciones que en el negocio de la oración le hace de sí, de las diferencias que hay, la principal es, que en esto que llamamos nacer, el espíritu de Cristo se ayunta con la esencia del alma, y comienza a ejecutar su virtud en ella, abrazándose con ella sin que ella lo sienta ni entienda. Y reposa allí como metido en el centro de ella, como dice Isaías : *Regocíjate y alaba, hija de Sión, porque el Señor de Israel está en medio de ti.* Y reposando allí, como desde el medio, derrama los rayos de su virtud por toda ella, y la mueve secretamente; y con su movimiento de él y con la obediencia del alma a lo que es de él movida, se hace por momentos mayor lugar en ella, y más ancho y más dispuesto aposento.

Mas en las luces de la oración y en sus gustos, todo su trato de Cristo es con las potencias del alma, con el entendimiento, con la voluntad y memoria, de las cuales, a las veces, pasa a los sentidos del cuerpo y se les comunica por diversas y admirables maneras, en la forma que les son posibles aquestos sentimientos a un cuerpo. Y de la copia de dulzores que el alma siente, y de que está colmada, pasan al compañero las sobras. Por donde estas luces o gustos, o este ayuntamiento gustoso del alma con Cristo en la oración, tiene condición de relámpago; digo que luce y se pasa en breve. Porque nuestras potencias y sentidos, en cuanto esta vida mortal dura, tienen precisa necesidad de divertirse a otras contemplaciones y cuidados, sin los cuales ni se vive, ni se puede ni debe vivir.

Y júntase también con esta diferencia otra diferencia: que en el ayuntamiento del espíritu de Cristo con el nuestro, que llamamos nacimiento de Cristo, el espíritu de Cristo tiene vez de alma respecto de la nuestra, y hace en ella obra de alma, moviéndola a obrar como debe en todo lo que se ofrece, y pone en ella ímpetu para que se menee; y así obra él en ella y la mueve, que ella ayudada de él obra con él juntamente; mas en la presencia que de sí hace en la oración a los buenos por medio de deleite y de luz, por la mayor parte el alma y sus potencias reposan, y él sólo obra en ellas por secreta manera un reposo y un bien que decir no se puede. Y así, aquel primer ayuntamiento es de vida, mas este segundo es de deleite y regalo; aquél es el sér y el vivir, aquéste es lo que hace dulce el vivir; allí recibe vivienda y estilo de Dios el alma, aquí gusta algo de su bienandanza; y así, aquello se da con asiento y para que dure, porque si falta no se vive; mas esto se da de paso y a la ligera, porque es más gustoso que necesario, y porque en esta vida, que se nos da para obrar, este deleite, en cuanto dura, quita el obrar y le muda en gozar. Y sea esto lo uno, y cuanto a lo segundo que decia, digo de esta manera:

Cristo nace en nosotros cuandoquiera que nuestra alma, volviendo los ojos a la consideración de su vida, y viendo las fealdades de sus desconciertos, y aborreciéndolos, y considerando el enojo merecido de Dios, y doliéndose de él, ansiosa por aplacarle, se convierte con fe, con amor, con dolor a la misericordia de Dios y al rescate de Cristo. Así que Cristo nace en nosotros entonces.

Y dícese que nace en nosotros, porque entonces entra en nuestra alma su mismo espíritu, que, en entrando, se entraña en ella, y produce luego en ella su gracia, que es como un resplandor y como un rayo que resulta de su presencia y que se asienta en el alma y la hace hermosa. Y así comienza a tener vida allí Cristo; esto es, comienza a obrar en el alma y por el alma lo que es justo que obre Cristo; porque lo más cierto y lo más propio de la vida es la obra.

Nombres de Cristo: Libro 3°,
' Hijo de Dios.'

PRÍNCIPE DE PAZ

Cuando la razón no lo demostrara, ni por otro camino se pudiera entender cuán amable cosa sea la paz, esta vista hermosa del cielo que se nos descubre ahora, y el concierto que tienen entre sí aquestos resplandores que lucen en él, nos dan de ello suficiente testimonio. Porque ¿qué otra cosa es, sino paz, o ciertamente una imagen perfecta de paz, esto que ahora vemos en el cielo y que con tanto deleite se nos viene a los ojos? Que si la paz es, como San Agustín breve y verdaderamente concluye, una orden sosegada o un tener sosiego y firmeza en lo que pide el buen orden, eso mismo es lo que nos descubre ahora esta imagen. Adonde el ejército de las estrellas, puesto como en ordenanza y como concertado por sus hileras, luce hermosísimo, y adonde cada una de ellas inviolablemente guarda su puesto, adonde no usurpa ninguna el lugar de su vecina ni la turba en su oficio, ni menos, olvidada del suyo, rompe jamás la ley eterna y santa que le puso la providencia; antes como hermanadas todas y como mirándose entre sí, y comunicándose sus luces las mayores con las menores, se hacen muestra de amor, y como en cierta manera se reverencian unas a otras, y todas juntas templan a veces sus rayos y sus virtudes, reduciéndolas a una pacífica unidad de virtud, de partes y aspectos diferentes compuesta, universal y poderosa sobre toda manera.

Y si así se puede decir, no sólo son un dechado de paz clarísimo y bello, sino un pregón y un loor que con voces manifiestas y encarecidas nos notifica cuán excelentes bienes son los que la paz en sí contiene, y los que hace en todas las cosas. La cual voz y pregón sin ruido se lanza en nuestras almas, y de lo que en ellas lanzada hace, se ve y entiende bien la eficacia suya y lo mucho que las persuade. Porque luego, como convencidas de cuánto les es útil y hermosa la paz, se comienzan ellas a pacificar en sí mismas y a poner a cada una de sus partes en orden.

Porque si estamos atentos a lo secreto que en nosotros pasa, veremos que este concierto y orden de las estrellas, mirándolo, pone en nuestras almas sosiego, y veremos que con sólo tener los ojos enclavados en él con atención, sin sentir en qué manera, los deseos nuestros y las afecciones turbadas que confusamente movían ruido en nuestros pechos de día, se van aquietando poco a poco; y, como adormeciéndose, se reposan, tomando cada una su asiento, y reduciéndose a su lugar propio, se ponen sin sentir en sujeción y concierto. Y veremos que, así como ellas se humillan y callan, así lo principal y lo que es señor en el alma, que es la razón, se levanta y recobra su derecho y su fuerza, y como alentada con esta vista celestial y hermosa, concibe pensamientos altos y dignos de sí, y como en una cierta manera se recuerda de su primer origen, y al fin pone todo lo que es vil y bajo en su parte, y huella sobre ello. Y así, puesta ella en su trono como emperatriz, y reducidas a sus lugares todas las demás partes del alma, queda todo el hombre ordenado y pacífico.

Mas ¿qué digo de nosotros que tenemos razón? Esto insensible y aquesto rudo del mundo, los elementos, y la tierra, y el aire, y los brutos se ponen todos en orden y se aquietan, luego que poniéndose el sol se les representa aqueste ejército resplandeciente. ¿No veis el silencio que tienen ahora todas las cosas, y cómo parece que mirándose en este espejo bellísimo, se componen todas ellas y hacen paz entre sí, vueltas a sus lugares y oficios, y contentas con ellos?

Es sin duda el bien de todas las cosas universalmente la paz; y así, donde quiera que la ven la aman. Y no sólo ella, mas la vista de su imagen de ella las enamora y las enciende en codicia de asemejársele, porque todo se inclina fácil y dulcemente a su bien. Y aun si confesamos, como es justo confesar, la verdad, no solamente la paz es amada generalmente de todos, mas sola ella es amada y seguida y procurada por todos. Porque cuanto se obra en esta vida por los que vivimos en ella, y cuanto se desea y afana, es por conseguir este bien de la paz; y este es el blanco adonde enderezan su intento, y el bien a que aspiran todas las cosas. Porque si navega el mercader y si corre los mares, es por tener paz con su codicia, que le solicita y guerrea. Y el labrador en el sudor de su cara y rompiendo la tierra, busca paz, alejando de sí cuanto puede al enemigo duro de la pobreza. Y por la misma manera, el que sigue el deleite, y el que anhela a la honra, y el que brama por la venganza, y finalmente, todos y todas las cosas buscan la paz en cada una de sus pretensiones. Porque, o siguen algún bien que les falta, o huyen algún mal que los enoja.

Y porque así el bien que se busca como el mal que se padece o se teme, el uno con su deseo y el otro con su miedo y dolor, turban el sosiego del alma y son como enemigos suyos que le hacen guerra, colígese manifiestamente que es huir la guerra y buscar la paz todo cuanto se hace. Y si la paz es tan grande y tan único bien, ¿quién podrá ser príncipe de ella, esto es, causador de ella y principal fuente suya, sino ese mismo que nos es el principio y el autor de todos los bienes, Jesucristo, Señor y Dios nuestro? Porque si la paz es carecer de mal que aflige y de deseo que atormenta, y gozar de reposado sosiego, sólo él hace exentas las almas del temer, y las enriquece por tal manera, que no les queda cosa que poder desear.

Nombres de Cristo: Libro 2°,
' *Príncipe de Paz.*'

VIDA RETIRADA

¡ Qué descansada vida
La del que huye el mundanal ruido,
Y sigue la escondida
Senda por donde han ido
Los pocos sabios que en el mundo han sido !

Que no le enturbia el pecho
De los soberbios grandes el estado,
Ni del dorado techo
Se admira, fabricado
Del sabio moro, en jaspes sustentado.

No cura si la fama
Canta con voz su nombre pregonera,
Ni cura si encarama
La lengua lisonjera
Lo que condena la verdad sincera.

¿Qué presta a mi contento,
Si soy del vano dedo señalado,
Si en busca de este viento
Ando desalentado
Con ansias vivas, con mortal cuidado?

¡Oh monte, oh fuente, oh río,
Oh secreto seguro, deleitoso!
Roto casi el navío,
A vuestro almo reposo
Huyo de aqueste mar tempestuoso.

Un no rompido sueño,
Un día puro, alegre, libre quiero;
No quiero ver el ceño
Vanamente severo
De a quien la sangre ensalza o el dinero.

Despiértenme las aves
Con su cantar sabroso no aprendido,
No los cuidados graves
De que es siempre seguido
El que al ajeno arbitrio está atenido.

Vivir quiero conmigo,
Gozar quiero del bien que debo al cielo,
A solas, sin testigo,
Libre de amor, de celo,
De odio, de esperanzas, de recelo.

Del monte en la ladera
Por mi mano plantado tengo un huerto,
Que con la primavera,
De bella flor cubierto,
Ya muestra en esperanza el fruto cierto.

Y como codiciosa,
Por ver y acrecentar su hermosura,
Desde la cumbre airosa
Una fontana pura
Hasta llegar corriendo se apresura;

Y luego sosegada,
El paso entre los árboles torciendo,
El suelo de pasada
De verdura vistiendo,
Y con diversas flores va esparciendo.

El aire el huerto orea,
Y ofrece mil olores al sentido,
Los árboles menea
Con un manso ruido,
Que del oro y del cetro pone olvido.

Ténganse su tesoro
Los que de un falso leño se confían;
No es mío ver el lloro
De los que desconfían
Cuando el cierzo y el ábrego porfían.

La combatida antena
Cruje, y en ciega noche el claro día
Se torna, al cielo suena
Confusa vocería,
Y la mar enriquecen a porfía.

A mí una pobrecilla
Mesa, de amable paz bien abastada,
Me basta, y la vajilla
De fino oro labrada
Sea de quien la mar no teme airada.

Y mientras miserable—
Mente se están los otros abrasando
Con sed insaciable
Del peligroso mando,
Tendido yo a la sombra esté cantando;

A la sombra tendido,
De hiedra y lauro eterno coronado,
Puesto el atento oído
Al son dulce, acordado,
Del plectro sabiamente meneado.

De la vida del cielo

Alma región luciente,
Prado de bienandanza, que ni el hielo
Ni con el rayo ardiente
Fallece, fértil suelo,
Producidor eterno de consuelo;

De púrpura y de nieve,
Florida la cabeza, coronado,
A dulces pastos mueve
Sin honda ni cayado
El buen pastor en ti su hato amado.

Él va, y en pos, dichosas,
Le siguen sus ovejas, do las pace
Con inmortales rosas,
Con flor que siempre nace,
Y cuanto más se goza, más renace.

Y dentro a la montaña
Del alto bien las guía, ya en la vena
Del gozo fiel las baña,
Y les da mesa llena,
Pastor y pasto él solo y suerte buena.

Y de su esfera cuando
A cumbre toca altísimo subido
El sol, él sesteando,
De su ato ceñido,
Con dulce son deleita el santo oído.

Toca el rabel sonoro,
Y el inmortal dulzor al alma pasa,
Con que envilece el oro,
Y ardiendo se traspasa,
Y lanza en aquel bien libre de tasa.

¡Oh son! Oh voz! Siquiera
Pequeña parte alguna descendiese
En mi sentido, y fuera
De sí el alma pusiese,
Y toda en ti, oh amor, la convirtiese.

Conocería dónde
Sesteas, dulce Esposo, y desatada
Desta prisión adonde
Padece, a tu manada
Viviré junta, sin vagar errada.

NOCHE SERENA

A Don Oloarte.

Cuando contemplo el cielo,
De innumerables luces adornado
Y miro hacia el suelo,
De noche rodeado,
En sueño y en olvido sepultado,

El amor y la pena
Despiertan en mi pecho un ansia ardiente,
Despide larga vena,
Los ojos hechos fuente,
Oloarte, y digo al fin con voz doliente :

Morada de grandeza,
Templo de claridad y hermosura,
El alma que a tu alteza
Nació ¿qué desventura
La tiene en esta cárcel baja, escura?

¿Qué mortal desatino
De la verdad aleja así el sentido,
Que, de tu bien divino
Olvidado, perdido,
Sigue la vana sombra, el bien fingido?

El hombre está entregado
Al sueño, de su suerte no cuidando,
Y con paso callado
El cielo vueltas dando,
Las horas del vivir le va hurtando.

¡Oh! despertad, mortales,
Mirad con atención en vuestro daño;
Las almas inmortales,
Hechas a bien tamaño,
¿Podrán vivir de sombras y de engaño?

¡Ay! levantad los ojos
A aquesta celestial eterna esfera,
Burlaréis los antojos
De aquesa lisonjera
Vida, con cuanto teme y cuanto espera.

¿Es más que un breve punto
El bajo y torpe suelo, comparado
Con ese gran trasunto,
Do vive mejorado
Lo que es, lo que será, lo que ha pasado?

Quien mira el gran concierto
De aquestos resplandores eternales,
Su movimiento cierto,
Sus pasos desiguales,
Y en proporción concorde tan iguales;

La luna cómo mueve
La plateada rueda, y va en pos de ella
La luz do el saber llueve,
Y la graciosa estrella
De amor la sigue, reluciente y bella;

Y cómo otro camino
Prosigue el sanguinoso Marte airado,
Y el Júpiter benigno,
De bienes mil cercado,
Serena el cielo con su rayo amado.

Rodéase en la cumbre
Saturno, padre de los siglos de oro ;
Tras él la muchedumbre
Del reluciente coro
Su luz va repartiendo y su tesoro.

¿ Quién es el que esto mira,
Y precia la bajeza de la tierra,
Y no gime y suspira,
Y rompe lo que encierra
El alma, y destos bienes la destierra ?

Aquí vive el contento,
Aquí reina la paz, aquí asentado
En rico y alto asiento
Está el amor sagrado,
De glorias y deleites rodeado.

Inmensa hermosura
Aquí se muestra toda, y resplandece
Clarísima luz pura,
Que jamás anochece ;
Eterna primavera aquí florece.

¡ Oh campos verdaderos !
Oh prados con verdad frescos y amenos,
Riquísimos mineros !
Oh deleitosos senos,
Repuestos valles, de mil bienes llenos !

INDEX

References to the selected texts have been made to the English versions only. Figures in *italic type* denote the pages of the introduction in which the author referred to is treated at length. **Clarendon type** is used to denote translated passages : the corresponding original versions can be found by consulting the table of contents. Where a work is mentioned by its Spanish as well as its English title, the reference is given under the English title only, the Spanish title being cross-referenced. Selected passages are denoted by inverted commas, books and complete works by italics. Footnote references to the books of the Bible are not included in this index.

PRINTED IN GREAT BRITAIN AT THE UNIVERSITY PRESS, ABERDEEN